Debt and Development in Latin America

Edited by
Kwan S. Kim and David F. Ruccio

UNIVERSITY OF NOTRE DAME PRESS
NOTRE DAME, INDIANA 46556

Library of Congress Cataloging-in-Publication Data

Main entry under title:

Debt and development in Latin America.

1. Latin America — Economic conditions —
1945-   — Addresses, essays, lectures.   2. Foreign
exchange — Latin America — Addresses, essays, lec-
tures.   3. Debts, External — Latin America —
Addresses, essays, lectures.   4. Latin America —
Economic policy — Addresses, essays, lectures.
5. Latin America — Dependency on foreign countries
— Addresses, essays, lectures.   I. Kim, Kwan S.
II. Ruccio, David F.
HC125.D374   1985   338.98   85-40598
ISBN 0-268-00855-8
ISBN 0-268-00856-6 (pbk.)

Manufactured in the United States of America

DEBT AND DEVELOPMENT IN LATIN AMERICA

Contents

Contributors   vii
Foreword, *Alejandro Foxley*   xi
Acknowledgments   xiii
Introduction   1

Part I: Crisis and Instability: The Structuralist Perspective

Power Relations and Market Laws, *Raúl Prebisch*   9
Social Disarticulation in Latin American History,
    Alain de Janvry   32
Wages and Employment in International Recessions:
    Recent Latin American Experience, *Victor Tokman*   74

Part II: Crisis and Instability: The Financial Side

Revisiting the Great Debt Crisis of 1982, *Albert Fishlow*   99
The External Debt Crisis in Latin America:
    Trends and Outlook, *Ricardo Ffrench-Davis*   133
Exchange Rate Regimes and the Real Rate of Interest,
    Larry A. Sjaastad   163

Part III: Strategies of Adjustment

Stabilization and Economic Justice: The Case of Nicaragua,
    E. V. K. Fitzgerald   191
Industrial Development in Mexico: Problems, Policy Issues,
    and Perspectives, *Kwan S. Kim*   205

Contributors

ALAIN DE JANVRY is professor of agricultural economics at the University of California, Berkeley. He received his Ph.D. from the University of California, Berkeley, and has since been active as an economic consultant and adviser for numerous development agencies and for governments of Third World countries. He is an internationally acclaimed specialist in rural development, agrarian reform, technological change and social equity, and has published extensively in these areas.

RICARDO FFRENCH-DAVIS is executive director of CIEPLAN, a Santiago-based policy research institute for Chile. Formerly, he was professor of economics at the University of Chile, and a visiting professor at the University of Boston and Oxford University. He is the author of numerous articles in professional journals, policy papers for Chile, and several books in the areas of international relations, North-South relations, and economic policies in Latin America and Chile.

ALBERT FISHLOW is professor of economics at the University of California, Berkeley. Dr. Fishlow is a distinguished specialist on Brazil and Latin America, having served as an adviser to the Brazilian Ministry of Planning for several years, Deputy Assistant Secretary for Inter-American Affairs, and an occasional consultant to the World Bank, Inter-American Development Bank, and several foundations. At present he serves on the editorial boards of *Foreign Policy*, *International Organization*, and *Latin American Research Review*. In addition to numerous articles in professional journals, he has authored several books concerned with issues of income distribution in Brazil and economic relations between industrialized and developing countries.

E. V. K. FITZGERALD is professor of development economics at the Institute for Social Studies in the Netherlands. He received his B.A.

vii

and M.A. from Oxford University and his Ph.D. in economics from Cambridge University. For many years he served as Assistant Director of Development Studies at Cambridge University and then in advisory posts in Peru, Mexico, Algeria, and Panama. At present he serves as senior economic adviser in the Presidential Office in Nicaragua. He is the author of three books, numerous chapters, and articles on Latin America, financial policy, public investment theory, and peripheral accumulation. He is editor of the *Journal of Development Studies* and serves on the editorial boards of *Latin American Research Review* and the *Bulletin of Latin American Research*.

KWAN S. KIM is an associate professor of economics and a Faculty Fellow of the Kellogg Institute at the University of Notre Dame. He received his Ph.D. in economics from the University of Minnesota. His career includes several years as visiting professor of economics in East Africa and Mexico, and two years as visiting scholar at the Agency for International Development. He has also occasionally served as an economic consultant for governments of developing countries and for international agencies. He has published extensively in the areas of trade and development, planning, and industrialization, with a special interest in East Africa, East Asia, and recently, Mexico.

RAÚL PREBISCH is currently director of the *CEPAL Review*, Special Adviser to the Executive Secretary of the Economic Commission for Latin America and economic adviser to the Argentine government. He graduated with a degree in economics from the University of Buenos Aires, and soon held a professorship in political economy at the same university. Dr. Prebisch served as Under-Secretary of the Argentine Ministry of Finance, Director-General of the Latin American Institute for Economic and Social Planning, Secretary-General of the United Nations Conference on Trade and Development, and Special Representative of the Secretary-General for the United Nations Emergency Operation. His special concern, as evidenced by his career work related to UNCTAD activities and his extensive publications, has been in the area of trade and development problems for Third World countries and North-South relations.

DAVID F. RUCCIO is assistant professor of economics and a Faculty Fellow of the Kellogg Institute at the University of Notre Dame. His Ph.D. in economics is from the University of Massachusetts-

Amherst. He is the editor of a book on multinational corporations in Portugal and has accumulated extensive research experience in Latin America. His publications concern theories of economic development and planning; his most recent writings focus on the external debt problem and the role of the state and planning in Latin American economic development.

LARRY A. SJAASTAD holds a professorship in economics at both the Univsity of Chicago and the Graduate Institute of International Studies in Geneva. He received his Ph.D. from the University of Chicago, and has had extensive experience in Latin America as a visiting professor at several Latin American universities and as a consultant for numerous federal and international organizations. His research interest is in the areas of monetary and fiscal policy with a focus on Latin America, and he has published extensively in professional journals.

VICTOR TOKMAN is director of the Latin American and Caribbean Regional Program of Employment in Santiago, Chile of the International Labor Office. He earned his Ph.D. at Oxford University and spent several years as a Research Fellow of the United Nations Institute for Economic and Social Planning. Dr. Tokman is a distinguished scholar, having published several books and numerous articles on the issues of technology, employment, and income distribution in Latin American countries.

Foreword

The last few years have witnessed a renewed interest not only by academics but also by the press and even the general public about economic trends and events in Latin America. To be sure this interest is to a large extent caused by the sudden awareness in the United States of the close interrelationship between the Latin American economies and the U.S. economy. This realization is old in Latin America. In fact, a whole school of economic thought was developed — the so-called "dependencia" theory — that purported to explain what was considered to be an asymmetrical but close interdependence between the economy of the United States and the rest of the continent.

The new awareness about the interdependent nature of economic problems has been triggered more than anything else by the so-called international debt crisis in Latin America and its possible devastating effect on U.S. banks and thus more generally on the U.S. economy. Since the crisis erupted in a way that caught almost everybody by surprise, information about the underlying factors behind the crisis has been mostly restricted to rather hurried press "background" reports. It is not that academic discussion has been absent since the crisis surfaced. But not much of that discussion has appeared in the form of books that go beyond short-term analysis of the factors that were responsible for its sudden, unexpected emergence.

Debt and Development in Latin America, edited by Professors Kim and Ruccio, represents a significant contribution in going beyond the current debt situation to discuss some of the structural factors that made Latin America more vulnerable than, say, the Asian economies, vis-à-vis the changed conditions of international finance. It brings together contributions of well-known economists both from the United States and Latin America and provides the reader with a balanced view of different perspectives on the current economic crisis in Latin America.

This book grew out of a lecture series jointly organized at Notre Dame by the Economics Department and the Kellogg Institute of International Studies. We were fortunate to engage in this project the distinguished economists whose contributions are here published. It is our conviction that the material they produced will be useful to a wide audience of academics, students in economics and the social sciences, and to the general public interested in learning about the underlying causes of economic instability in Latin America.

Alejandro Foxley
Kellogg Professor of Economics
and International Development

Acknowledgments

Our greatest debt is to the contributors for their enthusiastic participation in the Distinguished Lecture Series on economic development held at the University of Notre Dame, which forms the basis of this volume. Among a large number of individuals instrumental in making this symposium a success, special appreciation is due Rev. Ernest Bartell, C.S.C., Executive Director of the Helen Kellogg Institute for International Studies, and Professor Charles Wilber, Chairperson of the Department of Economics, for providing institutional as well as personal support in the preparation of this volume. We are also grateful to Michael Varga, Augusto de la Torre, Bruce Corrie, and Joseph Wilder for their much appreciated assistance in the technical editing of this volume, and to the members of the College of Arts and Letters steno pool at Notre Dame for their typing of the successive drafts of the various manuscripts. Finally, our thanks go to James Langford, Director of the University of Notre Dame Press, without whose support the final appearance of this volume would not have been possible.

Introduction

"The basis of the current crisis in economics today
is the contrast that exists between the 'elegance'
of economic theory and its practical relevance."
— A. Eichner

Not unlike other regions of the developing world, economic growth in Latin America has historically been unstable and uneven. However, the current pattern of growth among the Latin American countries gives evidence of structural imbalances that are more pronounced than elsewhere. Although the region as a whole has, until recently, enjoyed growth in national income that has been faster than that in population, this rising average income has been marred by sustained inflation, external payments disequilibria, and a deepening inequality in the distribution of income. These various tendencies reached such proportions that 1981–1982 was coined the year of the "Latin American crisis." Little if any amelioration in the conditions leading to that crisis has been witnessed since then.

The immediate roots of the crisis of the 1980s can be found in the preceding decade. In an attempt to overcome the global oil shocks of the early and again the late 1970s, many Latin American countries gambled on ambitious growth targets by borrowing heavily in international financial markets. For instance, Brazil responded to internal political pressures to expand at the expense of a deteriorating external payments position. The external debt of Chile and Argentina almost trebled over a few years, from 1978 to 1981. Mexico, based on the optimism of its newly discovered oil reserves, borrowed significant amounts from abroad for expansionary policies at home. This strategy of what Fishlow calls "growth-led debt" has led to the recent debt crisis, dramatically affecting Latin American countries in different forms.

Toward the end of the decade of the 1970s, the deepening world recession, combined with an ascent of real interest rates in the world capital market following anti-inflationary monetary policies in the industrialized countries, became a crucial factor, rendering adjustment more difficult for developing countries. All this occurred while their ex-

1

port demand was falling off, with a resulting deterioration in the terms of trade. It is noteworthy that the dimensions of these problems loomed much larger in the Latin American region, because of the distinct position of the Latin American countries in the world economy and their particular policy responses to the crisis.

Unlike many of the developing countries in Africa and Asia, a large number of Latin American countries are in the intermediate range of capitalist development, heavily dependent on foreign trade and multinational capital for industrialization. Other newly industrializing countries in Asia followed an industrialization path that accommodated to adverse external developments by a more immediate realignment of real wages and exchange rates in order to remain competitive in manufactured exports. Latin American countries generally pursued a more open capital market as an integral part of their international monetarist stabilization experiment in the 1970s.

Thus, during the early 1980s when the industrialized world was already showing signs of recovery from the recession, acute economic problems still remained unresolved in Latin America. In several Latin American countries, IMF-type stabilization policies have meant a virtual arrest in per capita income growth, delays in investment projects, and interruptions in anti-poverty programs.

It seems that unless the current world recovery turns out to be indeed a very strong one, the remainder of this decade will continue to be a period of stagnation and retrenchment for many countries in the region. In particular, the slow and import-efficient recovery of the industrialized world, coupled with the recent decline in the terms of trade observed for the Latin American region, will make it more difficult for the indebted Latin American countries to sustain a strong real growth in exports, even to pay for interest payments on outstanding debt. Furthermore, the prospects for sustained capital transfer from the creditors to the debtor countries are not promising. Already there is evidence to indicate that a reverse transfer of capital has been taking place from the borrowing countries to the lending countries, which of course means more difficulties for the region to meet debt service requirements. In the end, the financial pressures will likely build up to tempt the borrowing countries to impose import controls that could make these economies grow even more slowly.

Viewing the Latin American problems in this perspective, there are many unresolved issues worth considering: How relevant a factor is the international environment in affecting the setbacks and crises in the Latin American world? If domestic factors are a major cause of the problem, precisely what do they explain? Is it faulty economic theories that have misguided practice, or is it simply a bureaucratic inefficiency in implementing policies? Or are there other overriding socio-political constraints that impede progress in stabilization? Finally, what will be appropriate adjustment policies for responding to the recurrent economic crises witnessed in the region?

Each article presented in this volume concerns itself with some of these issues, addressing different aspects of the crisis and the varied manner in which the crisis has been confronted by different countries in Latin America. Some papers also explore the implications of these responses for the prospects of the region's future development.

The selection of the articles for this volume was based on our desire to allow the reader to examine alternative views of several leading Latin American and Latin Americanist development economists who have also been involved in controversial policy-fields in Latin America. The papers in the volume are divided into three parts: The first part, containing three papers, provides a spectrum of structuralist perspectives on the Latin American crisis; the second set of three papers focuses on the financial side of the crisis; the final part, comprising the remaining two papers, offers longer-term strategies for structural adjustment.

The first two papers by Prebisch and de Janvry examine from a historical perspective the causes of an unstable and ephemeral pattern of growth in Latin American countries that is basically attributable to the structural characteristics of a dependent capitalist, "underdeveloped" economy.

Prebisch provides an insightful overview of the international context in which trade and other economic relations take place between industrial centers and peripheral countries engaged in primary production. The world commodity and financial markets may serve the Latin American region as an essential catalyst contributing to the formation of capital and the acceleration of development in the region. Prebisch, however, sees asymmetries in this North-South relationship that tend to concentrate instability in the region, at the same time denying it access to an equitable share in the gains from a reciprocal trade. Pointing out the basic weaknesses of an untrammeled market system, he advocates a "regulatory mechanism" in the relations of the periphery with the centers.

De Janvry turns to the roots of political and economic instabilities historically observed for many Latin countries. Current development theories are considered in deep crisis, having failed to properly account for the causes of underdevelopment of the Third World countries. A Kaleckian framework of analysis for the characterization of alternative styles of development is provided, the key feature of which calls for the distinction between "social articulation" and "social disarticulation" in the growth process of a developing economy. "Disarticulation" occurs in the sense of a divergence between the production and domestic absorption of wage goods, implying a failure of an economic model to reconcile growth and equity. Thus, it leads to a growth process marred by periodic setbacks and crises and the consequent oscillation between democratic and authoritarian forms of government in Latin America.

Starting with a hypothesis that the recent world recession has induced the Latin American economies to reduce the level of economic activity, Tokman, on the other hand, turns to real-sector adjustments, examining all possible interactions among factor rewards, real exchange rates, terms of trade, employment and growth. Alternative policy options, as determined by the structural characteristics of the economy, are carefully explored on the basis of a typology of countries classified by the status of oil production and the "openness" to world markets. An interesting empirical result obtained concerns the behavior in the labor market: unemployment is correlated with the level of economic activity, not with real wages. This relationship contradicts the wisdom of conventional adjustment policies relying on real wage reductions as a means to equilibrate the labor market. He also draws a sharp distinction between the formal and informal sectors in the labor market. Given the complex working of the labor market institutions in Latin America, he questions the legitimacy of orthodox policies of unemployment and wage-repression for stabilization.

The papers by Fishlow and Ffrench-Davis address Latin American countries' debt and financial problems within the context of their stabilization measures. While Fishlow's paper traces the historical origins and evolution of the recent external debt problems in the Latin American region, examining at the same time their economic implications for the indebted countries, Ffrench-Davis focuses on the scope, composition and outlook of the external debt of the region. Both authors also question the adequacy of the existing international financial system in coping with the debt problems, and reject as inappropriate and counterproductive the current IMF adjustment policies of seeking an external equilibrium through restrictions of demand in a developing world in recession with high unemployment. Emphasizing the danger of overstating the prospects for global economy recovery, both foresee an asymmetry in the burden of adjustment, with the burden falling more heavily on the debtors, even with an industrialized country recovery. Thus, as a counteractive measure of Latin countries' responding to the current crisis, Ffrench-Davis argues for the "redynamization of import-substitution and the intensification of South-South cooperation in the field of production and trade."

Sjaastad's paper, in itself a contribution to the stabilization exchange rate regime literature, examines on both theoretical and empirical grounds the consequences of external exchange rate instability in the major currencies for a small developing economy integrated with world capital and product markets. Specifically, variations in the exchange rate of major currencies are shown to result in much larger variations in the corresponding instability of real rates of interest in the smaller, exchange rate-pegged economies. Thus, for countries such as Chile and Uruguay whose capital markets are highly integrated with that of the United States, the high real interest rates of the early 1980s that precipitated the latest recession in these countries were brought about by a sudden appreciation of the dollar under the Reagan administration. Sjaastad's conclusion is dismal: small open economies are essentially vulnerable to the instability of the world monetary system.

Fitzgerald's paper, based on the experience of Sandinista Nicaragua, provides an alternative strategy for adjustment as a response to the crises recurrent in a small, developing economy open to international capitalism. The crucial component in the stabilization package is provision of basic needs goods for the masses. This includes guaranteeing basic real wages and other strong incomes policy, and isolation of the basic goods sector from the nonbasic in an attempt to cushion any destabilizing external influence on basic-sector development. In the conceptual structure of the Nicaraguan model, money fails to become an important policy instrument for stabilization. Rather, financial adjustments should follow a real-sector adjustment only as a residual balancing factor in the stabilization policy equation.

The last paper by Kim deals with industrial development strategies for large Latin American countries with a significant potential domestic market. Based on a scrutiny of the historical experience of Mexican industry, he warns of the danger of unrestricted trade and foreign capital liberalization measures, and given the present uncertainties in international markets, the paper argues strongly for sectoral policies for industrial development that must be carefully orchestrated with overall macroeconomic policies.

Kwan S. Kim
David F. Ruccio

PART I

Crisis and Instability:
The Structuralist Perspective

Power Relations and Market Laws

Raúl Prebisch

In my younger years, I was a neoclassicist. I strongly believed in the Walras-Pareto theory of general equilibrium and was fascinated by its mathematical elegance. Under the free play of economic forces, according to that theory, resources would be allocated in the best possible way, both at the international and national levels, and the fruits of technological progress would correspond at the equilibrium point to the contribution of every factor to the production process.[1]

The world depression had a tremendous intellectual impact on me. I had to abandon the belief in free trade as well as in the positive results of the international division of labor. However, it took me many years to arrive at the conclusion that the free play of market forces was not conducive to the pattern of distribution supposed by the equilibrium theories.[2]

Let me first consider the problem of distribution in order to pave the way for explaining the question of the international division of labor between industrial centers and peripheral countries engaged in primary production.[3]

I am persuaded that conventional theories of development and income distribution have a great flaw due to the fact that they do not explicitly include in their reasoning the structure of society and its mutations, as well as the changing power relations emerging from these.[4]

1. Internal Dynamic Disequilibrium and Inflation

The concept of economic equilibrium in conventional theories is totally out of touch with reality, inasmuch as it overlooks the structural phenomenon of the economic surplus. I maintain that, however fully the rule of free market competition be observed, only part of the productivity increment attributable to technical progress is transferred to the labor force, while the rest is appropriated and retained as an economic surplus by the holders of the means of production, especially by the up-

9

per strata of society where the ownership and control of those means are concentrated.

The economic surplus plays a vital role in the dynamics of the system: it is the primordial source of reproductive investment which multiplies employment and productivity and continuously augments the surplus itself. It is also a source of the considerable expansion of consumption by the upper strata, increasingly stimulated by the techniques for the diversification of goods and services, which, it is true, also tend to augment the consumption by the lower strata as income increases.

During the past history of capitalism, it has been possible for the upper strata to appropriate the surplus by virtue of the passiveness of the labor force and the laissez-faire attitude of the State. The surplus is a historical category which is based essentially on social inequality; it corresponds to a specific power structure. In the course of structural change the labor force progressively, although unequally, develops its trade union and political power and struggles to obtain a larger share of the growth of productivity; the State does the same, in order to cover both its increasing social expenditure on behalf of the labor force and the outlays deriving from its own dynamics, which, in their turn, reflect the changes that have occurred in the power structure.

Insofar as the State, in order to cover the social services referred to as well as the expansion of other expenditures, resorts to taxation of which the burden has to be borne by the labor force, the latter tries to recuperate itself by means of wage increases. This tends to push wages up faster than productivity increases, thus weakening the growth rate of the surplus and therefore that of capital accumulation. Some of the taxes also fall on the surplus and adversely affect the development of reproductive investment and, consequently, of productivity, at least as long as State investment and expenditures do not counteract these effects.

Thus, as the passiveness of the labor force and the laissez-faire policy of the State are modified, the tendency for wages to increase faster than productivity and the slackening of the latter's rate of growth have consequences that are more and more disturbing, given the nature of the system.

Every increase in wages above the rate of productivity has the twofold effect of raising costs and boosting demand in such a way that the higher costs can be transferred to prices, at least insofar as the rate of increase of wages outstrips that of productivity. And hard upon this rise in prices follows a fresh wage increase, if the labor force has enough power to obtain it. This is an important source of the inflationary spiral, deriving from the pressure of costs and intensified by the upswing in rates of interest that succeeds the rise in prices.

The upward movement of prices is really due to the endeavor of enterprises to defend the appropriation and retention of the surplus. And there is no spontaneous mechanism whatsoever whereby the increase in costs can be absorbed at the expense of the consumption of the groups benefitting by the surplus so as not to weaken the rate of accumulation. This is not how the system functions. It tries to protect the appropriation of the surplus by the groups in question where both their consumption and their investment are concerned.

It should be taken into account, however, that if the real remunerations of the labor force are improved, a portion of them may be used for accumulation, thus offsetting, to some extent at least, the weakening of capital accumulation on the part of enterprises. But neither is there any mechanism that spontaneously leads to this sort of compensation. What is of essential interest to enterprises is to defend the surplus and use it freely for their own investment rather than to let it be drawn upon for accumulation by the labor force. The same might be said in general of accumulation by the State.

It is not so much a question of resolving the technical problem of accumulation in order to promote the dynamics of the system, as of preserving the appropriation of a large proportion of the fruits of technical progress by the owners of the means of production. The system's need to speed up the rate of accumulation in order to increase employment does not represent a responsibility intrinsically incumbent upon the social groups that appropriate the surplus. It is other elements that determine the rate of accumulation, above all a factor of a cultural nature: the degree of austerity of these social groups, or, in other words, their resistance to the pertinacious incitement to consumption, spurred by the ever-increasing diversification of goods and services. Whatever degree of austerity may have been practiced in the historical development of capitalism, it must be acknowledged that this is not a characteristic of peripheral capitalism.

Let us now revert to the defense of the surplus through price increases, which causes inflation to spiral when the labor force is no longer passive and the monetary authority allows the necessary creation of money. The growing distortions which accompany this amplification of the spiral sooner or later induce the monetary authority to restrict credit. The consequences are common knowledge: a decline or contraction of the growth rate, together with tighter and tighter compression of the surplus and a slump in employment.

It is precisely in the decrease in employment that the key to this monetary policy lies. Sooner or later it leads the labor force to accept a deterioration of its real remunerations until the wage squeeze permits a renewed increase of the surplus and, therefore, its dynamic role in accumulation as well as a rise in the consumption of the advantaged social groups.

Furthermore, a rise in interest rates, accentuated by a restrictive monetary policy, implies a substantial transfer of real income from productive activity (surplus and remuneration of labor force) to financial activity, and slows down the tempo of economic activity, which then contracts.

Such, in a few words, is the way in which a notable success in curbing inflation has been achieved, initially in the main dynamic center of capitalism itself. In a recent commentary on this fact, *The Economist* noted that this result had been effected by squeezing real wages in order to increase the profits of enterprises (i.e., to reestablish the surplus). This is a very laudable thesis, according to the periodical, which has gained a wide circulation both in the centers and in the periphery and which supports monetary policy as a means of combating inflation. Here are the terms in which its remarks are couched:

> Falling real wages, like falling oil prices, are correcting an imbalance that has harmed the world economy for 10 years. Too-dear oil and too-dear labor both helped to cause stagflation. Their demise could herald a new age of low unemployment and low inflation, especially if too-dear money also ended. When that happens, the world will enjoy many happy New Years.

The economic and social costs of a restrictive monetary policy are tremendous, as we have already pointed out. But according to its defenders, this is a cost that has to be incurred in order to restore the system to health, i.e., in order to correct what they consider to be excesses brought about by the exaggerated demands of the trade unions, as well as by the increasing social benefits that contribute to the hypertrophy of what is no longer a laissez-faire State. In fact, neoclassical economists generally accept with resignation (and not without a measure of complacency in some cases) the economic and social costs in question for the sake of remedying the consequences of the violation of market laws by the labor force, as well as by abusive exercise of power by the State.

This is a violation of market laws because, according to neoclassical theories, if the market is allowed to operate freely, with no extra-market interference whatsoever, the economic system will tend towards equilibrium. And given this equilibrium, workers, entrepreneurs, and capital will be remunerated in accordance with their contribution to the production process. Whence derives a conclusion of supreme importance in neoclassical theory (although it is not usually explicitly stated): the free play of market forces disseminates throughout society the fruits of technical progress which find expression in the steadily rising productivity of the system, when this is left to its own devices.

These arguments, of course, disregard the structural phenomenon of the surplus; not only does accumulation increase, but so does the privileged consumption of the social groups that benefit more by technical progress. It is precisely this manifest inequality in consumption that causes the twofold pressure for redistribution exerted by the labor force and the State. The system itself, given its *modus operandi*, precludes efficacious fulfillment of the goal of equitable distribution.

Let some thought be given to the significance of these facts. The labor force finds itself compelled to accept a compression of its real wages so that the system may recover its capacity for accumulation. And for that to happen, unemployment must increase. Can it be supposed that, if a reactivation of the economy and a rise in employment levels occur, the labor force will meekly renounce its aspirations in favor of accumulation and more lavish consumption on the part of the advantaged strata? Or will it be necessary to recognize that the system, in the present structural phase, is continually exposed to inflationary pressure, which weakens with unemployment and recrudesces with the reactivation of the economy?

There is nothing surprising, then, in the peculiar thesis of those who maintain that the regular operation of the system entails a certain coefficient of unemployment in order to moderate wage demands.

I believe I have reached a clear and categorical conclusion. It is not feasible to seek the social betterment of the less-favored groups through wage increases that raise enterprise production costs. A historical phase in the evolution of capitalism is coming to an end without a solution having been found for the fundamental problem of synchronizing the distribution of the fruits of technical progress and the accumulation of reproductive capital.

Moreover, to dream of resolving it by market laws would be a fatal illusion. The market, insofar as it operates correctly, is efficacious from the economic standpoint. But its social efficiency is partial and limited, as also is its ecological efficacy. It is not the market in itself that should concern us, but the underlying structure of society and the power relations inherent therein, as well as the ambivalence of technology. Nor must we labor under the delusion — much more dangerous still — that the abolition of the market will resolve these and other problems, since that would invest those who manage the system from the summit with a power which, besides jeopardizing the system's efficiency, would prove incompatible with the progressive democratization of society.

2. The Structural Imbalance Between the Periphery and the Centers

In this section I turn to the question of the free play of market forces at the international level, in the relations between the centers and periphery. The centers have always stubbornly refused to recognize their great structural differences from the periphery, which stem from the considerable lag in the latter's development. This lag is itself the consequence of the inherent dynamics of advanced capitalism: a centripetal type of dynamic that has always characterized the latter's development in the past and has not spread spontaneously to the rest of the world. The fruits of the increase in productivity due to their enormous technological progress have remained in the centers and have not spread further through the reduction of prices: a situation which has given impetus to the accumulation of reproductive capital and the unceasing innovations in the centers. For better or for worse, this is how the capitalism of the centers has developed, with the periphery playing only the role of an appendix. This explains the historical lag in the latter's development and its great structural differences from the centers. These differences are manifested in three main points worth mentioning briefly here: the structural disparities in demand; the economic and technological inferiority of the periphery, which makes protection necessary; and the characteristic division of the periphery into relatively small units, which calls for integration measures.

With regard to the first point, in order for a country to develop it is essential for it to change its structure of production in order to cope with the correlative changes in demand. These changes can be oriented mainly towards the interior or towards the outside world, and the attitude of the centers has a dominant influence in this. There can be inward-oriented changes involving import substitution, or outward-oriented changes involving the export of manufactures. The latter option has become increasingly necessary because of the relative slowness with which exports of primary commodities generally tend to grow.

The obstacles impeding the ability of import substitution to move beyond certain limits are well known. The limits in question depend on the availability of natural resources and on technological considerations, thus making it necessary to combine import substitution with the export of the manufactures.

To what extent can manufactures be exported? Over and above the question of the effort that a peripheral country is willing to make in this direction, this extent depends fundamentally on the receptiveness of the centers, which is influenced in turn by their rate of development and the intensity of their restrictions on imports from the periphery. As a general rule, it can be said that the greater the receptiveness of the centers in the light of these two elements, the less need there will be to substitute imports in the periphery.

This, however, covers only one aspect of the matter. The other aspect concerns the changes in the composition of demand, which, as noted earlier, go hand in hand with development. In view of the well-known disparities in the income-elasticity of the demand for imports, the demand for the latter, which come primarily from the centers, will tend to grow more quickly than the demand for the exports of the periphery by the centers.[5] Such is the effect of the technological innovations in the centers, which increasingly diversify goods and services, in contrast with the technological lag of the periphery. In order for the development of the latter to progress, it is essential that it should develop its exports of manufactures in order thus to correct the tendency towards an external structural imbalance caused by this disparity in elasticities. If it does not manage to do this, it will be forced to engage in import substitution, in view of the rate of development which it proposes to achieve.

Now, import substitution calls for a certain amount of rational and moderate protection. This is where we encounter a severe obstacle in the form of reciprocity, which is now being put forward once again as a condition for the centers to lower their levels of protection. It is worth going more deeply into this matter.

There is a fundamental difference which should not be overlooked: protection in the periphery is aimed at eliminating the tendency towards structural imbalance, whereas protection in the centers tends to aggravate this tendency, to the detriment of peripheral development. We have set forth our reasoning on this matter many times, but apparently we have not been persuasive enough. Reciprocity has been the most important reason why attempts have been made and continue to be made to extend the scope of GATT (General Agreement on Tariffs and Trade) to the peripheral countries, so that they can participate in the negotiations based on this concept. It is not recognized that there is in fact already implicit reciprocity, since the more the developing countries export to the centers, the more they will be able to import from the latter.

There is also another consideration which is often forgotten. No rational projection puts imports below the amount that is exported to the centers, taking account of financial remittances and other payments abroad: all that is changed is their composition. The difference is that protection is aimed to bring about a deliberate change in the composition of imports in order to promote change in the structure of production in line with the requirements of development. In the absence of such a policy, the composition of imports is determined by international market forces and the transnational corporations which predominate in them, so that the structure of production is determined from the exterior. This means that a country cannot develop faster than is permitted by the growth of its exports, that is to say, by the receptiveness of the centers.

Is protection really necessary, however, in order to achieve these changes in the structures of production? The original concepts under which GATT was set up, based on the old-fashion scheme of the international division of labor, did not accept this, nor do the economists who still continue to preach the virtues of the free play of market forces for the periphery. It is true that these economists recommend devaluation of the currency to carry out these changes without breaking these laws. However, in order to simplify the argument, let us pass over the fact that devaluation is also a kind of intervention. We are not talking, of course, about devaluation to bring the external value of currency in line with domestic inflation, which is fully justified; rather, we are referring to it as a tool of economic policy.

Applied with this criterion, devaluation has the virtue of making imports more expensive and thus promoting their substitution, and also stimulating the growth of exports through a reduction in their prices. It does this, of course, for the exports which require this stimulus; however it also affects the exports which were already competitive at the international level. That is to say, from their point of view, this type of change in the structure of production brings about a deterioration in the terms of trade when the growth of exports goes beyond certain limits. Thus, it would be counterproductive from the point of view of development. It is true that a tax on exports is also advocated in order to avoid this, but would not this represent interference by the State with the market laws?

Furthermore, devaluation means altering all prices and costs in order to achieve effects only on a relatively small part of the global product of the economy. This is not all, however. It is well known that when the labor force has sufficient power to gain compensation for price rises it will demand a rise in wages, which will eventually wipe out the effects of devaluation. Consequently, while protection and the corresponding subsidies seem to us to be inevitable, they must be rational and not arbitrary or excessive, as often happens.

In order to undermine the idea of protection, the old argument continues to be put forward that it is necessary to pay more for import-substitution products than imports would cost. This reasoning fails to take account of two points of decisive importance. First of all, there is the low income-elasticity of exports. If their volume is increased, their prices will go down, and after a certain point the periphery would experience a deterioration in the terms of trade, thus suffering heavier losses than the higher cost involved in the promotion of import-substitution activities. Second, these activities make it possible, within certain limits, to achieve a higher growth rate of the global product which more than outweighs the higher cost involved. Protection is thus an economically sound solution, provided it is applied in a rational manner, as it is always necessary to insist.

Of course, it is quite true that protection on the part of the periphery has infringed from the very beginning on the free play of the international market forces on which the original concept of GATT was based.

All the foregoing concerns the periphery, but it would seem that the most difficult problems lie with the centers. It is hardly surprising that these should resort to restrictions outside the ambit of GATT when they are suffering from serious unemployment. As already noted, however, they were very reluctant to liberalize their own trade, even during the years of prolonged prosperity and even in the case of countries suffering from a shortage of labor which threw wide their doors to immigrants. Nothing seems to indicate as yet that in the future, even when the current difficulties are overcome, the centers will be willing to make any really significant changes in their attitudes. I think that this is a fundamental problem whose true significance has not been made fully clear. Yet it is essential that this should be done if we are to find solutions capable of reconciling the interests of the centers and the periphery in increasing growth. It is therefore worth going into more detail on this subject.

As already noted, in the past development of the centers the fabulous increase in productivity has not been reflected in a steady decline in prices, but has been retained internally. This is a structural phenomenon which has constituted a very important factor in the accumulation of capital and in the carrying out of technological innovations. The periphery has only participated to a marginal extent in this process, except insofar as it has produced raw materials which the centers needed. It is doubtful whether capitalism would have been able to develop so vigorously if it had not been for this form of retention of the fruits of technical progress, especially in the upper strata.

The industrialization of the periphery was not a spontaneous consequence of this capitalist expansion, for the centers were only interested in investing in the periphery in order to obtain from it the primary commodities they needed: they had no intention of establishing industries there which could export anything other than primary products. For a number of reasons, they preferred to carry on industrial production in their own part of the world, and consequently the industrialization of the periphery was the result of its own decision in response to the severe crises in the centers: two World Wars and a Great Depression between them.

Be that as it may, the periphery, which had first been forced to industrialize through import substitution because of these critical conditions in the centers, gradually learned afterwards to export manufactures, thanks to the prosperity reigning in the centers and through the use of deliberate promotional measures. If this prosperity were to return in a few years, although not necessarily at the same level as before, the question would arise of whether the centers would be willing to follow a liberalization policy such as they have put into effect among themselves. Let us examine this very important aspect for a moment.

Up to now, the exports of manufactures from the periphery have been carried out only by a few countries and have accounted for a relatively small part of its potential. Would the centers be willing to liberalize their imports if this export effort reached large dimensions?

Let us reflect on the following fact. If success was achieved in the export of manufactures, this was because the exporting countries were capable of adopting techniques similar to those of the centers (although corresponding to less advanced phases of the latters' development) to produce goods for which the demand tends to grow less rapidly than the demand for the increasingly technologically advanced goods coming from the innovations made in the centers. It is hardly surprising that the possibility of access to advanced technologies and the lower level of wages have enabled the exporting countries to compete successfully with similar goods produced in the centers.

This fact could signify the beginning of a process of reversal of what has been occurring in the past development of the centers. It should be recalled that the fruits of technical progress have not been reflected in a corresponding reduction in prices, and that generally speaking the ability of the centers to open up external markets has not been due as much to lower prices as to the unceasing diversification of goods deriving from their technological innovations. It would appear, however, that this is not the way in which the exports of the periphery have been competing in the centers; instead, they have been exploiting their lower prices.

Although this reaction of the periphery to this historical process has still not reached large proportions, in view of the growing export possibilities it is necessary to think seriously about the possibile consequences of the accentuation of this phenomenon.[6] What will the centers do in the face of this process? Will they continue to maintain and increase their restrictions, as they have been doing so far outside GATT, or will they resort to the use of devaluation as an instrument, as the periphery has been recommended to do so many times?

As well as containing imports, devaluation would reduce the external prices of exports, even those which were already fully competitive. The reason we mention this is not because we believe that it is likely to occur, but merely in order to emphasize the difficult choice which the centers have to face. On the one hand, they would continue to violate the principle of GATT which they have defended so much; on the other hand, they would have to resign themselves to losing, through the lower prices of their exports, part of the fruits of their technical progress, with all the great disturbances that would imply.

In the meantime, a comment is called for which is not without importance. The centers have always proclaimed to the periphery the advantages of the international division of labor within the system of market laws. This attitude was completely in line with their interests, although it prejudiced the development of the periphery. Now that the periphery has begun to export, however, the centers are departing from those principles on which the existence of GATT is based.

To tell the truth, those principles, although they continue to be of great validity in the centers and in spite of the conjunctural phenomena mentioned elsewhere, have not been in keeping with the requirements of peripheral development in the past. Moreover, at present they actually militate against such development because they outlaw protection.

On the other hand, it cannot be denied that the centers will be exposed to growing adverse effects if, in this new stage of industrialization of the periphery, those principles continue to be fully valid. Let us recall the nature of the accumulation process, whose source lies in the increase in productivity which is not passed on in the form of reduced prices but is reflected in the displacement of demand to increasingly diversified goods and services. Obviously, increased competition from imports through a reduction in their prices, far from generating investment resources in the enterprises, reduces their surplus in the prejudice of accumulation. This competition thus generates unemployment and weakens accumulation. In contrast, when the unemployment is due to increased productivity, this increase produces an accumulation potential which, if utilized, enables the unemployment to be offset. This is the serious problem which is causing so much concern and which must be faced immediately if we are to find mutually advantageous solutions.

Clearly, it would suit the periphery much better to be able gradually to take advantage of the market of the centers without the need to resort to an exaggerated reduction of prices at the expense of the fruits of their technical progress. This would not suit the centers either. Up to now, without referring to the exports of the latter, we can say that they have tried to defend themselves through arrangements such as the Multifibers Agreement and so-called voluntary accords in order to limit exports from the periphery. As well as constituting discriminatory action — since they affect only the periphery and not the centers — these measures are not in line with the contractual system of GATT and are always subject to the threat of further unilateral decisions by the centers. Of course, the principles of GATT are not fundamentally applicable to these new tensions, which call for a new institutional system, as the UNCTAD (United Nations Commission on Trade and Development) Secretariat has suggested.

It is necessary, then, to explore other avenues which suit both the interests of the centers and those of the periphery. New ways of recognizing comparative advantages in practice are required. There can be no doubt that it is in the interests of the periphery to gain access to the markets of the centers for goods which are in line with their technological capacity. They would then be able to import the other technologically advanced goods produced by the centers, goods that would be very costly for them to substitute at the present stage of their technological development. This would also mean clear advantages for the centers, because of the ever wider field thus offered for the exploitation of their technological innovations. In other words, it would suit the centers to export goods with a high technological content in exchange for imports of goods with a lower technological content from the periphery. This would also be advantageous for the periphery itself.

Of course, I am not making concrete proposals, but simply stressing the need to explore these issues. What is needed is to reach formulas which gradually and progressively open up the markets of the centers without the risks of unlimited competition.

Clearly, the formulas should not be static but eminently dynamic. Exports of manufactures by the countries of the periphery, together with import substitution, will enable their industrialization to be made increasingly efficient and, at the same time, promote their technological development. It will therefore be understood that this advance would make it possible to increase the exports of goods which are at present not technologically accessible to the periphery. This has already happened in the case of countries which, although once peripheral, have finally attained technological homogeneity and become integrated into trade with the centers.

The peripheral countries which are advancing in their industrialization are passing through a transitional period which is more or less prolonged, in line with the big differences existing among them. If this process continues, there will be a steady expansion in actual fact, and not just in a formal manner, in the scope of the international division of labor within GATT and the mutually advantageous observance of its principles, including eventually that of reciprocity.

The role of the centers will be of considerable importance during this transitional period: up to what point will they be able to open themselves up substantially to the periphery? In the light of what has been said before, there would appear to be serious doubts about this: there is nothing to indicate that, even in the best of cases, the periphery could dispatch to the centers all the exports it would need to make in order to acquire the enormous amounts of goods required for this development.

There is no justification for placing exaggerated emphasis on exports to the centers while failing to give sufficient importance to exports of manufactures within the periphery itself. The main obstacle continues to be the economic division of the periphery, which is a clear manifestation of the way in which the centers, through the very dynamics of their own development, have left the periphery on the sidelines of industrialization.

According to the past system of the international division of labor, each peripheral country converged separately towards the centers, with very little intra-peripheral mutual trade. Import substitution used protection in a general manner, without establishing preferences among the developing countries. On top of the violation of conventional principles represented by protection in itself, such preferences would have added something which the centers would have rejected as open discrimination. Thus, import substitution was carried out in water-tight compartments and not much progress has been made in the arrangements arrived at over the course of time to try to do away gradually with these compartments.

One of the main reasons (although not the only one) why this division has lasted was the illusion, during the long years of prosperity in the centers, that the indefinite expansion of exports of manufactures made it unnecessary to continue with an active import-substitution policy combined with mutual exports within the periphery itself. Furthermore, the centers either actively opposed measures aimed at correcting the fragmentation of the periphery or, even in the best of circumstances, were indifferent to them and failed to give them the support which would have been of great significance in this respect. This was yet another of the consequences of the centripetal growth pattern which first of all prevented the periphery from industrializing and subsequently kept it on the sidelines of trade in industrial products.

It is worth repeating once again that this centripetal growth pattern is a primary factor in the centers' lack of any real interest in the development of the periphery, except inasmuch as it is important to their own development. I refer to the development of the periphery in all its social depth, that is to say, the process whereby the advantages of technical progress are spread throughout the structure of society and are not limited to a relatively small part of the labor force.

This assertion may seem surprising in view of the active role which the transnational corporations have played in the industrialization of the periphery in recent decades. At first, the centers opposed this development. However, once the process was well under way and appeared to be irreversible, they stimulated the participation of these transnationals, which thus took advantage of import substitution after having previously opposed it. It was claimed that the transnationals would be agents of the internationalization of production. Their most important role, however, has been to internationalize forms of consumption rather than those of production, since they have been an important factor in opening up the markets for the centers. In other words, without ignoring their technological contribution, the transnational corporations have nevertheless taken advantage of the industrialization of the periphery without making any serious contribution towards offering it international horizons.

Very important changes are now taking place in the world economy. Thus, we are at present witnessing, among other events which cause profound concern, the decline of productivity in the centers. The increase in productivity no longer seems to be a process which occurs automatically in the capitalist growth pattern. It must now be the result of a deliberate policy, in both the domestic and the international fields. It is therefore to be expected that new criteria should now be adopted in tackling the problem of relations with the periphery, including the question of comparative trade advantages. This problem must be approached, however, not in the previous ways, but in response to a situation which is very different from that which existed when the periphery began its industrialization. There is now no longer any doubt about the periphery's increasing capacity to achieve this, and it must therefore be allowed to participate in the sustained and growing process of comparative advantages, where it would make a notable contribution to increased productivity in the world economy.

3. The Appropriation and Retention of the Fruits of Technical Progress and the Distribution Struggle

Since we attached so much importance to the structural phenomenon of the surplus, the time has now come to explain, firstly how it comes about, next how it is retained, and lastly how the social struggle to share in the fruits of technical progress triggers the trend towards dynamic disequilibrium between the rate of expenditure and that of reproductive capital accumulation. This trend inevitably leads to inflation and cannot be contained by means of the monetary instrument without those huge economic and social costs which we stress above.

Let us begin, then, with a simple schematic explanation of the economic surplus. The surplus is closely linked to technical progress, which finds expression, thanks to capital accumulation, in a continous superimposition of new technical layers of increasing productivity on layers of lesser productivity. This is a process which is incessantly renewed.

It happens that when a technical layer is added in which productivity is higher than in those preceding it, the wages and salaries of the labor force thus employed do not improve correlatively with the increment in productivity. Within the play of market laws, an improvement will be obtained only by that part of the labor force which possesses the increasing skills that technical progress demands. The increase in productivity is the result of these skills plus capital accumulation in and through which technological innovations take shape. The wages of the rest of the labor force employed in new technical layers do not increase correlatively with productivity for a very simple reason: competition on the part of the labor force which is left behind in lower-productivity layers where income is less, and on the part of the labor force entering the market, prevents wages from rising at a rate equal to the increased productivity of the new technical layer.

I have applied the term surplus to the productivity increment which, not being transferred to the labor force, remains in enterprises and is appropriated by the owners of the means of production. A clear distinction must be drawn, moreover, between the surplus and the remuneration of those who organize the actual productive activity, whether they are the owners of the means of production or not.

The surplus has its origin, then, in structural heterogeneity, that is, in the diversity of technical layers, levels of productivity, and incomes of the labor force. It is conceivable that capital accumulation and the skills necessary to meet its requirements may tend to lead progressively to homogeneity, with similar levels of productivity and equal pay for equal skills. In that case, the surplus would peter out, as would likewise its dynamic role in accumulation, and other forms of capital accumulation would have to be put in its place. In any event, the process would be a relatively slow one, and would be threatened by the incessant diversification of goods and services which militates against reproductive capital accumulation, as well as by population growth, especially in the periphery.

Meanwhile, the redistributive power of the labor force and of the State gradually achieves what market laws are slow to accomplish. And as redistribution takes place, the expansion of expenditure which it involves is added to the ever-increasing expenditure of the social groups benefitting from the surplus. Thus, the system tends towards that dynamic disequilibrium between the rate of expenditure and the rate of reproductive capital accumulation which was mentioned above.

This tendency towards disequilibrium cannot be explained, however, without showing — likewise briefly — how the surplus is retained in enterprises, instead of being socially disseminated as the neoclassical theories assume, and how, in the course of structural changes in society, the redistributive power of the labor force and the State weakens the growth rate of the surplus, to the detriment of the rate of reproductive capital accumulation.

My interpretation is based on study of the dynamics of the production process and the various phases that occur during the period of time between the primary phase and the stage when the final goods (both consumer and capital goods, between which there is no difference where the production process as such is concerned) are launched on the market.

This introduction of the time factor is essential, as is likewise the growth of production. Otherwise, it would be impossible to explain how the increase in productivity which has been achieved in the various phases can be absorbed without a fall in prices. If enterprises do not transfer the whole of the productivity increment to wages, the demand stemming from their expenditures will be insufficient in relation to the growth in productivity.

Herein lies the significance of the time factor in the dynamics of the production process. In order to understand it, the various phases of production under way must be clearly distinguished from the final stage of output of final goods. Demand for the latter does not derive from the income that the enterprises have paid out formerly in the course of their production but from income earned during the process of producing new final goods, goods that will be offered on the market later on.

Such, in the dynamics of production, is the effect of the time factor. Because of it, the amount of goods in process of production, during a given period of time, is larger than the quantity of final goods in the same period. In other words, final goods lag behind current production. Thus, the increase in final goods, in any period in relation to the one before it could not be absorbed without the expansion of demand deriving from the income paid out by enterprises in the course of the production underway between those same periods.

The additional amount of final goods results both from the increase in employment and the rise in productivity. And if demand expands enough, the productivity increment stays in the enterprises in the form of a larger surplus (or an increase in profits, in a first approximation).

It should be explained that this larger surplus is not obtained in its entirety when the final goods are sold on the market; step by step it appears in each phase of the production process, in accordance with the demand expected by the enterprises concerned. Thus, partial surpluses emerge. If the demand for final goods is sufficient and confirms expectation, it can continue at the same rate for the whole of the production under way. Otherwise, adjustments in one or another direction will be necessary, according to whether the demand for final goods does or does not expand sufficiently to absorb the increase in those goods.

We are now in a position to introduce the creation of money into our argument. We were saying that the income paid out in the course of production generated the demand for final goods. If this demand is sufficient, enterprises in the final phase recover the income they paid out in due course and obtain their partial surplus. If production were static, the money thus obtained by enterprises would suffice for the purchase of goods produced during the preceding phase and for payment of their own labor force. And the same thing would happen in every phase. In the course of increasing production, on the contrary, the money obtained by enterprises in the various phases would not be enough both to step up their own employment and to purchase the goods in process of production in the preceding phase, the corresponding partial surplus included.

Thus, as production under way increases, enterprises have to resort to the creation of money by the bank system, except to the limited extent that they may have stocks of money available (for simplicity's sake, we shall eliminate this possible increase in the circulation of money, which makes no difference to our argument).

The role of the monetary authority, then, is to permit the creation of the money required for the growth of income in production under way, so that the increment in demand thus generated may be equivalent to the increase in output of final goods.[7] In this way, monetary stability can be maintained.

There are two principal sources of an increase in demand, namely, the growth of ongoing production, as has been explained, or the expenditure of the State, when its income does not suffice to cover its disbursements and recourse has to be taken to the creation of money. Inflation likewise has its origin in these two main sources.

We will now consider the inflation stemming from ongoing production. The additional income paid out by enterprises in the course of production corresponds to the increase both in employment and in salaries and wages. According to the playing out of market laws, wage increases are related in part to the rise in productivity that enterprises expect to achieve. However, it should be recalled that another part of productivity, that which is not transferred to the labor force, contributes to the growth of the surplus.

What happens when the labor force is no longer passive and acquires the necessary power to increase its wages at a rate higher than the growth rate of productivity, whether in quest of a genuine improvement or in order to recover losses incurred through taxation?

Obviously, in such a case the expansion of demand originating in production under way outstrips the increase in productivity, with a corresponding increase in the level of prices. Under these circumstances, what can the monetary authority do in order to maintain price stability? Here a restrictive monetary policy comes into the picture. If this policy is applied with firmness and continuity, it produces results that we all know. The rate of economic activity falls and unemployment appears or increases. The philosophy behind contractionary monetary policy is just to compel the labor force to accept lower wages and salaries. This philosophy is part and parcel of conventional neoclassical theories according to which the union and political power of the labor forces constitutes a departure from market laws; in this type of reasoning, unemployment is seen as a way of restoring not only the laws of the market but also the growth of the surplus. However, what these theories do not take into consideration is the sheer fact that, even under the full play of market forces, the fruits of productivity growth are not socially disseminated but are appropriated by the high social strata in the form of economic surplus.

In practice, while unemployment is seen as a way of reinstituting the play of market forces, the success in the use of this instrument depends initially on the intensity of the trade union and political power of the labor force. If this power is weak, it can be eliminated by unemployment. If, on the contrary, it is strong, the labor force will resist the decreases in their earnings. The result of the latter case is simply that enterprises, being deprived of an additional amount of money creation, have to divert their funds from capital accumulation to pay for higher wages and salaries. Naturally, this is detrimental to employment and gives rise to the phenomenon of stagflation, with which we are all familiar. In sum, in peripheral societies where the labor force has strong power, the monetary instrument tends to lose its efficacy. Its use often becomes counterproductive. Sooner or later, both enterprises and the unemployed exercise growing political pressures on the monetary authority, which finally has to yield and expand its credit creation in order to increase employment again. This not only enhances the political power of the labor force but also brings a new inflationary spiral with all its well-known adverse consequences.

Let us consider this phenomenon from another perspective. To the consumption of the high-income strata, one should add the consumption obtained by the labor force through its union and political power as well as the civil and military consumption of the State. Generally, in peripheral societies, these additional forms of consumption are not detrimental to the privileged consumption of high-income groups but are superimposed on it. As a result, a tendency to disequilibrium between the rate of expenditure and the rate of capital accumulation emerges, the final outcome of which is a new type of social inflation, one that cannot be attacked with the monetary instrument. The monetary authority in this situation is really dethroned.

It is true that if monetary restrictions are applied with great energy, even the best organized labor movement can be forced to yield, and correspondingly the rate of inflation may fall. But the economic and social costs of this type of policy are of such magnitude that eventually a monetary expansion will be called forth. With it, the power of the labor force will be restored and a new inflationary wave will be set into motion.

Those familiar with events in Latin America have witnessed the use of another instrument — other than monetary policy — in counteracting inflation. I refer to the instrument of force. One of the arguments given to justify the interruption or suppression of democratic processes has been the need to stop the inflationary spiral by eliminating the union and the political power of the labor force, so that the free play of market forces is restored and prices are allowed to attain their "own level." In this way, it is argued, the surplus will recuperate its dynamic. It so happens, however, that the instrument of force, instead of substantially stimulating reproductive capital accumulation, yields a greater impulse to the privileged consumption of the high-income strata of society. Furthermore, notwithstanding the control of remunerations and the freedom of prices, inflation generally continues due to external as well as internal factors. The latter correspond frequently to a budget deficit that is not corrected by orthodox fiscal policies, because its correction would require an increase in taxes falling on those groups which generally support the use of force by the State.

May I say in passing that the democratic process is sooner or later bound to be restored in those countries of Latin America where the use of force has suppressed it. It is all for the good. However, I have a great concern. I am afraid that in countries undergoing redemocratization the attempt to counteract inflationary forces will be utterly defeated, unless there is a transformation in the process of capital accumulation and income distribution. Indeed, given the existing pattern of capital accumulation and income distribution, the democratic process tends to devour itself. The enduring success of democratic processes crucially depends on a very serious change in the structure of political power. We cannot retreat to the past in order to assure the free play of economic forces in a social structure that is quite different. Nor can we continue with the disruptive process of appropriation and redistribution of the fruits of productivity. I do not see any other solution than the macroeconomic regulation by the State of the process of accumulation and distribution, and this implies very important institutional changes. If you wish to call this "socialism," I accept it, but it is a form of socialism combined with the play of the market forces. For economic as well as for political reasons, the market has to be preserved and purified. What is important is to deal with the structures and institutions that are behind the market. The time has arrived for a synthesis between socialism and liberalism.

4. Summary and Conclusions

Let me summarize now the main points elaborated in previous sections and offer some final reflections.

I do not deny the logical validity of neoclassical theories. However, they do not adequately explain the real phenomena of capitalist development in the periphery. Indeed, they omit from their reasoning the structure of society, its mutations, and the changes in power relations resulting from them. I have stressed that there is no tendency in peripheral capitalism to disseminate socially the fruits of development. This is due to the structural factors that lead to the appropriation of a large part of the fruits-of-productivity increases by the high social strata in the form of economic surplus.

This system of appropriation of the surplus could function well during the stage of development in which the power of appropriation prevailed, unchallenged by counteracting forces. Thus, under the full play of market forces, the dynamics of the system were based on a marked social inequality.

This stage was, however, temporary. The mutations of the social structure in the course of development have been accompanied by the appearance and strengthening of power-sharing by the labor force, which has interfered with the laws of the market. Furthermore, with the emergence of strong unions and the expansion and diversification of the functions of the State, the monetary instrument has tended to lose its efficacy. Why? Because under these new circumstances, the increment of global income paid to the labor force has the tendency to surpass the increment in productivity — a situation that is detrimental to capital accumulation and usually results in inflationary spirals. True, a sufficiently energetic contractionary monetary policy can correct the deviation of labor income growth from productivity growth, but it does so at the cost of unemployment and economic contraction, so much so that the pressure of labor and business finally prevails and the monetary authority is forced to expand credit. As this happens, the sharing of power by labor and the State is restored, and so is the danger of a new inflationary wave. The monetary authority thus becomes dethroned.

In the context of this struggle for sharing in the surplus, there is indeed no regulatory mechanism that assumes an adequate relationship between the increase in global nominal income and the increase in productivity. My firm conclusion is that the mutations in the structure of society and the corresponding changes in power relations make it impossible for the system to function satisfactorily and to avoid constant disequilibria. A macroeconomic regulatory mechanism compatible with the market system is required.

A regulatory mechanism is also indispensible in the relations of the periphery with the centers. The laws of the market were relevant during a stage of development when the centers and the dominant social groups in the periphery could reap the advantages of the international division of labor, to the detriment of peripheral industrialization and employment.

Industrialization came with a great historical delay. In the course of time, the periphery has been able to export manufactures with a lower technological content (in comparison with manufactures exported from the centers). But this is proving to have some disruptive effects that could be aggravated by further industrialization in the periphery. Here, again, we have to recognize the need to regulate. The free play of the market forces at the international level will not solve the problem, nor will it promote the vigorous reciprocal trade inside the periphery that is needed to correct its economic fragmentation.

These regulations in trade or in internal peripheral development are far from being easy, either politically or economically. But there are no alternatives. It is regrettable that the free play of the market forces cannot eliminate the external and internal constraints on development, as expected in the light of conventional theories. Although the market is of paramount economic and political importance, there is really no magic in the workings of the market.

EDITORS' NOTES

1. Extensive statements of Dr. Prebisch's critical assessment of neoclassical theories of development are found in various of his recent writings. In particular, "The Neoclassical Theories of Economic Liberalism," *Cepal Review*, no. 7 (1979); and "Dialogue on Friedman and Hayek. From the Standpoint of the Periphery," *Cepal Review*, no. 15 (1981).

2. Dr. Prebisch has retraced in more detail the stages in his intellectual journey in "Five States in my Thinking of Development," IBRD/The World Bank, Washington, 1982.

3. The central ideas outlined in this paper have been developed more fully by Dr. Prebisch in a series of articles published in the *Cepal Review* since 1976. In particular, the reader is referred to "A Critique of Peripheral Capitalism," *Cepal Review*, no. 1 (1976); "Socio-Economic Structure and the Crisis of Peripheral Capitalism," *Cepal Review*, no. 6 (1978); "Towards a Theory of Social Change," *Cepal Review*, no. 10 (1980).

4. For a recent article reviewing the sociological aspects in Prebisch's work see Adolfo Gurrieri, "La Dimensión Sociológica en la Obra de Prebisch," *Pensamiento Iberoramericano*, no. 2 (1982).

5. Dr. Prebisch articulated this thesis in his "The Economic Development of Latin America and Its Principal Problems" which made its appearance in mimeographed form in 1949, and which was fully reprinted subsequently in the *Economic Bulletin for Latin America*, vol. 7, no. 1, Santiago, Chile, 1962. This essay was baptized by Albert Hirschman as "the CEPAL manifesto." See A. Hirschman, "Ideologies of Economic Development in Latin American," in *A Bias for Hope* (New Haven, Conn.: Yale University Press, 1971), pp. 280–281. Prebisch's 1949 article along with his classic "Commercial Policy in the Underdeveloped Countries," *American Economic Review* 49, no. 2 (1959), constitute central building blocks to what came to be known as the "Prebisch-Cepal Doctrine." Prebisch's writings of the 1950s produced an uproar of critical responses among "orthodox" economists who focused principally on one aspect of those writings, namely, the question of the deterioration of the terms of trade. The most notable example was that of Gottfried Haberler (see his "The Terms of Trade and Economic Development," in H. S. Ellis, *El Desarrollo Económico y América Latina* [Mexico City: Fondo de Cultura Económica, 1957], pp. 325–51). For a discussion of the sense in which Haberler misunderstood Prebisch, as well as for an insightful examination of the ideas of Prebisch and of CEPAL, their evolution and their enduring contribution, see F. H. Cardoso, "The Originality of a Copy: CEPAL and the Idea of Development," *Cepal Review* (2d half of 1977): 7–40. A rather comprehensive bibliography of Prebisch's writings can be found in O. Rodriguez, *La Teoría del Subdesarrollo de la CEPAL*. (Mexico: Siglo XXI Editores, 1980).

6. On Prebisch's interpretation of the economic crisis of the early 1980s, its effects and historical meaning for the periphery, see his article "A Historical Turning Point for the Latin American Periphery," *Cepal Review*, no. 18 (1982).

7. The role played by the monetary authority in peripheral societies in connection with the process of appropriation and defense of the surplus has been discussed more extensively by Dr. Prebisch in his article "Monetarism, Open-Economy Policies and Ideological Crisis," *Cepal Review*, no. 17 (1982).

Social Disarticulation in Latin American History

Alain de Janvry

The history of many Latin American countries, and particularly those of the Southern Cone, has been characterized by an oscillation between democratic and authoritarian forms of government. Frequent changes of democratic regimes have led to economic destabilization and to political delegitimation resulting in the emergence of military regimes. While often able to engineer spectacular economic growth, military regimes have also run into economic and legitimation crises, allowing the return of constitutional forms of government. There is, as a result of these oscillations, an active debate among Latin American social scientists on the causes of both the failure of democracy and the exit from military regimes. Explanatory factors for both transitions have proved to be extremely weak. A systematic study of the rise of authoritarian regimes has failed to establish any stable association between economic and political factors (Collier, 1979). And the current analyses by social scientists of the process of redemocratization have focused almost exclusively on political factors: the delegitimation and repression by the military, the softening of ideological positions, and the formation of broad democratic class alliances (Garretón; Cavarozzi).

The thesis of this paper is that the cause for the long-run instability of democratic regimes originates in the failure of establishing an economic model able to translate productivity gains into wage gains and, hence, of reconciling growth with equity. Authoritarian forms of government are the political expression of patterns of growth that feed on cheap labor and on growing inequality in the distribution of income. The implication of this thesis is that redemocratization as a political process without a corresponding redefinition of the economic model implemented and of the class distribution of the benefits from growth is at best a temporary phenomenon. Countries to which this proposition applies most urgently are Argentina, Brazil, and Chile, which are all at political turning points between military and democratic regimes. In all cases, the stabilization of recently established or soon expected democratic regimes requires the urgent redefinition of the economic models to be implemented relative to the models that have led to the destabilization of democracy in the past or that were implemented under military surveillance. Without falling into the trap of presuming a linear determination of the economic by the political, I am arguing here that a broad correspondence needs to be established between the two levels in order for participatory forms of government to be given a chance of stability.

In the current context of international economic crises and exhaustion of the economic models followed in the past, such as import-substitution industrialization (ISI) and neoliberal export-led growth, new styles of development need to be defined and implemented. The crisis, in spite of its devastating social costs, thus can be seen as creating new opportunities for economic and political redefinition. What remains to be determined is a style of development that is consistent with the current international export pessimism, that is able to tie productivity gains in the sphere of production to real wage increases in the sphere of circulation in spite of structural unemployment, and that provides at least the objective (i.e., the necessary if not sufficient) basis for stable democratic forms of government.

My thesis is that the only style of development able to achieve these results in the current conjuncture is what I call "social articulation": namely, a growth path which is led by the production of wage goods and by the creation of effective demand for the domestic absorption of these wage goods, with trade serving as a handmaiden of articulation. To argue the case for this style of development, I will show that the failure to establish social articulation has been at the basis of the incapacity of democratic governments to remain in power in the Southern Cone countries and that its opposite, "social disarticulation," has been the style of development implemented by authoritarian regimes.

To defend this thesis, I will proceed in four stages, First, I will outline a theoretical framework useful to characterize and to analyze alternative styles of development. This will be used to establish the contrasted logic of accumulation under social articulation and disarticulation. Second, I will look at the different development theories that have been elaborated in or for Latin America in order to show how each theory conceptualizes, implicitly or explicitly, the question of social articulation and what type of programs it recommends in order to achieve social articulation. Third, I will review archetypical historical experiences of styles of development in particular countries and time periods in relation to the question of articulation and political regime. The purpose of this will be to understand the underlying causes of the reported failures to create social articulation as well as the contradictions of social disarticulation leading to the exit from this style of development. Finally, I will make some comments on a strategy of transition to social articulation based on the Latin American theoretical and historical experience.

1. A Framework for the Analyses of Styles of Development

A useful framework for the characterization of alternative styles of development can be derived from the work of Kalecki. According to him, the fundamental macroeconomic relationship that characterizes all economic systems is the necessary balance between expansion of the production capacity and expansion of the consumption capacity. Failure to maintain this balance will lead to crises of either underconsumption or inflation. In terms of styles of development, the central issue is that expansion of the production capacity can be obtained on the basis of several alternative economic sectors, while expansion of the consumption capacity can occur by creating effective demand in alternative geographical and social class locations.

Looking first at the production capacity of the economic system, let me call the "key sector of economic growth" that general production sector which has the highest gross rate of capital formation, i.e., that which is favored by new investments and that which consequently should have the highest rate of growth (de Janvry and Sadoulet, 1983). There are several alternative choices apparent immediately, each of which will correspond to a different style of development: key sectors can be directed at the production of exportables, luxury goods, or wage goods. The expansion of the production capacity of each of these alternative key growth sectors must correspond (following Kalecki's necessary relation) to expansion of the consumption capacity for the type of commodities they produce. This defines the geographical and social location of effective demand creation. It will be the international market if the key growth sectors produce exportables; the upper income classes, where income is derived from profit and rent and redistribution of part of these under the forms of salaries and transfers to numerous "subsumed" classes (Wolff and Resnick), if the key sector produces luxuries; and the working class if the key sectors produce wage goods. Note that the definition of luxury versus wage goods is, thus, not physical but economic, or more broadly, social: the same commodity, such as automobiles, for instance, can be a wage good in one country and a luxury good in another according to the level of wage income. This is precisely the drama of the current internationalization of consumption patterns: commodities which appear the same in a physical sense imply in countries at different levels of wage income, a completely different social logic in terms of Kalecki's necessary relation and the social location of effective demand creation.

Using this framework, we can identify three contrasted styles of development in terms of the choice of key growth sectors and of the geographical/social location of effective demand. These are export-led, luxury-led, and wage goods-led growth patterns. The first two are "socially disarticulated" in the sense that the necessary Kaleckian relation between production and consumption does not imply a relation between profits (the investment of which is the source of expansion of the production capacity) and wages. Consequently, accelerated disarticulated growth will tend to feed on cheap labor; and this type of development will be characterized by growth with increasing inequality in the distribution of income and usually repressive forms of government to contain wage demands in spite of eventually rapid productivity growth.

A wage goods-led development pattern, by contrast, will be "socially articulated" in the sense that the necessary Kaleckian relation implies a balance between profits and wages and, hence, between growth and equity. While all types of inequities can still exist under social articulation, such as labor market segmentation, sex discrimination, racism, corruption, etc., this style of development at least contains an objective logic for equitable growth and for participatory forms of government. While the conflictive claims of capital and labor in the division of the social surplus between profits and wages prevent the smooth meeting of Kalecki's balance at every point in time, and thus results in cycles and crises, that balance remains an inescapable macroeconomic requirement for the long-run growth path.

In practice, both articulated and disarticulated growth patterns tend to coexist in a given country, with one pattern dominating the other at a particular point in time. For one thing, a disarticulated growth path always implies the presence of articulation since the wages paid in the luxury and export sectors create an effective demand for wage goods. With surplus labor and fixed wages, the wage-goods sector expands under the pull of effective demand resulting from employment creation in the luxury and export sectors as well as in the wage-goods sectors to satisfy the demand for workers in the other two sectors (de Janvry, 1981).

More importantly, articulated and disarticulated patterns will coexist in a hierarchical fashion because they correspond to two patterns of class alliances with divergent economic logics. The first includes the wage-goods-producing bourgeoisie and organized labor; the second, the luxury and export-producing bourgeoisies usually closely associated with foreign capital. As will be seen, much of the political instability in Latin

America can be understood as the struggle between these two alliances for control over the state. Repeated failures at establishing social articulation reflect, in particular, the political incapacity of the "articulated alliance" to displace lastingly the "disarticulated alliance" from its historical hegemonic control of the state.

A word of caution is relevant here about the relationship between the economic and the political. I am not presuming a linear determination of the economic over the political but only establishing a broad correspondence, supported by both theory and history, between a pattern of accumulation (articulated or disarticulated) and a form of government (participatory or authoritarian). Enacting this correspondence can begin at the level of either the economic or the political. In the context of the current Latin American discourse on redemocratization, the point of this paper is that democracy without articulation is bound to be another of these ephemeral illusions that have marked the political history of that continent. Not that either could not hold without the other in the short run. But to think of a return to democracy as political scientists often do in terms of a shift in the pattern of class alliances without addressing the question of the key sector of economic growth and of the social and geographical location of effective demand can only be a myopic exercise in social delusion.

Using this framework for the analysis of styles of development, we can now look at the evolution of thought in development theory and ask how the different schools of thought that have prevailed in Latin America, explicitly and implicitly, have endorsed different styles of development.

2. Theories of Underdevelopment and Styles of Development

To contrast theories of development and to reveal the styles of development that each endorses we must analyze them at two levels: at the level of positive economics, we need to identify what is the theory of growth or stagnation and what is the theory of income and poverty that it contains. At the level of normative economics, we need to identify what is the growth strategy and what is the anti-poverty approach which it proposes.

In order to classify development theories, it is useful to begin from the great split in economic thought which originated with Adam Smith (Figure 1). His theory of the "wealth of nations" contains both a vision of harmony in the operation of the free market and a vision of exploitation in his understanding of the labor theory of value. Harmony and exploitation as guiding principles of economic relations were to be at the

basis of the great division between the Marshallian tradition of the
neoclassics and Keynes on the one hand, who rescued the principle of
harmony (Pareto optimality, comparative advantage, and factor rewards
according to their marginal products), and Marx and the structuralists
on the other hand, who adopted the principle of exploitation (class conflicts, surplus generation and extraction, contradictions, and dialectics).
In development economics this division gave rise to three grand schools
of thought: modernization theory deriving from the principle of harmony
and laissez-faire, the theories of imperialism and neostructuralism deriving from the principle of exploitation, and the theory of developmentalism (*desarrollismo*) that rejected both the possibility of laissez-faire
and the inevitability of exploitation.

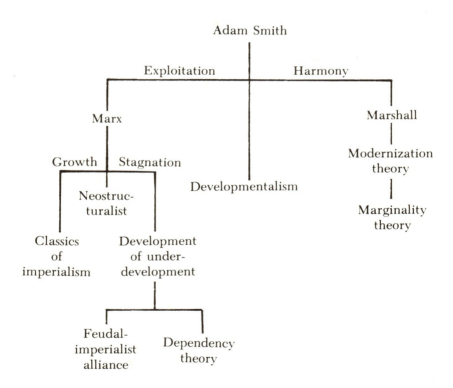

Figure 1: Genealogical Tree of Development Theories

Without entering into details, modernization theory and the interpretation it offers of growth and stagnation can be characterized by the following familiar snapshots: a vision of the linearity of history and of "normal patterns of growth" that can be decomposed into a succession of stages (Chenery and Syrquin, 1975; Kuznets, 1966; and Rostow, 1960); the existence of distortions relative to the norm of perfect competition as the cause of backwardness (Johnson, 1967); accumulation in the framework of socially articulated dualism (Jorgenson, 1969); traditional culture as a cause of low productivity (Schultz, 1964) and the key role of the diffusion of innovations, particularly technological, in the process of modernization (Rodgers, 1962); and specialization and trade according to comparative advantages resulting in a source of mutual benefits (Johnson, 1967). The theory of poverty is that of marginality: some individuals and regions have remained at the margin of integration in the market and in the other institutions of society. In a normative sense, the growth strategy that modernization theory advocates is that of liberalism: the promotion of technological change and human capital formation, a state that is passive in the marketplace, and the Chicago boys' triple motto: "Get those prices right, balance the budget, and open up!" The strategy to combat excessive forms of poverty, which could prove destabilizing to the existing social order, is that of social integration: acting from above to give access to the poor to the institutions of society.

From a liberal standpoint, ISI is severely criticized. Since a neoclassical world is assumed to prevail, distortions can be only antigrowth and self-defeating in the long run. And since countries are seen to end up with forms of state consistent with the chosen style of development, interventionism and distortions lead to centralization of the political system and nonparticipatory forms of government (North, 1979).

Developmentalism begins with the premise that Third World countries have structural characteristics that invalidate the assumption of modernization theory. Thus, a distinct theory of growth and stagnation is necessary — one that recognizes the existence of surplus labor and of socially disarticulated patterns of accumulation (Lewis, 1958) as well as of latent investment opportunities that can be activated by state intervention (Hirschman, 1981). Beyond recognizing the existence of an untapped employment creating growth potential and the fact that growth itself is a major force in the emergence of new social classes, developmentalism does not contain a theory of poverty. This failure, as we shall see, proved to be a serious limitation to successful implementation of developmentalist policies. In a normative sense, developmentalism advocates a growth strategy based on ISI promoted by active state intervention in the marketplace. Protectionism and subsidies, including overvaluation of the exchange rate to tax the primary export sector and subsidize imported capital goods, are to be used to create incentives to mobilize idle domestic resources and stimulate infant industries. Public investments are to be directed where linkages and big-push effects can be maximized. In terms of poverty, wages are expected to rise and the distribution of income is expected to improve once the "Lewis turning point" has been reached, i.e., once capital accumulation in industry has created enough employment to eliminate surplus labor. Via labor market effects, the Lewis turning point is to be a stage of transition from socially disarticulated to socially articulated growth since, once wages rise, industry finds an expanding market in the consumption of wage goods. In waiting for the Lewis turning point, however, the implicit developmentalist motto is "wait and repress (if needed)." As the emergence of military regimes with maturing developmentalist experiments has shown, this motto was unfortunately all too correct.

For the developmentalists, the liberal mode is seen to be tautological as it assumes the answer: it postulates that structural change, in some way, has already occurred and that the structural features of the Third World today are the same as those that prevail in the advanced countries. Social articulation, in particular, presumably has been achieved. Thus, structural change is not an issue in the liberal model while it is one for the developmentalists. Yet, the developmentalists see the need for structural change but not for structural reforms. For them, change will occur as a byproduct of growth itself, creating new social classes, undermining old privileges and the abuses of oligarchic and populist power, and establishing the basis for democratic forms of government. Articulation will be the product of growth. It is only the theories of development that derive from the concept of exploitation which will highlight the need for programs for structural change, by either reform or revolution, to establish social articulation.

There are basically four schools of thought in development economics that derive from the concept of exploitation. They can be contrasted in terms of the "law of uneven development" each portrays, i.e., accelerated growth or stagnation of the periphery relative to the center.

1. The classics of imperialism (Luxemburg, 1972; Lenin, 1973; and Bukharin, 1973) with a vision of the catching-up of the colonial relative to the advanced countries under the revolutionary transformation of capitalist expansion on a world scale.
2. The school of the development of underdevelopment which inverted the vision of the classics into one where capitalist expansion is a factor of underdevelopment and stagnation. This school, in turn, contains two contrasted versions:
   a. That of the "feudal-imperialist alliance" that attributes stag-

      nation to the permanence of feudal remnants associated with foreign capital, the extraction of an absolute instead of relative surplus value, and stifled partial transitions to capitalism (Kay, 1975; Weeks, 1977).

   b. That of dependency theory which, by contrast, sees capitalism everywhere in Latin America, ever since the beginning of colonial times, by defining it in the sphere of circulation and blames it for stagnation and poverty (Frank, 1969).

3. The neostructuralist school which looks at the possibility of eventual rapid growth in the Third World under conditions of "associated dependent development" and social disarticulation but with a tendency toward increasing inequality in the distribution of income and great instability over time (Cardoso, 1973; Marini, 1972).

For the sake of brevity, let me look here only at the styles of development advocated by dependency theory and neostructuralism — two schools of thought which are, of course, far from being internally unified.

Dependency theory is a theory of stagnation that looks at international surplus extraction between periphery and center as a cause of underdevelopment. Surplus is extracted via unequal exchange in trade (Prebisch, 1959; Emmanuel, 1972), via repatriation of profits by multinational corporations (Baran, 1957; Hymer, 1972; and Magdoff, 1969), via international labor migrations (Roemer, 1981), and via payment of interest on debt. There is no distinct theory of poverty which is seen to result directly from stagnation. The normative vision of styles of development falls into two categories — reformist and revolutionary. The reformists, basically represented by the Economic Commission for Latin America (Furtado, 1970; Sunkel, 1969), advocate selective delinking from the world economy to reject the international price system and an active role of the state in promoting reforms to enlarge the domestic market for wage goods, with land reforms and wage concessions as the key redistributive measures. While the style of growth advocated is one of social articulation by reform, this model is never fully spelled out, and reformist dependency theory ends up being more effective in denouncing obstacles than in providing a blueprint for development. This is even more clear in the revolutionary branch of dependency theory epitomized by Frank: capitalism is defined as production of commodities for profit and, thus, is seen omnipresent in Latin America since colonial times and held responsible for underdevelopment. A new style of development must emerge through a revolutionary transition to socialism with Guevara's "foco theory" as the strategy for change. But the postrevolutionary style of development is left unspecified.

The neostructuralist school emerges from the failure of dependency theory to explain the "economic miracles" that transformed many Latin American countries beginning in the mid-1960s. Luxury goods-led and export-led industrialization resulted in eventual rapid growth rates but with increasing inequalities in the distribution of income and great instability over time. The theories of growth and inequality that emerge are those of associated dependent development (Cardoso, 1973) and disarticulation (Marini, 1972). The theory of poverty is based on functional dualism and the articulation of modes of production between capitalists and peasants and artisans. The normative proposition is for styles of growth that are wage goods-led. Both liberalism and full-scale ISI are rejected: trade is to be made a handmaiden of articulated growth instead of a source of disarticulated accumulation. Social articulation will be obtained by profound redistributive reforms and by social incorporation of the popular sectors to allow them to engage in active defense of their economic interests at the level of the state.

In summary, we see that the question of social articulation has been central (if generally more implicit than explicit) to the Latin American debate on theories of underdevelopment and styles of growth. The neoliberals implicitly assume that social articulation has already been achieved and that growth should be export-led. The developmentalists argue that articulation will result from domestic market-oriented industrialization which, given the existing highly unequal distribution of income, implies a luxury-led pattern of growth as the engine of articulation. For both neoliberals and developmentalists, growth (even if it is to be obtained by very different routes) is seen as the instrument of development and the acceleration of growth the main policy implication. By contrast, the reformist *dependentistas* and the neostructuralists argue for social articulation as a result of reforms: control of the state over investment, and hence, over the choice of key growth sectors and income redistribution by land reforms and wage concessions to create the effective demand for wage goods. While the debate on theories of underdevelopment and styles of growth is yet to be resolved, the current crisis of development economics is nothing but the failure of theory to produce the anticipated results: the liberal model, which has been managed by the unholy alliance of the Chicago boys and the military, has lost credibility with the massive economic crises of the Southern Cone economies; developmentalism has failed to produce social change via growth, with industrialization resulting in sharply rising inequalities and authoritarian regimes instead of creating the basis for democratic forms of government; dependency theory, as a theory of stagnation, has failed to account for the economic miracles in many countries; and neostructuralism has yet to put forward a fully defined alternative to both ISI and export-led growth that can provide guidelines for the transition toward social articulation in the current context of global economic recession.

Thus, theory provides us with two approaches to the simultaneous achievement of growth and equity: articulation by growth and articulation by reform or revolution.

Articulation by growth is presumed to occur as a result of the tightening of the labor market through accelerated employment creation in the modern sector as a product of growth. In this case, the choice of the key growth sector is irrelevant: exports, luxuries, and wage goods will be preferred according to their respective capacities of sustaining rapid growth. If either of the first two is chosen, growth will be socially disarticulated and cheap labor will be the engine of growth until the Lewis turning point has been reached. This is the received doctrine of growth with equity via trickle-down effects. The strategy can fail, however: industrial growth may create insufficient employment to eliminate surplus labor due to the use of capital-intensive technology imported from the advanced countries; the rate of population growth may remain too high as poverty creates the logic for large families; and the rate of productive investment of capital income may be too low even if the share of capital in the industrial product is high. Since these conditions are characteristic of most Third World countries it is no wonder that the developmentalist's dream rarely materialized and served to justify, instead, poverty as an engine of growth.

Articulation by reform or revolution has been attempted following three alternative courses of action.

First, the redistribution of assets in private property in order to create, at the limit, the populist (Jeffersonian) vision of petty-bourgeois society where all households are simultaneously capitalists and workers. If social differentiation can be held in check, equitable growth should result. This is what Adelman advocates in her program of "redistribution before growth." To some extent, this is the basis on which equitable growth has been achieved in Taiwan and South Korea after extensive programs of redistributive land reforms, rural development to buttress the family farm with protective institutions, and human capital formation.

Second, the socialization of the economic surplus and the planning of its allocation between investment and personal incomes. If the emergence of sharp class distinctions based on control of the state apparatus or on unequal positions in the division of labor can be held in check, personal incomes can be egalitarian. With ups and downs, this is the long-run course that China has attempted to follow.

Third, the establishment of wage goods as the key growth sector. Even under conditions of surplus labor, the Kaleckian balance between production and consumption implies that wages must rise as per capita industrial production increases with constant factor shares. Achieving this structural condition requires the necessary reforms to gain control over investment in order to establish wage goods as the key growth sector, control over trade to tailor export performance to the capital goods and intermediate product import needs of the wage goods sectors, and control over the distribution of income to create an effective demand for wage goods commensurate with increasing per capita production. The experience of Latin America depicts that conceptualizing the economics of social articulation is a complex matter specific to each particular country and time period. In spite of several attempts, such a transition has never been successfully completed on that continent.

3. Styles of Growth in Latin American History

In reviewing the rich experiences of the attempts at alternative styles of development in Latin America, the thesis I want to defend is that they have all equally failed, either wittingly or unwittingly, in establishing social articulation. As a result, growth has been ephemeral and has resulted in a deepening of income inequalities, especially when growth has boomed.

There is a great deal of heterogeneity in styles of development across countries so that it is not possible to set time periods for the whole of Latin American history by stages that correspond to styles of development. What can be done, instead, is to analyze particular countries in particular time periods as archetypes of five styles of development that have occurred there since the 1930s: they are liberalism, populism, developmentalism, transition to socialism, and neoliberalism. I will characterize the experience of each of these archetypical styles of development by using five criteria:

1. choice of key sectors of economic growth;
2. social and geographical location of the market and the purpose of trade;
3. class structure and the form of government;
4. growth performance; and
5. social performance, especially changes in the distribution of income.

The first two criteria identify the style of development with respect to the articulation-disarticulation feature. Key to the third is how the articulated and disarticulated class alliances are posited relative to the state and what is the nature of their conflicts and power relations. The last two criteria characterize the growth and development outcomes of the period and the economic and social contradictions of its style of development.

Liberal Period: Argentina, 1860–1930

This period started with the victory of the free traders in 1806 and continued up to the Great Depression of 1930 when growth, based on integration in the international division of labor, came to a grinding halt with collapse of the world market. The key growth sectors were beef and grain production for export to the European markets, particularly to food-deficit England. Imports were principally luxury consumption goods of industrial origin and capital goods for investment in the agro-exporting sectors (railroads, godowns, and agroindustries). The dominant class alliance included a small group of cattlemen, financiers, and exporters, giving evidence of control of the state by the disarticulated alliance. The state itself was managed according to the principles of liberal democracy but with participation largely restricted to the members of the dominant class alliance.

The growth performance was strong (averaging an annual growth rate of 4.9 percent between 1850 and 1928) but also unstable, with phases of growth and stagnation amplifying the growth cycles of the industrialized economies. The level of prosperity reached on that basis was spectacular: in 1929, Argentina's GNP per capita was 40 percent of that of the United States compared with 20 percent in 1977. However, the benefits of that growth were largely concentrated in the hands of the upper classes able to enjoy European-style consumption patterns. The high degree of concentration in landownership both allowed 5 percent of the active population in agriculture to capture 70 percent of the gross income derived from agricultural production (Ferrer, 1967) and kept marginalized immigrants from access to land, forcing them to work as tenant farmers or as workers with wages held low by pervasive unemployment even in periods of economic prosperity. In addition, inflation and weak urban and rural labor organizations led to a steady worsening in real wages and in the distribution of income. This export-led pattern of disarticulated growth had as the principal contradiction a strong external dependency, which conditioned the stability of growth, and worsened social inequalities.

Populism: Argentina under Peron, 1946-1955

Following a meteoric political career that began with the military coup of 1943, Peron was elected president in 1946 with a program that marked the explicit rejection of the socially disarticulated, export-led style of development that Argentina had followed from the victory of the free traders in the 1860s to the Great Depression of 1929. Peron's program was oriented, instead, toward national independence, industrialization, and the redistribution of income. To acquire and conserve power he relied upon the support of organized labor which Peron himself had helped win political recognition and economic advantages during the period when he served as labor minister for the military government. Few leaders have influenced the political life of Argentina as deeply as Peron; and political alignments today are still defined in relation to what is presumed to be Peronist ideology.

The thesis I will defend here is that Peronism was a highly contradictory regime in that it attempted to promote social articulation by reform through ISI in wage goods while preserving the social structure of disarticulation in the agroexporting sector and, thus, also inducing ISI in luxury goods production. The result was an open contradiction in economic policy between the needs of the articulated and disarticulated alliances resulting in stop/go cycles. In the final analysis, Peronism failed to resolve the distributional conflict between the two alliances and to submit the external sector, controlled by the disarticulated alliance, to the needs of articulated growth resulting in economic destabilization and military intervention in favor of the disarticulated alliance.

Peronist populism was a late response to the hardships and humiliation that the Great Depression had brought to Argentina (Díaz-Alejandro, 1970). The economic crisis transformed the rural masses and the growing urban population into potentially explosive forces that the traditional parties were unable to organize. It is in this context that Peron launched his nationalistic program based on ISI, creation of the nationalized industrial sector, and income redistribution in favor of urban and rural workers, domestic industrialists, and bureaucrats and against rural landlords and foreign investors. This shift in policy orientation deeply affected the balance of power between urban and rural interests. There is, in fact, no country where the linkage between import substitution and urban sectors on the one hand, and pro-trade policies and rural interests on the other, is more sharply established. The result was a clear opposition of interests between articulated and disarticulated alliances. This opposition was the key contradiction in the Peronist attempt at achieving social articulation. Failure to resolve this opposition was to be the source of economic and political destabilization of the populist experiment in Argentina.

A number of reforms were implemented in order to stimulate investments and gain some control over them. The Central Bank was nationalized to allow public control over private deposits and investments, and several infrastructure services (railways and utilities) were purchased from foreign owners. Credit increased sharply with the industrial bank raising its participation in all industrial loans from 22 percent in 1946 to 78 percent in 1949. Import prohibitions and high tariffs discriminated differentially in favor of or against specific productive activities. Some industries, such as heavy intermediate products, suffered from negative effective protection. Meanwhile, light manufacturing was highly protected. The highest effective tariffs approaching 400 percent were designed to protect wage goods such as textiles, clothing and shoes, and food and beverages. Overvaluation of the peso by an average of 82 percent, relative to its value in the free market between 1946 and 1955, subsidized imports of capital goods and taxed agricultural exports. To cope with the drain on foreign exchange that this created, a clientelistic system of foreign exchange licensing was created.

The result was successful import substitution in wage goods where the percentage of imported value in GDP plus imports was 80 percent less in 1950–1954 than it was in 1937–1939. It was 52 percent in durable goods but much less successful in intermediate and capital goods with a reduction of only 41 percent. The key sector of economic growth thus became light industries oriented to the domestic market for both wage goods and luxury goods. The annual rate of growth of manufacturing was truly spectacular during the initial three years of Peron's regime. Beyond that, growth in manufacturing started to falter, reaching an average of 5.1 percent for the period 1946–1955. Agriculture, by contrast, only grew at 2.3 percent. This was due to a combination of cheap food policies implemented through government monopoly over exports via the state's trading organizations (IAPI), overvalued exchange rates without tariff protection of agriculture, and direct control over agricultural prices below the rate of inflation. These policies were meant to extract a surplus from agriculture via the terms of trade in order to support industrialization. External factors also worked against Argentine agriculture. The country's special relations with the Marshall Plan came to an abrupt end in 1948 when European and U.S. agricultural sectors recovered from World War II. This resulted in agricultural stagnation, a falling share of Argentine agricultural exports in world trade (from 43 percent to 20 percent in corn and from 35 percent to 19 percent in meat between 1945–1949 and 1950–1954), and strong opposition of the rural interests to Peron's rule.

On the side of effective demand, the domestic demand for luxuries existed through Peron's failure to address the question of landownership, in spite of a highly unequal land distribution, and through the income created in the agroexport activities. Peron's income policy was thus concentrated on the creation of domestic effective demand for the protected industrial wage goods. This occurred through favorable wage policies, income transfers through the institutions of a welfare state, and price controls over food terms.

Peron institutionalized collective bargaining and gave the loyal General Confederation of Workers (CGT) strong participation in the design of economic policy. As Table 1 shows, the share of wages and salaries in GNP increased from 37 percent in 1945–1946 to 44 percent in 1953–1955, and the share of Social Security contributions increased from 3 percent to 7 percent. While real per capita GNP increased by 3.6 percent between 1946 and 1955, real wage rates increased by 45.5

TABLE 1

Argentina: Real Wages and Gross National Product, 1943–1955

| | | | SHARES IN GNP | |
YEAR	PER CAPITA GNP[a]	REAL WAGE RATES[a]	Wages and Salaries	Social Security Contributions
1943	100	100	36.8	1.6
1944	108	111		
1945	101	106	37.0	3.0
1946	112	112		
1947	131	140	40.6	4.8
1948	130	173		
1949	116	181		
1950	113	173	43.7	5.8
1951	114	161		
1952	103	143		
1953	103	154	43.7	7.1
1954	111	165		
1955	116	163		

Source: C. Diaz-Alejandro (1970).
[a]Based on 1943 = 100

percent (Díaz-Alejandro, 1970). Even though there are no data on changes in the distribution of income during this period, the evolution of the share of wages and salaries indicates a sharp improvement in the distribution of income between 1946 and 1949 followed by unchanged inequality between 1949 and 1955.

In promoting simultaneously articulated and disarticulated growth and in failing to resolve the distributional conflicts between the corresponding two class alliances, Peron's economic program was bound to be highly contradictory. The growth performance became increasingly unstable due to recurrent balance-of-payment and inflationary crises, creating repeated stop/go cycles.

Balance-of-payment problems originated, in part, with the politically effective but economically costly programs of nationalization of foreign investments and repatriation of the foreign debt, resulting in a depletion of gold holdings by 89 percent between 1945 and 1948. But the basic source of difficulties with the balance of payments was, on the one hand, the rise of import demand to satisfy a process of ISI that neglected deepening toward capital goods and, on the other hand, severe discrimination against agricultural exports.

Imports increased by 97 percent in 1946 and 76 percent in 1947, resulting for the first time in a negative balance of trade during that year. With a large agricultural export potential, Argentina has the ability of rapidly rebuilding its balance-of-trade equilibrium through stabilization policies. This was done for the first time in 1948 and had to be repeated in 1950 and 1953, each time at an amplified scale, resulting in alternating cycles of industrial growth and agricultural export growth.

After the first two years of Peron's rule and after international reserves had been initially depleted, inflation began to rise, reaching 52 percent in 1951. The increase in the price level was the result of expansionary policies and sharp increases in real wages that went up by 21 percent annually during the first three years of Peron's regime (Table 1).

By 1952, inflation and trade deficits forced Peron to apply a strong stabilization program that, among other measures, required both freezing real wages for two years and restructuring the export sector. Peron relied on his charisma and control over organized labor to be successful with the first. The second required rebuilding the profit margin of farm producers by offering them prices higher than world market levels. Domestically, agricultural prices increased by 29 percent more than inflation in 1951 and 1952. Also, greater controls on imports and public expenditures were imposed.

Peron's stabilization measures were relatively successful as GNP grew at an annual average of 6 percent between 1953 and 1955, agricultural production by 11 percent, and manufacturing by 7 percent. By contrast, construction was totally stagnant due to reductions in both credits and public investments. Inflation was contained and positive trade balances restored. Yet, economic success was obtained at the cost of sacrificing articulation to the demands of the disarticulated alliance. Only a proudly overvalued peso, protection of the workers' gains in prior periods, and the basis of what never became a fully developed corporatist state remained from the glorious years.

Early ISI under populism thus resulted in an open clash between articulated and disarticulated alliances which Peron did not have the political power to resolve, particularly by questioning the structure of landownership. This resulted in a failed attempt at social articulation by reform as trade could not be subjected to the requirements of industry, resulting in balance-of-payment crises, and wage increases could not be tailored to productivity gains, resulting in inflationary crises.

What the experience of populism shows is that gaining control over investment to redefine the key growth sectors and over the distribution of income to create effective demand for these factors was necessary but not sufficient. Failure to deal with landlord power and, hence, to submit the external sector to the needs of articulated growth led to economic destabilization and eventually to military intervention in favor of the disarticulated alliance.

Developmentalism: Brazil under the Military, 1964-1979

Brazil between 1964 and 1979 provides a typical example of the *desarrollista* vision of expected articulation by growth and of the failure for this to happen in spite of eventually spectacular growth rates. As a result, Brazil became the archetype of authoritarian luxury-led social disarticulation and of the economic and social limits of this style of development. For almost 15 years (1965 to 1980), the average annual rate of GDP growth was 8.5 percent making Brazil the fourth fastest growing country (Knight and Moran, 1981). This growth performance was reached by a modernization strategy based on the production of durable goods with up-to-date technology thanks to favorable policies toward imports and foreign investment (subsidized import credits and overvalued exchange rates) and to the massive penetration of multinational companies. In 1972, for instance, foreign capital owned an average of 51 percent of the assets of the largest 300 manufacturing companies, reaching 78 percent in electrical machinery and appliances, 82 percent in transportation and cars, and 100 percent in rubber (Evans, 1979).

The Brazilian "miracle" started to fade away after 1974, not so much as a consequence of the negative impact of rising energy prices, as the "official" economists usually claim, but of the internal contradictions of the model. Market saturation for luxury consumption foods, in spite of increasing inequality in the distribution of income and attempts by government policies to stimulate demand, and mounting external debt associated with policies to stimulate the import of capital goods, led to both stagnation and delegitimation of the military regime.

At the political level, the Brazilian miracle took place under the leadership of civilian technocrats and the military, with a domestic bourgeoisie — both articulated and disarticulated — that was co-opted by sharing in the spoils of rapid growth (Faucher, 1981). The military was not brought to power in order to protect investments toward the capital goods sectors in an attempt at deepening ISI beyond its "easy" phase. Deepening had already advanced considerably before the coup. As Table 2 shows, the share of imports in consumer durables had been rapidly reduced between 1949 and 1965 but so had, with a lag, the share of imports in capital goods that declined from 64 percent to 8 percent. This "difficult" phase of ISI was prompted by stagnation of the export sector, that only grew at the annual rate of 0.85 percent between 1947–1948 and 1961–1962, making it impossible to sustain a sufficiently fast growth of capital goods imports (Serra, 1979). Military intervention was induced by an economic and social crisis brought about by the exhaustion of ISI on a joint articulated-disarticulated basis (as in Argentina under Peron) and the need to overcome an underconsumption crisis by concentrating the distribution of income and providing financing to upper income con-

TABLE 2

Brazil: Share of Imports in Total Supply,
    1949, 1955, 1962, and 1965 (percentage)

Year	Capital Goods	Intermediate Goods	Consumer Goods	
			Durable	Nondurable
1949	63.7	25.9	64.5	3.7
1955	43.2	17.9	10.0	2.2
1962	12.9	8.9	2.4	1.1
1965	8.2	6.3	1.6	1.2

Source: Serra (1979).

sumers in order to promote luxury-led disarticulation as the engine of growth. At the political level, populist demagoguery, social unrest, and the encouragement of the U.S. government and foreign investors, allied with the Brazilian industrial and commercial elite distressed by record inflation, pushed the military to end the Goulart government in March of 1964 (Wynia, 1978).

Key Sectors of Economic Growth

Among the different strategies to overcome the underconsumption crisis, the Costello-Branco government chose the one that not only politically but also economically seemed the most attractive from a technocratic-military point of view. Horizontal expansion of the market would have required a major income redistribution (articulation via reform) which was not appealing to the new government nor to the class alliance of which it had become the instrument. A further deepening of the import substitution strategy would have required a shift away from durables to intermediate and capital goods, and a consequent short-run decline in income due to problems of economies of scale and maturation of investments. The luxury durable goods sector was, thus, the logical choice to carry on another spurt of rapid growth but under the economic and social conditions implied by social disarticulation. Creating these conditions required a severe stabilization program to discipline workers' demands, reduce the rate of inflation, create a climate of confidence to attract international investment, and give a new role to government in economic activity.

After three years of stabilization programs the rate of inflation was reduced from 78 percent in 1963 to 28 percent in 1967, foreign capital and intermediate goods began to flow into the country, taxes were significantly reduced, and real wages fell. Annual growth rates of industry averaged 13 percent between 1967 and 1973. Growth was, however, unequal among sectors of industry. During the first phase of disarticulated growth (1966–1969), growth occurred mainly in the production of consumer durable goods while the capital goods sector stagnated (Table 3). This was not due to the incapacity to produce modern capital goods or to existing excess capacity but, as Serra explains, "the fact is that in response to the pressures from, and the advantages associated with external sources of financing, and because of the preferences of multinational corporations and of the desire to maximize the rates of short-term growth, economic policy began to discriminate against the industries that produced machinery and equipment, granting fiscal incentives only for the purchase of *imported* capital goods. . . . Between 1966 and 1969, capital goods imports grew by 20.5 percent annually, while domestic production rose only 7.1 percent." By the same token, both intermediate and nondurable consumer goods had poor performances. The overall result of this policy was to increase the share of imports from 6.8 percent in 1965 to 17.1 percent in 1979. As we shall see, this constituted one of the weakest economic aspects of the Brazilian miracle.

Only after 1971 did the military government, then under the leadership of General Medici, realize that an excessive dependency on foreign capital and intermediate goods was a brake to the overall sectoral articulation of the economy and an unsustainable drain on its balance of payments situation. This government tried to simultaneously maintain fast growth in the production of consumer durable goods and to induce, through a number of incentives, the production of capital and intermediate goods. At the same time, the state began a grandiose program of public works (stadiums, trans-Amazonian highway, etc.) that created the effective demand for the expansion of those sectors.

During the periods 1969–1973, consumer durable goods production, which continued under the control of private (mainly foreign) capital, grew at a record 22 percent a year. Significant improvements also occurred in the production of capital and intermediate goods. Nevertheless, the lack of sectoral articulation between the national production of capital and intermediate goods and the production of consumer durable goods, which relied mainly on imported inputs, made the proportion of imports in total supply and in the supply of capital goods increase.

The high performance levels of the Brazilian economy could not

TABLE 3

Brazil: Annual Rate of Growth of Manufacturing
by Major User Groups (percentage)

| PERIOD | CAPITAL GOODS | INTERMEDIATE GOODS | CONSUMER GOODS | |
			Durable	Nondurable
1959–1965	9.4	5.4	8.4	5.1
1966–1969	7.1	10.2	21.0	7.8
1969–1973	22.5	15.5	22.0	12.3
1973–1980	7.4	8.3	9.3	4.4

Sources: For 1959–1965 to 1969–1973, Serra (1979); for 1973–1980, Serra (1982).

have been possible without strong state intervention in supporting the accumulation process, both through incentives to the production of consumer durables (mainly the automobile industry) and capital and intermediate goods and through direct involvement in the production of those goods and services that the private sector did not consider profitable and in public works.

By 1974 the growth model was in deep crisis. Inflation, deficits in the balance of payments, and increasing inequality in the distribution of income were threatening both continued growth and social stability.

Social and Geographical Location of Effective Demand

On the demand side, the Brazilian economy based its growth process on a fast increase of exports, especially of industrial products and a diversified set of agricultural commodities, and on the rising consumption level of the upper strata of Brazilian society.

Brazil's income distribution in the 1960s was already tremendously unequal. While the wealthiest 10 percent of the Brazilian people received 40 percent of the national income, the poorest 50 percent only received 18 percent. (Table 4).

Since then, the situation has deteriorated for most of the population. The wealthiest 10 percent of the population has increased its share to 68 percent of total income. Meanwhile, the poorest 80 percent has lost its share of national income except for the poorest 10 percent that has kept constant its meager share.

The stabilization program, launched by the military government, had as an essential element the reduction in real wages. Minimum wages, as well as the actual wage index, fell in real terms (Table 5). The distribution of income among wage earners also worsened. After 1969 when wages began to rise the wages of the lowest paid workers increased by 10 percent between 1969 and 1974 while those of highly paid workers increased by 50 percent (Tavares and Souza, 1981).

As Table 6 shows, real salary increases were also far below productivity gains indicating a growing proportion of production for which no market was being created out of wages. Effective demand for these productivity gains had to be created through concentration in the distribution of income following the logic of disarticulated growth.

The socially disarticulated nature of the Brazilian model is clearly evident by looking at the social distribution of consumption. In 1975, the upper 22 percent of households in the distribution of income consumed 61 percent of the electrical appliances and 94 percent of the cars which were the key sectors of economic growth.

Effective demand for the key growth sector also expanded rapidly in the export market. The growth of manufacturing exports was spectacular averaging in current dollar terms an annual rate of 39 percent between 1964 and 1974 (Serra, 1979). The share of primary commodities in total export earnings fell from 75 percent to 42 percent between 1970 and 1980, while that of industrial products increased from 24 percent to 57 percent, with transportation equipment, machinery, and electrical products as the most important items (United Nations, *Economic Survey of Latin America*, 1980). This brilliant performance of manufacturing exports was due to several factors. One was the policy of export incentives that the new regime created; another was the containment of inflation that fell from 87 percent in 1964 to 17 percent in 1972 and the policy of minidevaluations that began in 1968; in addition, exceptionally favorable conditions for external demand prevailed during the period 1968–1973; and finally, the sharp reduction in real wages increased the competiveness of Brazilian exports.

TABLE 4

Brazil: Income Distribution, 1960, 1970, and 1980

	POPULATION DECILES	INCOME SHARES (percentage)		
		1960	1970	1980
Poorest	10	1.2	1.2	1.2
	10	2.3	2.1	2.0
	10	3.4	3.0	3.0
	10	4.7	3.8	3.6
	10	6.2	5.0	4.4
	10	7.7	6.2	5.6
	10	9.4	7.2	7.2
	10	10.9	10.0	9.9
	10	14.7	15.2	15.4
Wealthiest	10	39.7	46.5	47.9
Gini coefficients				
Fox		.50	.54	
Denslow-Tyler			.57	.59

Sources: Fox (1982) and Denslow and Tyler (1983).

TABLE 5

Brazil: Wage and Minimum Wage Indexes, 1960–1974
(1960 = 100)

YEAR	WAGE INDEX[a]	MINUMUM WAGE INDEX (Rio de Janeiro)
1960	100	100
1961	105	115
1962	105	96
1963	107	89
1964	103	89
1965	98	82
1966	92	76
1967	89	73
1968	92	74
1969	94	71
1970	95	70
1971	98	69
1972	102	71
1973	98	68
1974	107	69

[a]Wage index is based on data of 18 labor unions.

TABLE 6

Average Wage Index and Productivity, 1970–1974
(1970 = 100)

YEAR	AVERAGE WAGE INDEX	PRODUCTIVITY (per capita GNP)
1970	100.0	100.0
1971	103.2	109.3
1972	107.4	118.5
1973	112.7	131.8
1974	112.7	140.8

Source: Bresser (1983).

Yet, it is interesting that exports never represented a significant fraction of total demand for industry. On average between 1965 and 1975, the share of exports in industrial production was only 2.3 percent. Brazilian growth was clearly not export-led and effective demand for industry had to be created out of demand from the domestic upper income levels.

Contradictions of Luxury-Led Disarticulation

The Brazilian growth model performed well during the 1967–1979 period. Without active opposition, which was severely repressed by the successive military governments, Brazilian technocrats were able to implement a policy in which the real consumption of the masses was sharply reduced, public services were limited and managed according to pure "efficiency" rules (Dos Santos, 1980), income was accumulated by a small proportion of the population, and investments — both national and foreign — substantially increased. The key growth sector was the production of luxury consumption goods and effective demand was correspondingly being created in the upper social strata.

This pattern of accumulation entered into crisis in 1974. Since then, the high rate of industrial investment that was characteristic of the Brazilian miracle practically disappeared, falling from an annual growth rate of 26.5 percent during the period of 1967–1973 to only .1 percent during the period 1973–1980. Similarly, as we have shown in Table 3, the growth rates of all sectors of industry decreased dramatically. Inflationary tendencies, a consequence of both the increase in oil prices and the subsidy policies of the state which tried to protect the demand for consumer durables, reappeared reaching a rate of 60 percent for the 1974–1981 period in contrast to 19.5 percent during 1967–1973. The external market shrank because of the international recession, and the internal market for consumer durables concentrated in the upper classes was saturated.

Inflation in Brazil cannot be fully explained by the struggle among classes for the appropriation of surplus given the severe repression of labor demands. Bresser (1983) argues that inflation has been the consequence of the capitalist class attempting to increase, or at least maintain, its rate of profit during the downward phase of the economic cycle.

This argument is supported by two observations. One is the oligopolistic character of the Brazilian economy. Price increases were higher in the oligopolistic sectors than in the competitive ones. For example, in 1981, with an annual inflation rate for the February—July period of 105 percent, competitive sectors increased their prices by an average of 60 percent, while oligopolistic sectors increased their prices by 170 percent. The other is the set of state policies enacted to boost aggregate demand. The Brazilian economy is highly subsidized: subsidies are granted to industrial exports, durable goods consumption, capital goods production and imports, etc. As a consequence, an economy that in 1974 was working close to its growth potential had to end up with strong inflationary pressures. In addition, the state was involved in managing at a loss those necessary economic activities that were not profitable enough for private capital. Dos Santos (1980) refers to the case of electrical energy production which was passed over to the state at the initiative of the very multinational companies which controlled it and after they had received a juicy compensation.

The salary increases that the successive governments had to grant to keep a minimum social order contributed to the explosive inflation rate that occurred after 1974. For instance, between 1974 and 1979, with a 21 percent increase of productivity, real salaries grew by 37 percent (Bresser, 1983).

One element of the Brazilian miracle was the rapid expansion of industrial exports. But the production of modern consumer durables needs a large share of imported capital and intermediate goods. As we saw, the share of capital goods imports in total industrial supply grew from 15 percent in 1965 to 28 percent in 1974 (Serra, 1979). Exports were increasingly unable to balance the national requirement for imported industrial inputs.

External debt increased by almost fourfold during the 1969–1973 boom period. The Brazilian government was financing its industrial growth by reverting to easily accessible international credit. External debt growth was largely independent from the increase in oil prices. Before developmentalism, the balance of trade was positive so that it helped to keep under control the traditional deficits in the balance of services; since 1970, by contrast, trade deficits were systematic.

As Bresser (1983) explains, since 1973 Brazil has passed through several phases that have been contradictory to both the international and the national situations. The attempts at supporting the production of capital and intermediate goods without affecting the master line of the Brazilian miracle resulted in 1977 in an accumulated debt of 32 billion dollars and the interest on this debt was higher than 2 billion dollrs. This situation has worsened since 1979 when interest rates increased. By 1981, Brazil had a gross international debt of 61 billion dollars, and it paid 9 billion dollars (or 39 percent of the value of its exports) in interest. As

Bresser (1983) states, "between 1970 and 1976 Brazil's debt increased to increase accumulation and consumption; between 1978 and 1980 it increased to keep consumption levels; since 1981 Brazil's debt is to pay the interest on the debt."

The Brazilian accumulation pattern, however, was not exclusively an economic issue but also a social one. Its striking characteristic is not only the choice of luxury goods as the key growth sector but also its corresponding social policies in order to create the appropriate incentives to invest and the pattern of effective demand. Brazil's growth both reinforced and was fed by a deliberate policy of concentrating and increasing the consumption capacity in a few hands. In spite of this, a new underconsumption crisis (this time in luxury goods) could not be postponed forever. As Serra argued, "the inflection in the cycle was not a consequence of either demand patterns from the side of aggregate investment or of import supply restrictions. Problems sprang from the side of demand for durable and nondurable good consumption" (Serra, 1982).

Table 4 shows the extremely unequal income distribution and its deterioration over time since 1960. As a CEPAL report on poverty published in 1979 showed, Brazil is the third Latin American country in terms of absolute poverty with 49 percent of its families living below the poverty line (Iglesias, 1979). As growth slowed and inflation eroded wages, the regressive and exclusionary pattern of disarticulated growth could only lead to delegitimation of the military regime revealing the social limits of disarticulated growth with large masses of surplus labor. Luxury-led industrialization gave the short-lived illusion that social articulation could be achieved by rapid growth and without facing up to the issue of redistributive reforms.

Transition to Socialism: Chile under Allende, 1970–1973

Leading a broad coalition between the working class and the petty bourgeoisie, Allende came to power in Chile in November 1970. The Popular Unity (UP) program stated as a goal of its rule the replacement of the existing social order to initiate the construction of socialism. In doing so, two objectives were central: (1) to gradually socialize the key means of production and (2) to create social articulation by increasing the consumption capacity of the masses, especially the working class and the middle sectors. The first objective was essential if the state was to redefine the key sectors of economic growth. The second was both economically necessary to social articulation, and politically needed, since the "peaceful road to socialism" required gaining the majority of the popular vote and neutralizing the reactions of the upper class and foreign interests.

Allende's regime was all but homogeneous. A period of rapid growth and idyllic political performance during 1971 was followed by a period of economic chaos, political conflagration, and internal and external boycotts and aggression that put a bloody end to both the UP government and Allende's life on September 11, 1973. Both periods were directly related since, independent of the external factors and the purposeful manipulation of economic failures by the opposition, serious contradictions existed in the accumulation model the UP tried to implement.

Rise of the Popular Unity

The last years of Frei's regime were characterized by a deep economic and social crisis. Inflation rose from 22 percent in 1967 to 35 percent in 1970. Restrictive policies aimed at controlling inflation and the traditional pre-electoral investment contraction resulted in economic stagnation as well as an increasing level of unemployment (from 5.5 percent in December 1969 to 7 percent six months later) and social unrest. Multiple protests, not only by the traditional producers' association but also by such unexpected sectors as the judicial system and the military created among Chileans a widespread feeling of lack of power.

Nevertheless, as Bitar points out, the level of economic deterioration was only relative. Inflation was not at an unmanageable level nor was unemployment very high. The trade balance was highly favorable, and international reserves were bountiful as a consequence of the high copper prices during the Vietnam War. Idle capacity was high: 63 percent in the capital goods and consumer durables sector, 78 percent in the traditional mass consumption goods industry, and 86 percent in the intermediate goods industry, with an overall average for manufacturing equal to 75 percent (de Vylder, 1976). In such circumstances, Allende found a declining economy in process but with enough possibilities to address a new growth strategy.

Allende's program was not merely directed at economic recovery but also at replacing the current economic structure "ending the power of national and foreign monopoly capitalists and large owners in order to initiate the construction of socialism" (Stallings, 1978). This program implied an immediate threat not only to the national and foreign bourgeoisies with interests in Chile but also to the American political interests in the region. On September 16, 1970, Kissinger declared: "We must not deceive ourselves with the rise of Allende to power, thinking that this will not create massive problems for us and the democratic and pro-North American forces in Latin America and, in the end, for the whole Western hemisphere" (Bitar, 1979). From that time on, a number of actions were initiated or supported by the United States to destabilize the Chilean economy.

To be successful Allende had to be able to reactivate the economy and manage it in favor of those social sectors that had granted their support to the UP. Using Allende's words, "the political model towards socialism that my government is applying requires that the socioeconomic revolution take place simultaneously with an uninterrupted economic expansion" (de Vylder, 1976). The opposition, however, symptomizing the interests of the disarticulated alliance, was interested in just the contrary; that is, in demonstrating that socialism and anarchy were synonymous and, consequently, isolating the UP. It is therefore valid to contend that the economy was simultaneously a "backdrop and a battlefield for political struggle" (Ramos, 1979).

Chile was structured as a mixed economy with three sectors: (1) entirely controlled by the state (local plants of multinational companies except those providing essential goods and services, mineral resources, and banking and foreign trade); (2) mixed public-private enterprises where the state was dependent on the private sector's supply of technology; and (3) small private firms involved in retail sales. In agriculture, the UP stopped expropriating all farms larger than the equivalent of eighty irrigated hectares, using the Land Reform Law passed by the Christian Democracy. The National Worker's Confederation participated not only in the management of firms but also in the planning commission (ODEPLAN) and a number of other government bodies. As Ramos observed, the process of structural transformation was a complex one since planning failed to dominate, guide, and globalize the economic performance of the Chilean economy and was excessively influenced by immediate economic pressures.

An Attempt at Articulation by Reform

To assess the three years of UP government is complicated not only by the number of reforms the government attempted to implement in a short period of time, but also by the uneven performance of the economy in these three years. While 1971 was a record year for many socioeconomic variables, 1972 was the beginning of a process of decline that reached chaotic proportions in 1973. Economic goals explicitly spelled out included (1) redefinition of the key sectors of economic growth from luxury goods to basic consumer items; (2) guarantees of employment for all Chileans of working age at adequate salaries; (3) liberation of Chile from subordination to foreign capital by expropriating some firms and setting conditions for the operation of others; (4) rapid economic growth;

(5) development of exports and new markets, reduction of technological dependency, and the ending of devaluations; and (6) control of inflation and rationalization of commerce and distribution (Stallings, 1978). All these goals, as well as the necessity of incorporating the middle class into the political process, relied on four conditions: sustained economic growth to satisfy the foreseeable expansion of working and middle class demands; efficient performance of the public sector so that it could not only control the overall economy but also accumulate enough surplus to finance the expansion of public works and employment creation; increased exports to pay for capital and consumer good imports; and sustained agricultural output to avoid an increase in food imports. As Wynia (1978) emphasizes, the overall model was plagued by hazards. The failure of any of these conditions could cause the program to fall apart with inflation, trade deficits, bottlenecks and shortages, and finally delegitimation.

During the first year, a program to "solve the immediate problems of the large majority" was launched (Ramos, 1979). It consisted of a Keynesian-type program of short-term demand reactivation through real income expansion, increased public expenditures, and easy monetary policy. In early 1971, several laws were passed attempting to increase not only the participation of wages and salaries in total national income but, also, redistribute them in favor of the poorest segments of society. The law contained three essential points: to restore the purchasing power of all Chileans, except the highest paid, to the level of January 1970; to give additional salary increases to the lowest paid workers; and to begin a process of standardization and leveling of all social benefits. The official policy of favoring salary increases and supporting workers in negotiating salary increases made average income per employed worker increase by 55 percent as against the 40 to 45 percent envisaged by the government and the 1970 inflation of 35 percent (de Vylder, 1976; Table 7). The participation in GNP of payments by producers to individuals grew from 72 percent in 1970 to 78 percent in 1971 (Mamalakis, 1978). This redistributive process lasted during all of Allende's period so that the Gini coefficient decreased from .55 in 1970 to .47 in 1972 (Stallings, 1978).

In order to prevent the monetary gains of the working class from being offset by inflation, the government reinforced the existing system of price controls. The assumption of the Chilean government was that the profit squeeze, created by its price stabilization policies, would be compensated by an increase in production as a consequence of the expanding demand capacity of the economy.

Total government expenditures, including spending by public institutions and public enterprises, increased by almost 80 percent in current prices (de Vylder, 1976). Special attention was given to those projects that could reduce employment and address social needs. In this fashion, construction was a priority sector: 71,000 new units were begun by the public sector alone in 1971 in contrast with a total (public and private) of 23,700 in 1970. Simultaneously, monetary policy supported the overall economic program. Low interest rates and easy credit made the amount of liquidity in private hands grow from 11 percent of GDP in 1970 to 17 percent in 1971. The most relevant difference with the Frei period, however, was the marked shift in credit distribution away from the private and toward the public sector, as the share of the latter in total credit created by the banking system increased from 23 percent in 1970 to 60 percent in 1971.

With substantial increases in both population purchasing power and means of payment for firms, the government was able to mobilize the

TABLE 7

Chile: Real Wage and Salaries, 1970–1973

YEAR		INDEX (1969 = 100)	PERCENTAGE CHANGE
1970	June	112.8	
	April	113.4	.5
	July	114.6	1.0
	October	116.0	1.2
1971	June	126.1	8.7
	April	144.9	14.5
	July	148.9	3.1
	October	151.3	1.6
1972	June	153.9	1.7
	April	146.3	– 4.9
	July	147.6	.9
	October	137.9	– 6.6
1973	June	149.9	8.7
	April	137.0	– 8.6
	July	124.0	– 9.5
	October	59.1	– 52.3

Source: Based upon data from International Bank for Reconstruction and Development (1980).

underused productive resources and increase supply. The result was an economic boom in 1971. Taking advantage of the existing industrial idle capacity, the reserve labor force (the unemployment rate in greater Santiago was 8.3 percent in December 1970), the large reserves of foreign exchange (442 million U.S. dollars at the end of 1970 — enough to pay for 44 percent of total import demand in that year), and the large stock of consumer goods, GNP grew by an impressive 7.7 percent, unemployment dramatically decreased to 3.8 percent, and the rate of inflation was reduced by 20 percent from a rate of 33 percent in 1970.

Indeed, it seemed that the impossible had been achieved and that reactivation had occurred without inflation. But the mass demand-led reactivation had created huge disequilibria: social articulation had been achieved on the side of effective demand without a corresponding capacity in mobilizing new investments to expand the key sectors of economic growth. Consumer expenditure grew more rapidly than did GNP so that this gap had to be filled using the already existing stocks, increasing imports, and financing imports against existing reserves. The rapid growth of public expenditures was not matched by a parallel increase in government revenues: while government income decreased by 1.5 percent, expenditure grew by 31.9 percent. Expansionary policy had to be financed through treasury indebtedness given the systematic rejection by the opposition-controlled Congress of passing any tax reform proposed by the executive branch. This congressional opposition proved to be highly detrimental to Allende's program since it prevented financing the improvements in living standards of the masses and the creation of effective demand for wage goods through income transfers from the wealthier.

Another weak point of the Allende model was the foreign sector. Copper prices fell and so did export revenues. The total value of imports did not grow significantly, but the composition of imports changed. Capital goods imports declined dramatically while that of consumer goods (especially foodstuffs) increased. Between 1970 and 1972, the share of consumer goods in total imports increased from 24 to 43 percent and that of food from 13 to 31 percent, while the share of capital goods declined from 29 to 15 percent. This foreign sector behavior was the consequence of the increasing consumption capacity of the Chilean population and the use of the exchange rate as an anti-inflationary instrument. Contrary to the earlier administration, which followed a policy of minidevaluations of the currency to adjust the balance of payments — but, also, contributed to a certain degree of inflation — the UP began a policy of fixed exchange rates in order to protect the consumption capacity of Chileans via both price stability and the absence of shortages.

Lessons for the Transition to Social Articulation

The success of Allende's strategy of articulation by reform depended upon its ability of adjusting the production capacity to expansion of the consumption capacity. During the first year of the regime, production could be expanded using the existing excess capacity and through heavy public investments. Nonetheless, even though public investment increased by 7 percent, total investment decreased substantially as private investment declined by 68 percent during that year, representing only 20 percent of total investment in contrast to 43 percent the previous year (Stallings, 1978). Total investment, consequently, declined by 24 percent in 1971 and again by 45 percent in 1972.

The Chilean model of transition to articulation was, thus, consumption-led. As Foxley and Muñoz (1976) demonstrated, this development strategy was erroneous in the sense that a redistribution of income from the wealthier to the poorer sectors could only be possible if consumption and investment were kept in balance, a relationship that we attributed to Kalecki in characterizing styles of development at the beginning of this paper. In the Chilean case, this could be possible only through greater participation of the public sector in the overall economic surplus. If income were redistributed in favor of the groups with a higher propensity to consume and if no new investment were to compensate for this, consumption would grow faster than production so that inflationary tendencies and/or imports and/or deficits would have to grow.

By the middle of December 1971 the Millas-Matos team launched a program of "stabilization at a higher level." It consisted mainly in permitting drastic once-and-for-all price increases, hoping to reestablish the equilibrium between supply and demand for those commodities in short supply. But pressures over prices were too strong, and equilibrium was impossible to reach except through a politically unacceptable reduction in the consumption capacity of the masses. The stabilization program was, thus, doomed to fail as it could not address the roots of the problem.

In an attempt to correct the distortions that the policy of fixed exchange rates created in the foreign exchange market, the government adopted in December 1971 a policy of multiple exchange rates. The structure of exchange rates was oriented toward discriminating against imports of luxury consumption goods and at maintaining subsidies to the import of wage goods. Between 1970 and 1973, the exchange rate for food and fuel increased from 12 to 20 while that for luxury consumption goods increased from 12 to 240. Yet, these measures failed to reduce the deficit in the balance of payments which kept on growing through the period.

By 1973, the UP government was in deep political and economic crisis. On the one hand, the opposition was sufficiently organized to exploit to its advantage the uneasiness of a middle class threatened by real or provoked bottlenecks and scarcities while, on the other hand, the parties of the UP were divided among themselves as to how to confront the crisis. Meanwhile, the economy was at rock bottom. The austerity measures that the government applied in 1973, including a reduction in real wages and salaries, came too late to top the inflationary spiral. State finances were exhausted, and international credit to Chile had vanished.

Both internal contradictions and external pressures were thus to blame for the downfall of Allende's attempt at articulation by reform. From the point of view of extracting lessons for a theory of the transition to social articulation, it is essential to keep in mind that both investment in the key sectors of economic growth and effective demand creation have to be managed simultaneously. If, as was the case in Chile, the domestic and international private investors react to the redistributive measures by boycotting investment, the public sector has to overcome this deficiency by gaining greater control over investment — in particular, by redistributing income not only from the upper to the lower classes but, also, by increasing the participation of the public sector in the redistributed surplus.

Neoliberalism: Chile under Pinochet, 1973–1984

Following the liberal doctrines of the Chicago boys, the military regime that seized power through the coup of September 1974 set out to reorganize the ideological and the economic context of Chile to stage a return to the model of export-led social disarticulation that had prevailed until the 1930s. For that purpose, the first three years of the regime consisted of an attempt to stabilize the economy and to erase the prevailing socialist ideology and institutions. To reduce the rate of inflation that had reached 606 percent in 1973, aggregate demand was drastically curtailed. Real wages fell by 35 percent between 1972 and 1975, and the share of wages in national income was reduced from 54 percent to 34 percent (Table 8). Prices were freed for virtually all items, and the peso was devalued by 230 percent. The fiscal deficit was reduced from 23 percent of GDP in 1973 to 3 percent in 1975. In spite of this, inflation was still 343 percent in 1975, and it took until 1978 for it to fall to 37 percent. To dismantle the remnants of socialist ideology, the opposition parties were banned and many of their leaders were exiled or eliminated. The union movement was depoliticized and severeley restricted in its legal rights. Union activity was confined to the level of the firm, and the dura-

TABLE 8

Chile:Social Indicators, 1970–1982
(1970 = 100)

YEAR	REMUNERATIONS			PER CAPITA GOVERNMENT SOCIAL EXPENDITURES	UNEMPLOY- MENT RATE[a]	PER CAPITA GDP
	Wages	Pensions	Family Allowances			
1970	100.0	100.0	100.0	100.0	5.7	100.0
1971	122.7	141.7	135.1	128.1	3.8	105.8
1972	96.1	95.5	105.6	105.6	3.1	104.0
1973	80.4	55.3	49.0	b	4.8	98.6
1974	65.0	59.3	69.5	91.8	9.2	97.9
1975	62.9	52.0	67.1	75.0	16.5	83.8
1976	64.9	56.3	61.8	71.2	20.2	85.3
1977	71.4	60.9	57.6	78.8	18.6	92.1
1978	76.0	67.0	56.0	79.0	17.9	98.0
1979	82.3	75.9	54.2	82.8	17.3	104.4
1980	89.3	82.8	54.4		17.2	110.3
1981	97.3		54.0		15.6	114.2
1982	96.4[c]		52.9[c]		27.0[c]	97.1[c]

[a]Includes workers in the Plan of Minimum Employment.
[b]Blanks indicate data not available.
[c]Preliminary.
Source: Cortazar (1982).

tion of strikes was limited to 60 days after which workers had to accept the employers' conditions or lose their jobs. The school and media were used to actively promote a new ideology of individualism, consumerism, and social submissiveness.

The economy then was fully and rapidly opened to international competition following the principles of the shock treatment. Tariffs, which had averaged 94 percent in 1973, were brought down to a uniform rate of 10 percent by 1979. Incentives were given to inflows of foreign capital. And foreign loans could come in freely, allowing bankers to capture the large differential between international and domestic interest rates, the latter having climbed from 49 percent at the beginning of 1975 to 178 percent at the end of the same year.

With stabilization and the opening up of the economy actively pursued, the third item on the policy agenda was the privatization of the economy. Two-thirds of the land that had been expropriated under the Land Reform Law was either returned to its former owners or auctioned off to the public. The remaining third, which had been organized in cooperatives, was distributed to private family farms with the right of selling and accumulating land. By 1979, about half of these farms had been sold by the original beneficiaries. The commercial lands of the Mapuche Indians were largely enclosed and privatized based on the current pattern of usufruct. More important from a macroeconomic standpoint, the government sold 437 of the 507 state enterprises at prices which were extremely low in the context of the 1975–76 recession. This allowed a few economic groups (Vial, Cruzat) to acquire a large number of firms and to consolidate enormous economic power. Privatization of the land and industry thus led to rapid concentration in all sectors of the economy. A further aspect of the privatization of the economy was the reduction in size of the government sector. Government expenditures as a share of GNP fell from 41 percent in 1970 to 34 percent in 1979 (Cortázar, 1982). This led to a decline in the level of social expenditure per capita of 17 percent (Table 8).

Under protection of a severely authoritarian military regime, the bureaucrats trained in the principles of liberal economics were able to induce what appeared to be a definitive take-off between 1977 and 1980. The average annual growth rate in real GDP during these years was 8.5 percent, while the rate of inflation declined to 31 percent. In agriculture, the sectors able to grow rapidly were those with international comparative advantages, especially fruits and forest products. Manufacturing grew at the annual rate of 8 percent. Yet, a closer look at sectoral rates of growth indicates the artificial nature of this boom. Expansion was largely based on an increase in external debt and investment remained depressed. The high growth rate sectors were financial services (21 percent annual growth), commerce (17 percent) and construction (14 percent) indicating the speculative nature of expansion and its bias towards nontradeable goods. In spite of rapid growth, the rate of unemployment remained at an average of 18 percent, indicating the structural incapacity of the neoliberal model to absorb surplus labor. The share of employment in the informal sector of the economy increased from 26 percent in 1970 to 29 percent in 1980 (García and Wells, 1983). With opportunities for urban migration limited by unemployment, the peasant sector expanded rapidly as a refuge alternative and a reservoir of poverty. Between 1965 and 1979, the number of farms under twenty hectares of irrigated land increased by no less than 50 percent (Jarvis, 1981). The distribution of income also grew sharply more unequal following the logic of social disarticulation. Between 1969 and 1978, the real income of the poorest 60 percent of the population decreased by 18 percent. Absolute poverty increased as well with 59 percent of the population below the poverty line in 1979 compared to 35 percent in 1968.

In 1979, the Chicago boys were at the peak of their economic power, and they set out to attack the one remaining variable which required adjustment: reducing the rate of inflation from 38 percent down to that of the dollar. To do so, they adopted the dramatic measure of pegging the peso to the dollar at a "forever" fixed exchanged rate, following the theory of the monetary approach to the balance of payments. While this was effective in bringing inflation down to zero in 1982 through a massive contraction of economy activities, the fact that this did not occur immediately led to an overvaluation of the peso by nearly 100 percent in 1982. Rapid capital inflows, induced by high interest rate differentials, allowed the financing of the growing current account deficit and thus the peso did not have to be devalued for a full three years. The results were devastating to the Chilean economy. Imports increased rapidly and depressed the production of tradeables, bankrupting large segments of industry constructed painstakingly over 50 years of import substitution industrialization. The articulated alliance was thus given a death blow by the bureaucrats of liberalism. The rapid inflow of foreign funds through debt created monetary expansion which encouraged the production of nontradeables. Land speculation, financial services, commercial activities, luxury imports, and construction became the key sectors of economic growth. By contrast, agriculture, manufacturing, and mining were stagnant.

By the end of 1982, the disaster was fully apparent. The rate of growth of real GDP in 1982 had fallen by 15 percent. Real income per capita had declined by 4 percent relative to 1970 and per capita industrial production by 25 percent. Inflation was back at 30 percent (Edwards, 1982). The foreign debt was the highest in Latin America on a per capita basis amounting to 80 percent of the GNP and its service absorbing 80 percent of the value of export earnings. Most of the large financial groups had been bankrupted by the incapacity of many businesses and individuals to pay their debts in a context of recession, rising interest rates, and devaluation (about half of the domestic debt was held in dollar terms). The government had to nationalize these financial institutions with the result that it now controls virtually the whole financial sector and most of the real sector of the economy as well.

The social costs were devastating. Unemployment had reached 33 percent (including people receiving the miserable wage of 1 U.S. dollar per day as part of the Plan of Minimum Employment). The share of wages in total income had dropped by 15 percent between 1974 and 1982 (Cortázar, 1982). Pensions and family allowances had fallen by 35 percent and 40 percent, respectively, relative to 1970 (Table 8). In Santiago, the level of consumption by the 20 percent poorest households declined by 31 percent and that of the poorest 60 percent by 19 percent between 1969 and 1978. By contrast, the consumption level of the wealthiest 20 percent increased by 2,072 percent (Cortázar, 1982). The distribution of wealth and income had worsened, and absolute poverty increased for the poor relative to 20 years before. Food dependency in wheat had increased from 30 percent in 1973 to 63 percent in 1982. And devaluation of the peso by more than 100 percent in one year following June 1982 was pushing upward the level of food prices, squeezing further the consumption levels of the poor.

Economic collapse resurrected political activity, this time directed against the military regime. Opposition initially took the form of a broad democratic alliance dominated by the Christian Democracy. Yet, the failure of negotiating concessions with the military is leading to a weakening of this center alliance and to increasing polarization of the opposition, paving the way toward the escalation of violence in the face of stubborn resistance of Pinochet's one-man rule.

The lesson is clear in terms of social disarticulation. By returning to the liberal model of export-led social disarticulation that prevailed in Latin America before the Great Depression, Chile (and other Southern Cone countries) demonstrated, once more, the lack of long-run viability and the high social costs of this style of growth in spite of its theoretical attractiveness in the textbooks of orthodox economic teaching.

4. Conclusion

Political and economic instability in Latin America can usefully be analyzed in terms of the contradictions of disarticulated growth and the struggles between articulated and disarticulated alliances in repeated attempts at social articulation. While articulation by growth has proved to be illusory, articulation by reform has failed to be properly achieved either due to lack of adequate conceptualization of the necessary reforms involved or to lack of sufficient political power to carry through these reforms. We have studied in some detail the experiences of Argentina, Brazil, and Chile with articulation by growth or by reform. Other relevant Latin American experiences also should be analyzed, in particular the attempts at articulation in Peru in 1968 and Ecuador in 1972 as well as the Cuban and Nicaraguan models.

In terms of strategies of transition to social articulation, the historical experiences we have studied reveal how much more difficult it is to gain control over investment and trade in order to redefine and expand the key sectors of economic growth than it is to create the necessary expansion of domestic effective demand for wage goods. In the latter, both the Peronist and the Popular Unity regimes became successful too rapidly. The implication is the need to postpone satisfying popular pressure for increased consumption of wage goods until productivity gains in the production of these goods have been firmly obtained. Increasing wage goods consumption on the basis of the mobilization of excessive capacity alone is an invitation to subsequent destabilization. Neglecting the key role of the external sector in providing access to the raw materials and capital goods for the wage-goods industries as well as in importing those wage goods for which the country does not have natural comparative advantages is also a sure path to destabilization.

The transition to social articulation thus requires enough political power to postpone demands for increased consumption of wage goods until permitted by appropriate gains in productivity and to curtail the entrenched habits for internationalized consumption patterns in the upper classes. The hard task of this transition is to use the power of the state to redirect investment and to submit trade to the needs of articulation. However arduous the task, there seem to be few alternatives to this approach if stable and equitable styles of development are at last to be part of Latin America's future.

REFERENCES

Baran, P. *The Political Economy of Growth*. New York: Prometheus Books, 1957.
Bitar, S. *Transición, Socialismo, y Democracia*. Mexico: Siglo XXI, 1979.
Bresser, P. L. "Auge e Declinio nos Anos 70," *Revista de Política Económica*, vol. 3, no. 2 (1983).

Bukharin, N. *Imperialism and the World Economy*. New York: Monthly Review Press, 1973.

Cardoso, F. E. "Associated-Dependent Development: Theoretical and Practical Implications." In *Authoritarian Brazil*, edited by A. Stepan. New Haven: Yale University Press, 1973.

Cavarozzi, M. "Political Opposition and Transition to Democracy in Latin America: The Argentinian Case." Paper presented at the Latin American Studies Association Meeting, Mexico, September, 1983.

Chenery, H., and M. Syrquin. *Patterns of Development, 1950–1970*. London: Oxford University Press, 1975.

Collier, D. *The New Authoritarianism in Latin America*. Princeton: Princeton University Press, 1979.

Cortázar, R. "Chile: Distributive Results, 1973–1982." Santiago: CIEPLAN, November, 1982, mimeographed.

de Janvry, A. *The Agrarian Question and Reformism in Latin America*. Baltimore: The Johns Hopkins University Press, 1981.

de Janvry, A., and E. Sadoulet. "Social Articulation as a Condition for Equitable Growth," *Journal of Development Economics*, vol. 13 (1983), pp. 275–303.

Denslow, D., and W. Tyler. "Perspectives on Poverty and Income Inequality in Brazil." World Bank Staff Working Paper no. 601. Washington, D.C.: World Bank, July 1983.

de Vylder, S. *Allende's Chile*. Cambridge: Cambridge University Press, 1976.

Díaz-Alejandro, C. *Essays on the Economic History of the Argentine Republic*. New Haven: Yale University Press, 1970.

Dos Santos, T. "Economic Crisis and Democratic Transition in Brazil," *Contemporary Marxism* (1980).

Edwards, S. "Economic Policy and the Record of Economic Growth in Chile in the 1970's and the 1980's." Department of Economics, University of California, Los Angeles, November 1982, mimeographed.

Emmanuel, A. *Unequal Exchange*. New York: Modern Reader, 1972.

Evans, P. *Dependent Development: The Alliance of Multinational, State, and Local Capital in Brazil*. Princeton: Princeton University Press, 1979.

Faucher, P. "The Paradise that Never Was: The Breakdown of the Authoritarian Order." In *Authoritarian Capitalism*, edited by T. Bruneau and P. Faucher. Boulder, Colorado: Westview Press, 1981.

Ferrer, A. *The Argentine Economy*. Berkeley: University of California Press, 1967.

Fox, L. "Income Distribution Analysis in Brazil: Better Numbers and New Findings," January 1982 (unpublished).

Foxley, A., and O. Muñoz. "Income Distribution, Economic Growth, and Social Structure: The Case of Chile." In *Income Distribution in Latin America*, edited by A. Foxley. Cambridge: Cambridge University Press, 1976.

Frank, A. G. *Capitalism and Underdevelopment in Latin America*. New York: Modern Reader, 1969.

Furtado, C. *Economic Development in Latin America*. Cambridge: Cambridge University Press, 1970.

García, A., and J. Wells. "Chile: A Laboratory for Failed Experiments in Capitalist Political Economy," *Cambridge Journal of Economics*, vol. 7 (1983), pp. 287–304.

Garretón, M. A. "Political Opposition and Transition to Democracy in Latin America: The Chilean Case." Paper presented at the Latin American Studies Association Meeting, Mexico, September 1983.

Hirschman, A. O. *Essays in Trespassing: Economics to Politics and Beyond.* Cambridge: Cambridge University Press, 1981.

Hymer, S. "The Multinational Corporation and the Law of Uneven Development." In *Economics and the World Order from the 1970's to the 1990's*, edited by J. Bhagwati. New York: Collier-Macmillan, 1972.

Iglesias, E. "Latin America: Broadening the Social Impact of Growth," *IFDA Dossier*, Geneva, 1979.

International Bank for Reconstruction and Development. *Chile: An Economy in Transition.* Washington, D.C.: World Bank, 1980.

Jarvis, L. "Small Farmers and Agricultural Workers in Chile, 1973–1979." PREALC, Working Paper no. 210. Santiago, September 1981.

Johnson, H. *Economic Policies Toward Less Developed Countries.* Washington, D.C.: Brookings Institution, 1967.

Jorgenson, D. "The Role of Agriculture in Economic Development: Classical versus Neoclassical Models of Growth." In *Subsistence Agriculture and Economic Development*, edited by C. Wharton. Chicago: Aldine Publishing Company, 1969.

Kalecki, M. "The Marxian Equation of Reproduction and Modern Economics," *Social Science Information*, vol. 7 (December 1968), pp. 73–79.

Kay, G. *Development and Underdevelopment: A Marxist Analysis.* New York: St. Martin's Press, 1975.

Knight, P. and R. Moran. "Bringing the Poor Into the Growth Process: The Case of Brazil," *Finance and Development* (1981).

Kuznets, S. *Modern Economic Growth: Rate, Structure, and Spread.* New Haven: Yale University Press, 1966.

Lenin, I. V. *Imperialism: The Highest Stage of Capitalism.* Peking: Foreign Languages Press, 1973.

Lewis, A. "Economic Development with Unlimited Supplies of Labor." In *The Economics of Underdevelopment*, edited by A. Agarwala and S. Singh. London: Oxford University Press, 1958.

Luxemburg, R. *The Accumulation of Capital: An Anti-Critique.* New York: Monthly Review Press, 1972.

Magdoff, H. *The Age of Imperialism.* New York: Modern Reader, 1969.

Marini, R. M. "Dialéctica de la Dependencia," *Sociedad y Desarrollo*, no. 1 (January–March 1972), pp. 5–31.

Mamalakis, M. *Historical Statistics of Chile.* Greenwood Press, 1978.

North, D. "A Framework for Analyzing the State in Economic History," *Explorations in Economic History*, vol. 16 (October 1979).

Prebisch, R. "Commercial Policy in Underdeveloped Countries," *American Economic Review*, vol. 49, no. 2 (May 1959), pp. 251–73.

Ramos, S. "Inflation in Chile and the Political Economy of the Unidad Popular Government." In *Chile, 1970*–73, edited by S. Sideri. The Hague: Martinus Nijhoff, 1979.

Rodgers, E. *The Diffusion of Innovations*. New York: Free Press of Glencoe, 1962.

Roemer, J. "Unequal Exchange, Labor Migration, and International Capital Flows: A Theoretical Synthesis." Univerisity of California, Department of Economics, Working Paper no. 172. Davis, July 1981.

Rostow, W. *The Stages of Economic Growth*. Cambridge: Cambridge University Press, 1960.

Scultz, T. W. *Transforming Traditional Agriculture*. New Haven: Yale University Press, 1964.

Serra, J. "Three Mistaken Theses Regarding the Connection Between Industrialization and Authoritarian Regimes." In *The New Authoritarianism in Latin America*, edited by D. Collier, Princeton: Princeton University Press, 1979.

_____."Ciclos e Mudanças Estruturais na Economia Brasileira do Aposguerra: A Crise Recente," *Revista de Economía Política*, vol. 2, no. 3 (1982).

Smith, Adam. *An Inquiry Into the Nature and Causes of the Wealth of Nations* (2 vols.). Edited by Edwin Cannan. London: Metheun & Company, 1930.

Stallings, B. *Class Conflict and Economic Development in Chile, 1958*–1973. Stanford: Stanford University Press, 1978.

Sunkel. O. "National Development Policy and External Dependency in Latin America," *Journal of Development Studies*, vol. 6 (October 1969).

Tavares, M. C., and P. R. Souza. "Emprego e Salarios na Industria," *Revista de Economía Política*, vol. 6, no. 1 (1981).

United Nations, *Economic Survey of Latin America, 1980*. Santiago de Chile: United Nations Publication, 1982.

Weeks, J. "The Sphere of Production and the Analysis of Crisis in Capitalism," *Science and Society*, vol. 41, no. 3 (Fall 1977), pp. 281–320.

Wynia, G. *The Politics of Latin American Development*. Cambridge: Cambridge University Press, 1978.

Wolff, R. and S. Resnick. "Classes in Marxian Theory," *Review of Radical Political Economics*, vol. 13 (Winter 1982), pp. 1–18.

Wages and Employment in International Recessions: Recent Latin American Experience

Victor E. Tokman

Latin America and the Caribbean, as well as the rest of the world, have gone through several international crises during the last decade which have made it necessary to introduce economic adjustment policies. Adjustment is inevitable since the national economies must adapt themselves to the reduced availability of real resources. Nevertheless, there is more than one possible adjustment policy, and given this diversity as well as the varying modes of application, different results emerge.

In the first place, as regards the period required to produce results, there is a difference between policies that affect the level of expenditure and policies that operate through changes in relative prices as the principal mechanism for shifting resources from the production of goods for domestic utilization to the production of tradeables. Yet, the trend in the reduction of domestic expenditure should be to concentrate on the level of consumption rather than on that of investment, so as to avoid adverse effects upon economic growth. At the same time, adjustment to the international recession has coincided with inflation in most Latin American and Caribbean countries, making it necessary to apply both adustments simultaneously. The final result is that adjustment policies have ceased to be neutral and have significantly affected wages and the employment level: wages, because they are usually regarded as the key variable for stabilization of the price level, for fostering an improvement in international competitiveness, and for inducing the contraction of the level of consumption; the employment level, because a lower level of domestic expenditure generates a higher level of open unemployment.

The current world crisis, like the one suffered at the beginning of the 1970s, is different from other international fluctuations to which the economies of the region and the developing world have been subjected. In fact, the magnitude and depth of these recent crises affect not only developing countries but also those at the center. In this connection, a comparison needs to be drawn between the present recessive conjuncture and that experienced in the 1930s.

There are at least two important differences between the two periods. First, the role currently played by the rise in oil prices and whether a country produces oil or not establishes a first major differentiation among countries, irrespective of whether it is located in the North or in the South. In Latin America and the Caribbean, this differentiation can be seen in the dissimilar performance in the present crisis of the oil-exporting economies as compared with the rest of the continent.

Second, in contrast to the 1930s, the present and previous international recessions have been accompanied by inflation in the developed world. This has at least two direct implications. On the one hand, the deterioration in the terms of trade of non-oil-exporting countries of the region is at present greater than that observed in the 1930s. The terms of trade of Latin American countries decreased at annual rates of 6.7 percent between 1930 and 1933, whereas this deterioration attained a negative annual rate of 8.4 percent in the 1974–1975 crisis and of 9.6 percent from 1978 to 1981 in the non-oil-exporting group. Even so, and perhaps because of the policy of relative expansion pursued in the developed countries in contrast to the situation during the 1930s, the decline in the purchasing power of the region's exports has been less severe; in the current crisis the expansion of exports in quantum has more than compensated for the fall in the terms of trade.

On the other hand, the policies pursued in the central countries and especially in the United States during the present recession have entailed a substantial rise in nominal interest rates at a time when foreign indebtedness in the countries of the region has increased significantly. The rise in nominal interest rates exceeds the rate of growth in export prices on non-oil-exporting Latin American countries, amounting between 1978 and 1981 to an increase of 47.5 percent in the prime rate and of 32.6 percent in the rate applicable to Euro-dollars, both in real terms.

The aim of this paper is to review the relationships between the aforementioned variables which summarize the effects of international recessions on the economy in the region and the behavior of wages and employment. To this end, special attention will be paid to the periods 1974–1975 and from 1979 to the present. On the basis of this review, different reactions of the region's countries to the international situation can be identified as well as the extent to which the latter has affected wages and employment. Given the difficulties in analyzing all countries of the region, a broad typology of situations will be made for an analysis of particular cases. The discussion, moreover, will necessarily be restricted since a more comprehensive analysis of the adjustment process would take us beyond the limited scope of this paper.

We start with a working hypothesis that although the international recession necessarily entails adjustments that imply a relatively lower level of activity, there have been alternative options that have in fact been applied by different countries in the region. These options are in part determined by the structural features of the economy but they also depend on the policy package that is applied. In this context, wage policy comes to play an important role in short-run adjustments and in effect determines the distribution of the costs involved in the adjustment among different groups of the population.

Two other aspects will also be considered. The first is the impact of the rise of the rate of interest on Latin American economies; this is a distinguishing factor of the present crisis. The second is the adjustment of the labor market and its implications for shifts in income levels and income distribution.

1. External Adjustment and Wages

The Case of Small and Open Countries

There is a first group of countries in the region of small size which have a ratio of exports to gross national product fluctuating between 20 and 30 percent. They shared these same structural features already in the 1930s and when faced with the international crisis at that time they had to remain tied to the gold standard while waiting for the automatic adjustment to operate. On that occasion, they suffered a considerable cost as a result of not being able to design policies that would attenuate the effect of the international crisis. The present situation seems to be basically the same. The full impact of world recessions falls upon these economies which must inevitably absorb the deterioration in the terms of trade and reduce real wages whenever an international situation of this sort occurs.

Central America and the Caribbean provide numerous examples of this type of an economy, where the possibility of an autonomous policy is limited. In particular, if we examine the performance of Costa Rica and Honduras in the 1973–1975 crisis and in the present one, we can see that in both countries the fall in the terms of trade has brought with it a decline in real wages. Thus, in Honduras the first recession implied a loss of nearly 6.3 percent in the rate of growth of output owing to the fall in the terms of trade and a reduction of 2.9 percent in industrial-sector real wages during the same period. The present recession has meant a fall in the growth rate of output of around 8.2 percent and of 8.1 percent in industrial real wages (see Table 1).

In Costa Rica there are similar links between the negative effect of the terms of trade and the decrease in real wages during the two international crises. In this country there is also a further reduction in real wages stemming from an upsurge of inflation in an economy that had not previously experienced high inflation rates. The 1973–1975 recession coincided with an inflation rate of 25 percent, while in the 1978–1981 crisis the annual inflation rate averaged 30 percent, and the rate for 1981 reached 65 percent.

The Case of Medium-Sized and Large Countries

During the recession of the 1930s and to a greater extent in more recent international crises, several countries of the region retained a certain degree of autonomy which enabled them to reduce the impact of international crises. This group of countries comprises those of larger size, which are generally less open to international trade and have a higher degree of urbanization and modernization. Hence, exports hardly exceed 10 percent of their gross national product, the proportion of formal-sector, urban activities in employment reaching between 50 and 60 percent of the total labor force with employment in modern industry accounting for between 20 and 28 percent of the non-agricultural labor force. It is precisely in this group of countries that wages come to be a representative variable, given the greater extent of wage-labor as a direct result of the higher degree of modernization. Included in this group are the Southern Cone countries (Argentina, Chile and Uruguay), Brazil, Colombia, Mexico and Venezuela, among others.

To begin with, it is convenient to review the performance and the economic policies of these countries during the crisis of the 1930s.[1] These countries were relatively unaffected by the crisis of the 1930s compared to other countries of the region and the United States and Canada. In general, their economies grew more rapidly than these two countries in the period following the crisis (1932–1939): they recovered sooner (in 1932); their contraction was not so pronounced as in North America; and manufacturing industry, which became the leading sector in these economies, grew steadily at an annual rate of between 8 and 13 percent whereas in the United States the manufacturing sector remained stagnant.

The policies pursued by this group of countries during the 1930s were characteristically heterodox, in defiance of the conventional prescriptions of monetarist experts at the time ("money doctors," according to Carlos Diaz-Alejandro). Concerning the balance of payments, there were exchange rate devaluations, and multiple-exchange systems were established with a higher rate for imports, a medium rate for exports, and a preferential rate for servicing the external debt. Likewise, most of these countries renegotiated their debt unilaterally, with only Argentina, Haiti, and the Dominican Republic continuing to service the debt on its original terms. The effect of devaluation was not inflationary and helped to increase competitiveness through a change in the relation between the exchange rate and wages, basically through an increase in the former while the latter remained stable in real terms. These measures were accompanied by exchange controls and tariff adjustments that increased the level of protection.

The monetary and fiscal policies employed at that time had a clear expansionary effect. The supply of real money increased due to the decline in nominal prices and to the increase in the stock of money against bonds (independently of the gold standard that had been in force up to that time). In several countries, a moratorium on the internal debt was declared and financial institutions were supported to prevent bankruptcy by means of diverse measures ranging from special rediscount lines to, in some cases, the freezing of savings deposits. Fiscal policy acquired distinct anti-cyclical features; there was no attempt to balance the budget and a deficit was financed by delays in payments and an increase in short term borrowing. Likewise, public expenditure increased, thus avoiding a contraction of economic activity.

Finally, the combined effect of these measures was to produce a far-reaching structural transformation which characterizes the economies of these countries up to the present. This transformation basically consisted of a rapid expansion of the manufacturing sector together with a higher degree of state intervention in economic activity.

At present, the group of countries that already enjoyed some autonomy in the 1930s has begun to develop differences mainly because of the range of impacts of oil price hikes in the more recent international crises. Hence, a distinction must be made among oil-exporting countries, those which are largely dependent on imported fuel, and those which have some degree of autonomy owing to their being relatively self-sufficient. Ecuador, Mexico and Venezuela are among the oil-exporting countries; Brazil, in particular, is heavily dependent on fuel imports; and, finally, in the group of countries relatively self-sufficient a distinction must be made between those which in the past decade have applied structural policies of price stabilization and external openness (basically, those of the Southern Cone) and those which have pursued more conventional policies, such as Colombia.

Oil-Exporting Countries

These countries which benefited from the rise in the price of oil through improvement in the terms of trade, expanded their export volume. This was particularly the case of Ecuador, Mexico and Venezuela, which were able to apply a policy of real wage increases owing to a favorable international situation. Hence, a close correlation between the rise in the terms of trade and increases in real wages can be observed. (see Table 1).

However, there was a growing tendency in these countries to overexpand domestic expenditure and to increase the money supply as a result of the aforementioned oil boom, resulting in accelerated inflation and/or balance of payments problems. These results can be judged as paradoxical since these economies had not only historically exhibited low rates of inflation but also had combined their boom in the recent decades with a balance of payments deficit. They were compelled to resort to adjustment policies involving a reduction of expenditures and wage controls, as in Mexico and Venezuela during the period 1971–1979. As a result, real wages tended to contract despite improvements in the terms of trade.

In effect, although during the period 1973–1981 wages benefited from the oil boom, their improvement diminished due to the aforesaid internal disequilibria and the nature of the policies applied. This was reflected in the acceleration of inflation in economies having little previous experience of it and those lacking systems of wage indexation. Thus, in Venezuela between 1973 and 1981, despite an expansion in output on the order of 28 percent attributable to improvements in the terms of trade, real wages in the industrial sector increased by only 14 percent during the same period.

Non-Oil-Exporting Countries

Countries Dependent On Oil Imports

By far, the most important country in this group is Brazil, an economy relatively autonomous in the design of economic policy but heavily dependent on oil imports. This country made active use of its possibilities to increase the external debt in order to cushion the economy from the recessionary impact associated with a pronounced fall in the terms of trade.

As a result of these policies, during 1974–1975 Brazil was able to raise industrial real wages by around 12 percent, despite the fact that the terms of trade fell by approximately 21 percent. Even so, in the face

TABLE 1

External Adjustment, Wages and Prices in Some Latin American Countries

	TERMS OF TRADE[a]	DEGREE OF OPENNESS[b]	EFFECT ON PRODUCT[c]	PURCHASING POWER OF EXPORTS[a]	WAGES[a]			DOMESTIC PRICES[d]
					Urban Minimum	Industrial	Construction	
Group A: Oil-exporting countries								
Ecuador								
1973–1975	36.3	18.1	6.6	16.5	3.3	7.3	n.d	17.1
1975–1978	8.7	12.4	1.1	27.7	-8.0	8.4	n.d	11.6
1978–1981	31.1	11.4	3.6	28.1	111.3	22.9	n.d	13.7
1973–1981	94.4	14.0	13.2	96.0	112.5	43.0	n.d	13.7
Mexico								
1973–1975	3.6	7.3	0.3	2.5	16.9	8.6	5.8	15.8
1975–1978	12.2	7.0	0.8	82.3	7.9	8.0	9.1	21.3
1978–1981	47.6	7.4	3.5	140.6	-8.4	-1.7	1.6	26.1
1973–1981	71.5	7.2	5.1	349.8	15.6	14.0	17.3	21.7
Venezuela								
1973–1975	97.6	14.3	14.0	30.0	-9.3	13.1	n.d	9.8
1975–1978	-13.9	9.5	-1.3	-20.4	-19.6	2.1	n.d	7.3
1978–1981	114.2	8.1	9.3	77.2	17.7	-1.1	-5.2	17.8
1973–1981	264.4	10.6	28.0	102.3	-14.2	14.2	n.d	11.8
Group B: Medium-sized and large countries								
1. Oil-dependent								
Brazil								
1973–1975	-21.2	6.9	-1.5	14.7	-2.3	12.1	6.9	32.5
1975–1978	2.6	6.2	0.2	24.7	3.5	13.3	12.0	42.0
1978–1981	-42.7	7.0	-3.0	6.3	1.1	8.1	-1.9	87.3
1973–1981	-53.7	6.5	-3.5	16.0	2.3	37.3	17.4	54.8

2. Relatively self-sufficient

a) With substantial economic policy changes

Argentina

1973–1975	5.5	-30.0	-1.7	-45.9	-8.9	1.7	33.3	173.8
1975–1978	9.2	-19.2	-1.8	87.2	-50.4	-54.9	-55.9	211.5
1978–1981	8.1	-8.4	-0.7	-3.3	6.3	14.7	3.2	118.2
1973–1981	7.5	48.2	-3.6	24.0	-52.0	-20.6	-43.1	163.9

Chile

1970–1975	15.3	-46.8	-7.2	-28.7	-41.1	-41.8	-18.3	233.1
1975–1978	21.2	-0.6	-0.1	27.1	29.9	44.3	4.2	80.1
1978–1981	24.6	-14.0	-3.4	13.7	-1.5	38.0	27.0	25.9
1970–1981	20.4	-57.2	-11.7	3.0	-24.7	15.9	8.1	98.9

b) Without substantial economic policy changes

Colombia

1973–1975	14.8	-19.9	-2.9	0.4	16.4	-8.0	7.3	22.3
1975–1978	7.4	64.7	4.8	51.7	9.4	13.3	5.1	24.2
1978–1981	6.9	-32.4	-2.2	-23.8	17.6	7.2	17.6	27.7
1973–1981	9.7	-7.4	-0.7	16.1	49.7	11.7	32.6	25.0

Group C: Small open countries

Costa Rica

1973–1975	27.6	-9.2	-2.5	-7.1	-7.4	-9.0	-6.1	25.4
1975–1978	21.2	40.1	8.5	55.2	25.3	31.3	34.9	5.9
1978–1981	21.8	-29.2	-6.4	-10.5	-8.3	-12.2	-11.2	30.1
1973–1981	23.5	-9.8	-2.3	29.7	6.3	4.9	12.7	19.3

Honduras

1973–1975	27.1	-23.1	-6.3	-20.2	-7.2	-2.9	-31.9	10.4
1975–1978	24.1	23.3	5.6	60.5	-15.6	12.0	77.5	6.2
1978–1981	27.1	-23.7	-8.2	-1.0	-6.2	-8.1	-24.4	14.3
1973–1981	26.1	-27.6	-7.2	32.2	-26.5	0.0	-8.6	10.2

Source: Elaborated by PREALC on the basis of national data.

[a] Changes between the initial and final year of each period.
[b] Relation between exports and gross domestic product.
[c] Obtained by multiplying the change in the terms of trade by the coefficient of openness.
[d] Annual cumulative rates referring to changes December to December.

of a further fall in its terms of trade from 1978 onwards, the growth in real wages has considerably decelerated (see Table 1).

It is clear that Brazil gradually lost flexibility in the management of international crises which took the form of internal imbalances witnessed by the inflationary upsurge of recent years and the increased indebtedness associated with the rise in real interest rates. Thus, if the growth in the nominal interest rate applied by commercial banks to best customers (prime rate) as well as that applied to short-term deposits in Euro-dollars is compared with the growth in the price of Brazilian exports, it will be seen that the former rose during 1978–1981 by 59 percent and the latter by 43 percent, both in real terms. Given that 86 percent of Brazil's external debt has been contracted at variable interest rates and that it constitutes around 30 percent of gross national product, and taking into account that the rate prevailing in 1978 was around 10 percent, it can be estimated that the rise in international interest rates has produced a deterioration of around 1. 3 percent in output. This decline in output is equivalent to about 43 percent of the deterioration in output attributable to the fall in the terms of trade during the period 1978–1981.

Nevertheless, despite the unfavorable situation confronted by Brazil, the analysis of the period 1973–1981 shows that although it had to face a deterioration in the terms of trade that implied a decrease in the rate of growth of output of around 3.5 percent, domestic policies were used that not only prevented wages from a general decline, but permitted a rise of around 37 percent in the average real wage paid in the industrial sector. This is undoubtedly a clear illustration of policies capable of coping with the international recession without shifting the full burden of the adjustment to wages and which, on the contrary, allowed their expansion despite the adverse conditions in the international market.

Countries Not Dependent On Oil

Countries Without Substantial Changes In Economic Policy. A case that illustrates this type of situation is Colombia. Its terms of trade were adversely affected both in the 1973–1975 crisis and again in 1978. Despite the adverse impact of the international situation, its economic policies fostered an expansion in the quantum of exports, neutralizing the adverse effect of international prices and permitting a substantial rise in real wages during the period. Thus, in the face of a potential decline in output of around 1 percent between 1973 and 1981 that could be attributed to the decline in the terms of trade, urban minimum wages rose by 50 percent, industrial wages by 12 percent and those in construction by 33 percent, all in real terms during the same period (see Table 1).

Countries With Substantial Changes In Economic Policy. This group includes Argentina, Chile and Uruguay,[2] which during the decade pursued policies of price stabilization and external openness in their economies. It is outside the scope of this paper to comment on these policies.[3] We shall concentrate instead on the degree of autonomy concerning the management of this domestic policy and on the consequences of such policies.

First, the fact that these countries possess some degree of autonomy in their economic policy decisions and are not entirely subject to international fluctuations is clearly illustrated by the case of Argentina, which during the 1973–1975 crisis succeeded in raising wages in real terms despite a deterioration in its terms of trade of nearly 30 percent. Similarly, Chile in the recession beginning in 1978 succeeded in preventing the deterioration in the terms of trade from being transferred to wages. It should be noted in this case that the increase in real wages during the recent period was largely due to the slowdown in the inflation rate, which in an indexed economy automatically amounted to a rise in real wages.

Secondly, wages became a basic variable in the economic and social policies adopted by these countries. Wage control was a basic policy instrument in the effort to achieve price stabilization and an improvement in international competitiveness; especially during periods when fixed exchange-rate policies were in force or more generally, an overvaluation of the local currency was maintained with a view to achieving through reduced wages, a shift of resources towards the production of tradeables. Wage control was also used as an instrument to discipline the labor force, since in both countries the governments sought to avoid social pressures that might challenge their economic and political policies. In particular, this economic strategy led to a disarticulation of the trade union movement that resulted from an anti-industrial and anti-occupational bias present in the policy.[4] This permitted reductions in real wages without major resistance arising from within the system.

The result of these policies was a reduction in wages that apparently exceeded the cost that would have been incurred in absorbing the deterioration of the terms of trade. Thus, in Argentina between 1973 and 1981 the decline in the terms of trade implied a reduction in the growth of output of nearly 3.6 percent but wages in the industrial sector fell during that period by nearly 21 percent. In Chile between 1970 and 1975, the negative effect of the terms of trade implied a fall in output of around 7 percent, but industrial wages contracted by over 41 percent (see Table 1).

To summarize the analysis of this section, the experience of different countries in the region suggests that although in the face of adverse international developments the countries have no option other than to adjust their economies, this adjustment implies adopting incomes policies that result in a fall of real wages. This has automatically occurred only in a small group of countries which because of their size and degree of openness do not possess the autonomy to change the situation. On the other hand, a number of countries in the region have in the past shown a certain degree of autonomy to control the domestic adjustment to international recessions by influencing the distribution of the cost of adjustment, and by other mechanisms through which the national economies adjust to external crises. Experience also shows that some countries have succeeded in applying an expansive wage policy under circumstances of adverse international conditions, just as others have accentuated the cost of adjustment by introducing substantial changes in their economic policies at the same time. Finally, the oil-exporting countries are a special case in which internal and sometimes external imbalances are likely to follow with the consequence that wages actually rise much more slowly than theoretically expected.

2. The Increase in International Interest Rates

The present world recession differs from the earlier ones in that it has not only produced a major fall in the region's terms of trade but also has been accompanied by a rise in the interest rate applicable to servicing the external debt. Between 1978 and 1981 the rate applicable to best debtors by North American banks (prime rate) rose 72.3 percent and the rate applicable to short-term deposits in Euro-dollars rose 54.9 percent. The trend during the first half of 1982 indicates still higher levels than those prevailing towards the end of 1983.

This considerable increase in nominal interest rates entails an additional outflow of financial resources for the countries of the region. It has been estimated that in 1981 each additional percentage point in the nominal interest rate meant an increase in interest payment of 2.25 billion dollars for the region as a whole. This payment is equivalent to 2.6 percent of the total value of Latin America's exports, which in countries like Mexico approached 3.3 percent, and in Argentina and Brazil, about 3 percent of this export revenue.

To assess the pressure on resources implied by the increase in the nominal interest rate, it is necessary to examine the evolution of export prices in the region during the same period. When this comparison is made, the results seem to reflect the particular features of each country. In the region's oil-exporting economies, export prices grew faster than the increase in the nominal interest rate during the period and the variation in the real interest rate has consequently been negative. In the remaining countries of the region, the effect of the change in the real interest rate affects output growth differently according to the evolution of export prices, of the external debt as a percentage of gross national product, and the portion of the debt contracted at variable interest rates.

First, in some countries the rise in nominal interest rates was accompanied by a fall in export prices as the external debt rose to a larger percentage of gross national product. This is typically the case of Central American countries, in particular Costa Rica and Honduras. As a result of the rise in real interest rates, the possibility of growth diminished at least by 2 percent in Costa Rica and in Honduras by 1.6 percent during the period 1978–1981[5] (see Table 2). Secondly, there is another group of countries where the rise in nominal interest rates combined with virtually stationary export prices and where the percentage of the external debt in national product is near 25 percent but is largely contracted at variable interest rates. In this group we find Brazil and Colombia, where the effect of a potential loss in output growth approximates 1 percent during the same period. Finally, there is a group of countries in which the increase in nominal interest rates was largely offset by an improvement in export prices, but high coefficients of the external debt as a percentage of the national product were exhibited. The average size of the coefficient was about 40 percent, of which some 80 percent has been contracted at variable interest rates. This is the case of Argentina and Chile, with a potential loss in output of 0.4 percent in the former and of 0.7 percent in the latter.

On the other hand, to gain an approximate idea of the effect of the rise in real interest rates in relation to that attributable to the deterioration of the terms of trade, it is convenient to relate both effects to the potential growth in national product. This shows that the size of the effect associated with real interest rates during the period 1978–1981 varies among different countries between 19 and 56 percent of the terms-of-trade effect. In one extreme case we find Argentina and Colombia, where the real interest-rate effect is around 50 percent of that linked with the terms of trade. We next have an intermediate group including Brazil and Costa Rica, where the effect of the former is around 30 percent of the latter. A third case exists in countries like Chile and Honduras where the same relation is nearly 20 percent (see Table 2).

Lastly, it should be noted that the most significant change in the structure of the region's external debt in recent years is an increase in the proportion of private funds in the total, as regards both their origin and their destination. There is a considerable increase in the proportion

TABLE 2
Effect of the Change in International Interest Rates, 1978–81

	$\dfrac{i_1}{\dot{p}_x}$ (1)	$\dfrac{i_2}{\dot{p}_x}$ (2)	$\dfrac{i_1}{\dot{p}_i/t_c}$ (3)	$\dfrac{i_2}{\dot{p}_i/t_c}$ (4)	PERCENTAGE OF THE EXTERNAL DEBT — In National Product[a] (5)	PERCENTAGE OF THE EXTERNAL DEBT — Subject to Variable Interest Rates[b] (6)	EFFECT ON POTENTIAL OUTPUT GROWTH DUE TO INTEREST RATES[c] (7)	RELATION OF THE EFFECTS ON OUTPUT GROWTH DUE TO INTEREST RATES AND TERMS OF TRADE[d] (8)
Argentina	5.9	17.8	-57.3	-47.5	41.1	80.0	-0.39	56.0
Brazil	42.9	58.9	26.1	40.3	24.9	84.0	-1.07	36.0
Chile	22.1	35.8	-14.4	-4.8	35.6	65.6	-0.68	20.0
Colombia	68.1	86.9	7.2	19.2	22.8	58.3	-1.03	46.8
Costa Rica	56.0	73.6	99.4	125.5	49.3	62.4	-1.99	31.1
Honduras	49.9	66.7	8.0	20.2	59.6	45.8	-1.59	19.4

Source: Elaborated by PREALC on the basis of information from the countries.

i_1 = variation in the interest rate in Euro-dollars at 90 days.
i_2 = variation in the prime interest rate.
$\dot{p}_x$ = changes in exports prices.
$\dot{p}_i$ = changes in domestic prices.
t_c = changes in the exchange rate.

[a]Refers to 1980.
[b]Refers to the average for the period 1978–1980.
[c]Calculated by applying the mean variation in the real interest rate (1) and (2) to the percentage of the debt subject to variable interest rates.
[d]Relation between (7) and the effect of loss due to the terms of trade estimated in Table 1.

of private sector credits without public sector guarantees. This has brought about a change in the characteristics of external indebtedness, which has increasingly been contracted at variable interest rates, reaching 85 percent of the total of 1981. The recipient countries have clearly become more vulnerable to the rate variations in international markets.

From a distributive point of view, the effect of increased nominal rates should be related to the evolution of those particular prices relevant to private lenders. For them, the relevant prices are given by changes in domestic prices in relation to changes in the exchange rate. From this comparison, it will be seen below that the effect of the rise in nominal interest rates has not generally been passed on to national private lenders; this is because most of the countries in the region exhibit either a fixed exchange rate with increase in domestic prices or exchange-rate depreciation lagging behind domestic inflation.

A clear example of fixed exchange rates with domestic inflation is the group of oil-exporting countries, especially Mexico and Venezuela; in addition such small and open economies as Honduras maintained a fixed exchange rate against positive variations in domestic prices. From the standpoint of those countries incurring debts in dollars, this is likely to imply a negative real interest rate. The same occurs in Argentina and Chile since (during this period) both countries applied stabilization policies which made use either of a fixed exchange rate or lagging devaluation as instruments for reducing inflationary pressures. In these two cases, the real interest rate for dollar debtors is also negative. In Brazil and Colombia, where lags in foreign exchange depreciation are also found but to a lesser degree than in the countries mentioned above, the effect was to reduce the increase in the real interest rate by about half in Brazil and by one-ninth in Colombia. Lastly, there were countries such as Costa Rica, where the rise in the nominal interest rate was accompanied by an appreciation in the real exchange rate, resulting in a positive real interest rate that was higher for the private debtor than for the country as a whole.

In summary, it is clear that the rise in the international nominal interest rate amounts to an additional substantial burden for the countries of the region, which at the same time are forced to adjust their economies to a recessionary situation. Nevertheless, on comparing the effects of the rise in real interest rates, the situation of particular countries is found to differ according to the evolution of their export prices, the weight of the debt in relation to national product, and the proportion of the debt subject to variable interest rates. Finally, the actual incidence of the increase in nominal interest rates upon national private sectors depends on the exchange rate policy of the country and on the evolution of domestic prices. The result shows in most cases a lesser burden than that determined by the variation in the interest rate in international financial markets, and in some countries indicates the transformation of this burden into an actual subsidy.

3. Economic Adjustment and the Labor Market

In implying that open unemployment is determined by high wages, conventional adjustment policies pursue the decrease of real wages as a way to equilibrate the labor market. This line of argument can be questioned on theoretical grounds but we will restrict ourselves to discuss its empirical validity in the case of Latin America.

In analyzing the variation in wages (whether the urban minimum, those in manufacturing or in construction) in relation to the changes in open unemployment during two periods of the last decade, the results clearly show that no such relationship exists. The information for twelve Latin American countries in the period 1975–1978 and 1978–1981, selected because of the different international situations prevailing in each one, clearly confirms this (see Table 3).

Thus, during the first period only in one country (Venezuela) was the fall in urban minimum wages accompanied by a significant decrease in the rate of open unemployment. But even in this case the same relationship did not hold in connection with the change in industrial wages. Moreover, there was no country in which an increase in real wages was associated with a significant rise (over one percentage point) in open unemployment. On the contrary, in six out of the twelve countries considered we found the opposite association; that is, increases in real wages were accompanied by significant decreases in the open-unemployment rate or decreases in the former operated with a significant rise in open unemployment.

In the period 1978–1981 only two countries showed a simultaneous fall in real wages and open unemployment when both urban minimum wages and industrial wages were considered. Similarly, when sorting out movements in the same direction (i.e., increases in real wages together with increases in open unemployment) the number of cases is three for the urban minimum while there were no significant cases in relating wages in industry and construction. On the other hand, we had a great number of countries showing opposite movements in real wages and the rate of open unemployment, no matter what type of wages were being considered.

The evident incapacity of changes in the real wage to account for changes in open unemployment, and indeed the appearance of con-

Table 3

Real Wages, Activity Level and Open Unemployment

	1975–1978					1978–1981				
	GROWTH OF PRODUCT[a]	CHANGES IN WAGES[b]			CHANGES IN OPEN UNEMPLOYMENT[c]	GROWTH OF PRODUCT[a]	CHANGES IN WAGES[b]			CHANGES IN OPEN UNEMPLOYMENT[c]
		w_m	w_i	w_c			w_m	w_i	w_c	
Argentina	1.6	-50.4	-54.9	-55.9	0.2	0.2	8.9	19.9	—	0.7[d]
Brazil	6.6	3.5	13.3	12.0	0.6	3.5	-10.2	-6.3	-15.5	1.7[e]
Colombia	6.1	9.4	13.3	5.1	-2.0	4.1	20.3	7.4	14.3	-0.8
Costa Rica	6.9	25.3	31.3	34.9	0.4	0.6	1.8	0.7	1.4	3.3
Chile	7.2	30.0	20.6	44.4	-1.7	6.7	-0.6	18.1	23.6	-4.3
Jamaica	-2.1	-17.2[f]			4.0	-3.8[d]	-12.0[f]			5.0[d]
Mexico	6.6	7.9	8.0		-0.3	8.5	-9.0	-5.7		-2.4
Panama	3.6	-11.7	—	-11.7	1.0	5.0	2.1	—	-2.5	2.0[g]
Peru	0.5	-32.0	-27.4	-38.6	0.5	3.9	13.8	2.6	2.6	-1.2
Trinidad & Tobago	9.9	8.8			-1.7	4.9[d]	5.1[d]			1.8
Uruguay	4.1	-16.8[f]	-26.3	-25.9	1.6	4.1	-15.1	-15.0	-13.6	-3.4
Venezuela	6.1	-19.6	2.1	—	-3.2	-0.1	-3.0	-12.8	—	1.9

Source: PREALC figures on the basis of information from the countries.

[a]Annual growth rates.

[b]w_m: urban minimum wages.

w_i: manufacturing-industry wages.

w_c: wages in construction. Percentage variation during the period.

[c]Changes in percentage points between the first and the last years.

[d]Refers to 1978–1980.

[e]Preliminary estimation.

[f]Refers to total wages.

[g]Refers to 1978–1979.

siderable evidence to the contrary, necessitates the investigation of other determinant factors. In particular, changes in the level of economic activity can induce variations in the open-unemployment rates. This is based not only on an important current of theoretical interpretation but also the available evidence for short-term variations seems to suggest the existence of a high correlation of this sort. On relating information on the growth of gross domestic product with changes in the rate of open unemployment (see Table 3), it is observed that in the period 1975–1978, in five of the twelve countries for which information is available, there is a positive correlation between accelerated growth and decreases in the unemployment rate, or between a contraction in output and an increase in the unemployment rate. Again, in the period 1978–1981, this relationship holds in five of the twelve countries. It is clear that there is in the short run an appreciable degree of correlation between the level of economic activity and the rate of open unemployment, though in some cases a high growth rate can be associated with a constant unemployment rate.

In order to verify this association quantitatively, some simple econometric exercises were carried out. First, an analysis of simple correlation between changes in the open-unemployment rate and the rate of growth of output or of wages (urban minimum, industrial and in construction) was made. Secondly, multiple regression was used in an attempt to analyze the causal impact of the growth rate of output and changes in real wages upon variations in open unemployment, introducing different definitions with respect to wages. The results can be seen in Table 4. They corroborate the conclusions shown by the previous table in the sense that regardless of the definitions used, real-wage changes had little effect on the variations of the open-unemployment rate since the coefficients in general are not significant. On the contrary, variations in the level of activity clearly influence the level of open unemployment and the coefficients obtained, whether by simple correlation or by multiple regression, are always significant.

The data suggest then that the open-unemployment rate appears to be more responsive to changes in the activity level than to variations in real wages. Even so, the attempt to explain changes in the labor market through the mere observation of variations in open unemployment is indeed limited for economies like those of the region where there is a significant amount of underemployment. Adjustment in heterogeneous labor markets may take various forms: changes in open unemployment, variations in underemployment or a combination of the two. Let us illustrate the reaction of the labor market to a recessionary conjuncture in four Latin American countries presenting different conditions.

TABLE 4

Changes in Open Unemployment and Their Possible Determinants

	Constant	Changes in Activity Level[a]	Changes in Real Wages[b]	R^2
Subperiod 1975–1978[c]				
Equation 1	2.88633	−0.57945	0.03423	0.60273
		(−3.40988)*	(1.41288)	
Equation 2	0.79168	−0.24174	−0.11179	0.16458
		(−0.46913)	(−0.02459)	
Equation 3	0.04078	−0.77355	−0.01619	0.21569
		(−0.01496)	(−0.43274)	
Equation 4	4.75109	−0.18935		0.31080
Equation 5	−5.41725		−3.67836	0.29916
Equation 6	−5.10346		−6.64900	0.36598
Subperiod 1978–1981[c]				
Equation 1	2.25356	−0.62411	0.01137	0.56503
		(−3.41731)*	(0.20000)	
Equation 2	1.87016	−0.69292	−0.02299	0.66087
		(−3.37861)*	(−0.47701)	
Equation 3	3.67456	−1.03945	−0.01178	0.50647
		(−1.77369)	(−0.15435)	
Equation 4	3.40546	−0.90710		0.75039
Equation 5	1.31256		0.01373	0.37023
Equation 6	0.63197		−0.61773	0.12523

Source: Table 3.

[a]Defined as the annual cumulative rate of growth of gross domestic product.

[b]Equation 1: includes urban minimum wages; equation 2: includes industrial wages; equation 3: includes wages in construction; equation 5: includes urban minimum wages; equation 6: includes industrial wages.

[c]In all the equations the dependent variable is the changes in percentage points in open unemployment and the figures in brackets indicate the T = test.

*Significant.

For this purpose, we chose Argentina in the period 1974–1980, Chile during the past decade and Venezuela and Costa Rica since 1978. The first two cases were selected because they combine external adjustment with deep changes in economic policy, mainly directed to achieve price stabilization and a higher degree of openness. The third case illustrates the experience of an oil-exporting country combining an oil boom with economic policies aimed at correcting some internal disequilibria which were observable in an inflationary upsurge compared with previous historical patterns. The last case illustrates the small open economy facing balance of payments problems with inflationary pressures.

As can be seen in Table 5, the four cases present common features. On the one hand, the rate of growth of output is low, and even negative in Venezuela. On the other hand these economies exhibit inflationary problems in differing degrees. In Costa Rica and Venezuela, although price increases might be considered relatively moderate, annual rates were recently four and even five times as high as the historic inflation rate. Finally, during the periods under analysis real wages declined in all four cases. These common features reflect similar decisions of economic policy designed to control domestic demand and wages with a view to reducing price increases.

However, the labor market reacted quite differently in each case. In Argentina, the adjustment took place via an increase in the proportion of those employed in the urban informal sector, while the open-unemployment rate remained constant throughout the period. In Chile and Costa Rica, on the contrary, the adjustment proceeded almost entirely through a rise in the open-unemployment rate, while the proportion of the urban informal sector remained constant or even decreased. The labor market in Venezuela adjusted in an intermediate manner, showing a rise both in the open-unemployment rate and in the proportion of those employed in the urban informal sector. The first case illustrates an adjustment entirely achieved through an increase in underemployment, Chile and Costa Rica through an increase in open unemployment, and in Venezuela the adjustment through both open unemployment and underemployment.

One might ask what it is that determines these distinctly different types of adjustment in the labor market. Given the similarity between the four countries in respect to the magnitude of the informal sector, the difference might be traced to the average level of income prevailing in this sector. Both in Argentina and in Venezuela the average income obtained by informal sector workers shows a small difference in relation to occupations in modern activities. In Chile and Costa Rica the same difference is as high as 30 percent. This implies that those who are unable

TABLE 5

Three Types of Labor Market Adjustment

	Annual Rate of Growth of Output	Annual Rate of Growth of Prices	Variation in Real Wages[a]	Changes in[b]			Ratio of Incomes in the Informal Sector to Modern Sector[c]
				Open unemployment	Share of urban informal sector	Non-agricultural EAP	
Case 1							
Argentina (1974–1980)	1.9	156.3	-46.9	-0.3	4.0	0.6	1.03
Case 2							
Venezuela (1978–1981)	-0.6	16.9	-6.7	15.7	6.4	4.5	0.86
Case 3							
Chile (1970/1–1980)	2.7	79.1	-21.4	14.5[d]	0.1	2.7	0.73–0.80
Case 4							
Costa Rica (1978–1981)	0.6	30.1	-11.2	30.1	5.0	5.6	0.71

Source: Elaborated by PREALC on the basis of national statistics.

[a] Wages in the manufacturing industry.

[b] Refers to annual cumulative rates.

[c] As incomes disaggregated by these sectors are difficult to obtain, proxy variables were used depending on data availability. Argentina: ratio of incomes of non-professional self-employed to wage earners. Venezuela: ratio of income of non-professional self-employed and employees in establishments of less than 5 employees to non-professional wage earners. Chile: ratio of incomes of self-employed with less than 12 years of education and employers with establishments of less than 5 employees to wage earners. The variation reflects the inclusion or not of self-employed who are owners of real estate. Costa Rica: ratio of incomes of non-professional self-employed to wage earners.

[d] Includes those occupied in the Minimum Employment Programme (PEM).

to find work in the modern sector because of the adjustment in the labor market prefer to remain in active search for a job when the opportunities of alternative employment would entail a considerably smaller income. On the opposite side, when the difference is not so marked the option of working in the informal sector until the labor market becomes normal is a valid alternative.

Finally, it is interesting to compare the adjustment of the labor market in developing countries like those analyzed above with one developed country, say the United States, during the same period. For this country the data show that the non-agricultural population grew at 2.8 percent per year between 1978 and 1981, that the number of unemployed rose by 10.5 percent per year and that the non-professional self-employed and unpaid family workers diminished by 6.3 percent per year. It is clearly a case of adjustment through increases in the open-unemployment rate. If income differentials in the U.S. are small, or at least smaller than in Argentina and Venezuela, one would have *a priori* expected also an expansion of non-wage occupations; but the difference lies in the existence of unemployment insurance which in the U.S. covers more than 40 percent of the unemployed. For these people, unemployment does not mean zero income, but the guarantee of some percentage of their income while actively searching for new jobs.

Apart from illustrating differences in types of adjustment of the labor market, the comparative analysis above suggests that the distributive effects in each case are different. Indeed, the existence of unemployment insurance with wide coverage at normal income levels minimizes the direct effect on the distribution of income. At the other extreme the increase in the number of unemployed without any welfare aid, as in Chile and Costa Rica, drastically deteriorates income distribution, while the intermediate cases of adjustment through expansion of less renumerated occupations also negatively affect the distribution of income but in a milder way. In this latter case, the reduction of average income of those in self-employment plays the role of a collective unemployment insurance, constituting, in fact, a second best solution from a welfare point of view.

NOTES

1. The analysis of the performance and policies during the crisis of the 1930s closely follows the work of C. Díaz-Alejandro, *Latin America in the 1930s* (New Haven: Yale University, Economic Growth Center, 1981).

2. It should be noted that the three countries have different degrees of dependence on imported oil. Argentina is practically self-sufficient while Uruguay is highly dependent. Chile's position is intermediate.

3. See, for example, PREALC, *Políticas de estabilización y empleo en América Latina*, series Investigaciones sobre empleo/22 (Santiago: PREALC, 1982).

4. R. Lagos and V. E. Tokman, *Global monetarism, employment and social stratification*, series Occasional papers/47 Rev. 1 (Santiago: PREALC, 1982).

5. The method used to calculate this result consisted of estimating the proportion of the debt subject to variable interest rates in relation to gross domestic product and applying to this coefficient the rate of growth of the interest rate in real terms, defined as the variation in the international interest rate deflated by the variation in the export prices of the respective country.

PART II

Crisis and Instability: The Financial Side

Revisiting the Great Debt Crisis of 1982

Albert Fishlow

In the aftermath of the Mexican and Venezuelan reschedulings in the fall of 1984, and in the glow of upward revisions in the expansions of world trade for 1984, the debt crisis seems to have taken another giant step toward oblivion. It is only a matter of time before Brazil also comes to terms with the banks for a multi-year restructuring. Even Argentina and the International Monetary Fund (IMF) have recently reached agreement on a letter of intentions spelling out the policies that will satisfy creditors and change its status from intensive care to convalescence.

These developments seem to confirm the optimism of those who forecasted the stability of the financial system and the ephemeral quality of the debt problem. Before the experience of the past decade is forgotten and its lessons discarded, however, another look is in order. Developing country debt of over 800 billion dollars at the end of 1983, amounting to more than a third of gross domestic product, is not a trivial sum. The corresponding burden on export earnings of interest alone came to 13.2 percent in 1982, and close to 20 percent for major borrowers. The thirty or so countries forced to reschedule their debt payments since 1981 make clear the broad swath of the difficulties. Balance of payments shortfalls have thus not been an isolated phenomenon.[1]

Yet, it is also a mistake to ignore their regional concentration. In many ways the debt crisis is almost exclusively a Latin American crisis. It was the dramatic inability of oil-rich Mexico to meet its obligations in August 1982 that first transformed dry statistical accounts of external debt found in the obscurity of financial pages to bold headlines. Mexico was the second largest developing country debtor at 80 billion dollars, and with proven oil reserves of seemingly unlimited value. If it could not service its debt, what of other countries similarly burdened but less favored? Those other countries prominently included Brazil and Argentina, with Chile and Peru not far behind. Latin America countries had been among the largest borrowers, accounting for some 40 percent of the total debt in the early 1980s. Latin America was also the region whose debt burden relative to export earnings was greatest, and where, after 1980, the debt problem most rapidly deteriorated. Hemispheric coun-

99

tries represented about half of all countries forced to reschedule, and were responsible for over 90 percent of the bank debt restructured.[2]

In understanding the characteristics of the crisis, therefore, as well as the prospects for the future, a regional dimension is useful. It permits greater specificity in defining the effects of world economic recovery. Rising exports from Hong Kong do not alleviate the debt problem of Chile. A regional thrust has the further advantage of introducing new elements of political realism, international as well as internal. Latin American debtors have organized into the Group of Cartagena, and talk of debtors' cartels is largely a regional, rather than a generalized Third World, export. At the same time, the region can be discussed only within the context of the broader problem.

In this paper, I focus on three aspects of the debt crisis of 1982. First, I examine its origins in the disequilibrium of the international economy in the 1970s and in the responsive domestic policies of the developing countries. From that basis, I consider the possibility of industrialized country recovery as a solution. Latin America is given special but not exclusive treatment. Finally, by way of conclusion, I evaluate the adequacy of the existing institutional framework for coping with the debt problem and satisfying future financial requirements.

1. From Debt-led Growth to Growth-led Debt

The expansion of the Euro-currency market in the 1960s was, on the whole, of little significance to developing countries. European central banks and transnational corporations were the principal transactors. Only as the decade was drawing to a close, largely under the impulse of a recession-induced declining conventional demand for loans, did money center banks begin to search out new prospects. They found a hitherto untapped clientele among the rapidly growing countries of the developing world that later would be christened the "newly industrializing countries" (NIC's): Brazil, Mexico, and Korea, among others. Not surprisingly, because of their middle-income status, their larger manufacturing sectors, and their greater economic ties to the United States, Latin American countries were especially favored.

Capital began to flow to finance the increased imports required by accelerating economic expansion. Such loans, and not merely export promotion, were the basis of a more elastic supply of foreign exchange facing these countries, and permitted a more aggressive and accelerating growth strategy. For Brazil, in particular, its economic miracle was characterized by such debt-led growth.

The sudden injection of petro-dollars into world financial markets in 1974 altered both the pace and the purpose of borrowing. OPEC exporters realized a current account surplus in that year of almost 70 billion dollars as a result of the quadrupling of oil prices, and placed much of it in short term deposits with commercial banks. Those dollars were loaned for a longer term to countries that were importers of oil in order to finance their much larger balance of payment deficits. Amid predictions of impending doom and disaster, private financial markets found a way not only to keep the global economy afloat but, with short order, to fuel renewed expansion. That way was an unprecedented increase of external debt, especially on the part of the developing countries.

Countries did not have to borrow at the time. They could have reduced their purchase of oil or, failing that possibility, have restricted other imports. But such responses would have implied passing along the oil tax not only in the form of lower real incomes, but also of probable diminished output and employment as economies adjusted. That was an unpopular choice for most Latin American governments, especially when many were taking credit for improved economic performance. The other option was to accelerate the growth of exports to offset the increased cost of imports; while no less a reduction of real income, such a strategy at least promised to be less contractionary than policies aimed primarily at import reduction. That choice again seemed dubious when recession in the industrialized countries was slowing aggregate trade growth in 1974 and 1975. If countries in the region had resisted export promotion strategies in favor of the domestic market when world demand was favorable, they were even less inclined to radical responses under uncertain international conditions.

More gradual, debt-financed adjustment was therefore especially attractive to Latin American countries, an option rendered the more alluring by its cheap cost. They had the good fortune of being eligible. Those that had the luxury of borrowing to offset the rise in oil prices were predominantly the ones that had already established prior links to the market: they turned from debt-led growth to growth-led debt. In the earlier period, they could count on an elastic supply of foreign capital and could, and did, set ambitious growth targets independent of a foreign exchange constraint. In the later period, they operated under greater restriction. Although they borrowed more, countries were not facing unlimited supplies of credit: their growth rates had to be set more modestly, with larger debt financing the larger needed import requirements.

Not all eligible countries chose such a path. Taiwan and Singapore, for example, accepted a more immediate adjustment and realignment of real wages to remain competitive in exports. Korea borrowed, but in order to sustain investment in a manufacturing sector more and more oriented to exports. The more dependent economies were upon their exports, the more inclined they were to favor aggressive efforts to expand market shares rather than to accept continuing debt-financed balance of payments deficits. In such open economies, import substitution was not a prominent part of medium-term adaptation, and export competitiveness was best accomplished by short-term flexibility and medium-term efforts to find new competitive niches.

Enough countries opted for deficit finance to permit financial markets to sustain world demand. By making money cheap, the banks induced borrowers to maintain and expand their imports to offset the export surplus of the oil producers. In this fashion, a classic potential over-savings, non-full-employment solution to the surplus problem was averted, and global recovery could build upon the continuing growth of the middle-income developing countries. Increased indebtedness thus had positive externalities.

From a national perspective, debt also produced favorable results. The select group of countries that were able to borrow experienced better economic performance. The poorest countries, on the other hand, had to adjust immediately and painfully, despite large official lending mobilized on their behalf. As a consequence, a wider gulf opened between the middle-income and the low-income countries in the 1970s, even as it narrowed between semi-industrialized and industrialized countries. Per capita income grew between 1970 and 1980 at an annual rate of 3.2 percent in the middle-income countries, 2.4 percent in the industrialized, and not at all in the low-income countries other than India and China.[3]

Table 1 confirms this dominant role of the NIC, and of the Latin American countries, in credit markets in the immediate aftermath of the oil price shock. The NICs accounted for almost two-fifths of the increase in all developing country debt between 1973 and 1976. Mexico and Brazil, together, accounted for about a quarter. All low-income countries could manage little more than 10 percent, almost exclusively from official sources. Five of the non-surplus oil exporters virtually matched that participation.

For some of the borrowers, especially in Latin America, the new credits became habit-forming, even after real prices of oil began to be eroded and industrial country growth recovered after 1975. Balance of payment deficits declined only gradually, as bank willingness to continue to lend opened up new possibilities for public spending. Table 1 reveals a continued high level of participation of the NICs in total borrowing, and an expansion of the role of the oil-exporting countries. Although borrowing had its origins in the oil crisis, it took on a life of its own, a life influenced not merely by the higher price of oil but also that of manufactured imports.

Since banks preferred guarantees, and these could more readily be given on public loans and indirect borrowing of state enterprises, private international credit markets imparted a significant bias toward public sector expansion. This, too, favored those middle-income countries with a more pervasive network of state enterprises and interventionist tradition. Once again, this asymmetric supply condition reinforced the demand of Latin American countries. They found the speed and less exigent requirements of the private banks a welcome contrast to the rigidities of official loans, and their implicit interventionism.

Commercial banks, on their side, found their new customers an important source of profits. They made their money on the higher upfront commission fees and spreads for loans to developing countries; and low real interest rates, or even negative rates, were no worry. Indeed, they were welcome in minimizing the debt servicing problems of the developing country borrowers. As long as bank depositors were willing to accept negligible returns, and surplus oil producers had such a preference for liquidity that they were accepting such returns, the arrangement was quite satisfactory. In addition, the banks benefited from access to domestic banking facilities in the largest borrowers. These added significantly to the profits earned from international loans, which helps to explain the willingness to lend at modest, and declining, spreads. Citicorp's Brazil operations, for example, generated 20 percent of all corporate earnings in 1982.[4]

As a result of these influences, all developing country debt grew at a rate of about 20 percent a year from 1973 to 1978, increasingly weighted by the floating loans of banks. For Latin America, the rate was an even greater 22 percent. Lenders bore the risk of a mismatch between overnight deposits and six- or eight-year loans; borrowers bore the risk of changing interest rates and had their costs pegged to the London Interbank Offer Rate (LIBOR). In addition, countries were exposed to the high rates of loan turnover implicit in the short maturity structure of commercial loans. This translated into debt-service ratios that far exceeded previous conventional standards, without providing comparable access to increased real resources.

A relatively small number of countries, almost exclusively Latin American, thus embarked on a strategy of growth-led debt in the 1970s, subject to special vulnerabilities. They were financing medium- and long-term capital formation on the basis of short-term credits with an uncertain and variable price. Inherent in any debt strategy was an inability

Table 1
Developing-Country Debt[a] (billions dollars)

	1973	1974	1975	1976	1977	1978	1979	1980	1981	1982	1983
Non-Oil Countries	130.1	160.8	190.8	228.0	280.3	334.3 / 300.7[c]	354.5[c]	421.4[c]	492.6[c]	551.3[c]	585.6[c]
NICs[b]	51.3	66.2	82.3	101.5	122.7	149.5 / 115.9[c]	135.0[c]	160.9[c]	184.5[c]	211.9[c]	217.7[c]
Brazil	13.8	18.9	23.3	28.6	35.2	48.4	57.4	66.1	75.7	88.2	97.0
Mexico	8.6	12.8	16.9	21.8	27.1	33.6					
Republic of Korea	4.6	6.0	7.3	8.9	11.2	14.8	20.5	26.4	31.2	35.8	42.0
Southern Cone	10.1	12.4	12.7	13.0	14.9	19.2	27.5	38.3	51.3	55.2	60.0
Argentina	6.4	8.0	7.9	8.3	9.7	12.5	19.0	27.2	35.7	38.0	42.0
Chile	3.7	4.4	4.8	4.7	6.2	6.7	8.5	11.1	15.6	17.2	18.0
Low-Income Countries	26.4	30.9	34.6	40.1	48.6	54.8	62.7	71.4	75.2	81.8	88.0
Selected Oil Exporters	15.4	17.9	21.2	27.3	35.3	47.1	58.2[c] / 99.0	65.2[c] / 119.0	70.5[c] / 137.5	78.3[c] / 160.3	90.0[c] / 173.0
Algeria	2.9	3.3	4.5	5.8	8.3	12.7	14.9	15.1	15.3	14.8	17.0
Indonesia	5.7	7.1	8.9	11.0	12.8	14.5	14.9	17.0	18.0	21.0	23.0
Mexico							40.8	53.8	67.0	82.0	83.0
Nigeria	2.2	2.2	2.1	1.8	1.9	3.6	4.7	5.6	7.9	11.2	17.0
Venezuela	4.6	5.3	5.7	8.7	12.3	16.3	23.7	27.5	29.3	31.3	33.0
Total[d]	145.5	178.7	212.0	255.3	315.6	381.4	453.5	540.4	630.1	711.6	758.6
Total, All Developing Countries					329.3	398.2	472.0	559.9	646.5	724.8	767.7

[a]Short and long-term debt, including private, non-guaranteed debt. Excludes loans from the IMF.

[b]Newly industrializing countries, here equivalent to IMF category of "major exporters of manufactures," excluding Argentina but including Mexico.

[c]Excludes Mexico.

[d]Sum of Non-Oil Countries and Selected Oil Exporters.

Sources: 1973–76—Non-Oil Countries, NICs, and Low-Income Countries from IMF, *World Economic Outlook* (Washington, D.C.: 1983); for NICs and Low-Income Countries, estimated short-term debt—excluded in the source—has been added by the author.

1973–82—Brazil, Mexico, Republic of Korea, Argentina, Indonesia, and Venezuela from William R. Cline, *International Debt and the Stability of World Economy* (Washington, DC.: Institute for International Economics, 1983). Algeria and Nigeria estimated from Morgan Guaranty Trust Company, *World Financial Markets*, June 1983, and World Bank, *World Debt Tables* (Washington, D.C.: various years). Chile from Morgan Guaranty, *World Financial Markets*, June 1983, and R. Zahler, "Recent Southern Cone Liberalization Reforms and Stabilization Policies: The Chilean Case, 1974–1982," *Journal of Interamerican Studies and World Affairs*, vol. 25, no. 4 (November 1983), pp. 509–62.

1977–83—Non-Oil Countries, NICs, Low-Income Countries, and Total, All Developing Countries, from IMF, *World Economic Outlook* (Washington,- D.C.: 1984).

1983—Brazil, Mexico, Republic of Korea, and Argentina from OECD, *External Debt of Developing Countries, 1983 Survey* (Paris: 1984); Chile and Venezuela from *Euromoney*, March 1984; Algeria from *Quarterly Economic Review* (*The Economist Intelligence Unit*), no. 1, 1984; Nigeria from *Wall Street Journal*, February 21, 1984; and Indonesia estimated by the author from 1983 borrowing data provided in *Quarterly Economic Review* (*The Economist Intelligence Unit*), no. 1, 1984.

to know its real return because the uncertain future prices of exports were an important determinant of the potential benefits. Compounding the problem in this case was an unpredictable cost of debt, and a vulnerability to future capital market supply conditions.

Yet, up to the second oil price shock, the gamble was worth taking. Export growth was sustained in world markets at favorable prices, despite worries about protectionism. As a consequence, the ratio of debt outstanding to export proceeds was more favorable for all non-oil developing countries in 1979 than in 1970–1972 (although assisted by rising oil revenues for some new exporters in the group). Debt service, even if claiming a larger share of exports than earlier as grace periods expired and interest rates crept upward, was still a modest 19 percent for the group as a whole. Short-term loans were not yet much in evidence and posed no cash-flow problem. The ratio of reserves to debt outstanding at the end of 1979 was a third more satisfactory than the level in 1970–1972. Latin American borrowers, although subject to debt-service ratios twice as large as for the aggregate, had also accumulated reserves and seemed equally immune from adverse effects.

Instead, as noted earlier, those developing countries with access to the financial market succeeded in sustaining their rates of growth far more effectively than those forced to do without. They did so because they utilized increased foreign savings to finance higher levels of investment. Evidence on the consumption behavior of a number of the major debtor countries is reported in Table 2.[5] It confirms the productive application of the much larger foreign capital inflows in the period after 1973.

In the first place, despite the acceleration in borrowing, the propensity to consume out of net foreign proceeds in 1973–1978 was not statistically significantly greater than in the prior period. If foreign resources were not all applied to investment, neither were they diverted to consumption in proportions different than they had been. Second, the share allocated to savings from foreign borrowing in 1973–1978 was significantly greater than the allocation from gross national product for Korea; for both Brazil and Mexico, the deviations are in the right direction although falling short of statistical significance. Indeed, for these three largest debtors, the savings coefficients from net capital inflow are high enough that the hypothesis that all borrowing was saved cannot be rejected. At the margin, for these countries, debt translated more than proportionally into investment. Third, even after the second oil shock in 1979–1980 provoked further uncertainties and reduced growth and investment, there was no systematic tendency toward greater consumption out of borrowing. Some countries did show a rise, Brazil most prominently, but the only statistically significant change was Mexico's in the direction of greater saving. Finally, the pattern of expenditures in a non-debtor country like Colombia is not much different from that in the largest debtors.

This conclusion of no gross displacement of domestic saving is corroborated by IMF studies comparing changes in average ratios of saving to GNP with relative changes in the current account between the late 1960s and the 1970s. Taking into account as well simultaneous invest-

TABLE 2[a]

	Marginal Propensity to Consume from National Product	Marginal Propensity to Consume from Foreign Capital	
		1965–1978	1979–1981
Argentina	.76	.82	1.02
	(21.39)	(2.49)	(1.20)
Brazil	.79	-.02	.90
	(48.24)	(.04)	(1.91)
Chile	.86	.95	.51
	(33.92)	(2.84)	(1.62)
Colombia	.73	.69	.20
	(35.68)	(2.67)	(.50)
Indonesia	.67	1.00	.76
	(37.80)	(6.84)	(4.63)
Korea	.68	.20	.48
	(34.87)	(1.82)	(1.97)
Mexico	.76	.43	-.51
	(36.26)	(1.30)	(1.54)
Venezuela	.46	.54	.38
	(1.16)	(7.40)	(1.72)

Source: Data on national accounts from *International Financial Statistics*.

[a]*t*-values in parentheses.

ment increases, the "increases in external deficits can in most cases be accounted for by expansion of investment (relative to total output) rather than by growth of consumption."[6] The cross-section methodology leads to the stronger result that debt had its principal application in investment, not true in our sample for such borrowers as Argentina, Chile and Indonesia. What seems clear is that countries did not borrow in order to increase their consumption ratios, although their absolute consumption may have risen.

Although some countries encountered difficulties and were forced to reschedule, and while some analysts remained skeptical of the magic of the market, the consensus judgment about developing country debt until the second oil shock was a positive one. Rapidly growing debt was a solution rather than a problem. Capital outflows that would later cause the growth of debt to exceed substantially the growth of resources domestically applied were not yet a major concern. Even in 1980, an IMF occasional paper could read:

> In sum, the overall debt situation during the 1970s adapted itself to the sizable strains introduced in the payments system and, in broad terms, maintained its relative position vis-à-vis other relevant economic variables. Though some countries experienced difficulties, a generalized debt management problem was avoided, and in the aggregate the outlook for the immediate future does not give cause for alarm.[7]

A Changed International Environment

Even as those lines were being written, the bases for its optimism were being eroded by a deteriorating global economy. In the first instance, oil prices soared again under the impulse of uncertain supplies as war broke out in the fall of 1979 between Iran and Iraq. After considerable volatility in the spot market, the new average 1980 oil price settled at a level almost two-and-a-half times greater than its 1978 value of 12.83 dollars a barrel. The immediate impact, reminiscent of the first oil price shock, was a large OPEC surplus offset by a large non-oil developing country deficit.

Once again there was a recession in the industrialized countries, as contractionary policies sought to contain inflation, but this time more seriously. The impact on developing country exports and terms of trade was to prove longer lived. Finally, there was a new element in the formula: real interest rates began an upward ascent. Where before the capital market facilitated deficit finance, it now penalized not only the flow but also the stock of past debt contracted on a floating basis.

Table 3 quantifies the approximate contribution of each of these

TABLE 3

Sources of Deterioration in the Current Account of Non-Oil Developing Countries, 1979–1982 (billions of dollars)

	1978	1979	1980	1981	1982	CUMULATIVE 1979–82
Actual Trade Balance	−36.6	−51.3	−74.3	−79.6	−52.2	—
Adjusted Trade Balance[a]		−46.3	−57.3	−47.8	8.8	—
Oil Effect[b]		5.0	17.0	18.6	14.8	55.4
Recession Effect[c]		—	—	13.2	46.2	59.4
Export Volume[d]		—	—	—	23.2	23.2
Terms of Trade[e]		—	—	13.2	21.3	34.5
Interest Payments on Debt Service (gross)	−19.4	−28.0	−40.4	−55.1	−59.2	—
Interest Rate Effect (gross)[f]		−1.1	.5	11.4	23.0	33.8
Interest Rate Effect (net)[f]		−.5	.2	6.5	14.0	20.2
Actual Current Account	−41.3	−61.0	−89.0	−107.7	−86.8	—
Adjusted Current Account[g]	−41.3	−56.5	−71.8	−69.4	−11.8	—

Source: Actual trade balance and actual current account from IMF, *World Economic Outlook* (Washington, D.C., 1983)

[a] Adjusted Trade Balance: Actual trade balance minus sum of oil and recession effects.

[b] Oil Effect: Actual cost of net imports of oil (using import price of industrialized countries) minus estimated cost using oil price that varies after 1978 with export prices of oil-importing countries.

[c] Recession Effect: Composite of terms of trade and volume effects (does not add because of interaction).

[d] Export Volume: Non-oil export value times cumulative negative percentage deviation between actual export volume of oil-importing countries and volume predicted by 3.2 percent industrialized-country growth in 1980–82.

[e] Terms of Trade: Cumulative negative percentage deviation between actual non-oil terms of trade (export prices of non-oil, oil-importing countries; import prices of oil-exporting countries in 1973–74, 1979–80, non-oil countries in other years) and terms of trade predicted by 3.2 percent OECD growth and deceleration of industrialized-country inflation at 1 percentage point per year beginning in 1979.

[f] Interest Rate Effect: Based on difference between the 1975–78 average real interest rate and actual real rates. For short-term interest payments, the U.S. prime rate was used. Interest on long-term and medium-term loans was calculated by using the real U.S. prime rate with a weight of 1/3 and the OECD long-term fixed interest rate with a weight of 2/3, corresponding to portfolio weights reported in OECD, *External Debt of Developing Countries*, 1982. Rates were applied to average annual debt, obtained by using average of year-end debts. Net interest effect includes the offsetting earnings from short-term assets. This method approximates well the actual gross and net interest payments in IMF, *World Economic Outlook* (Washington, D.C.: 1983).

[g] Adjusted Current Account: Actual current account minus sum of oil effect, recession effect, and net interest effect.

three adverse factors to the current account deficit realized by the group of non-oil developing countries as a whole. The role of the oil price shock, even allowing for the favorable impact on such countries as Mexico, Peru, Egypt, and a few others, is paramount in timing and magnitude. In second place is the recession-induced reduction in export earnings, the result of both slower growth in volume and deterioration in price. This negative influence is most pronounced in 1982. By this time, the severity and length of the slowdown in the industrialized countries produced a volume, as well as an increasing cumulative price, effect. It is not suprising that by 1982 countries found themselves in more and more balance of payments difficulty.

The counterpart Latin American calculations using the same method are found in Table 4. There are important differences in the findings. There is no net oil effect for the region, excluding Venezuela, because imports and exports approximately cancel out. Indeed, by 1981 the region is a beneficiary of the oil shock. Table 4 also shows a modest recession effect, owing exclusively to swings in the terms of trade. Latin America bore a larger part of the brunt of declining commodity prices than did other middle-income countries less reliant on exports of primary products, but in compensation expanded the volume of its exports at a higher than predicted rate. Hence the actual volume of exports over the period 1979–1982 was greater than the hypothetical level without the recession.

Higher interest rates are, however, the distinctive hallmark of the region's vulnerability. Debt was not only relatively larger compared to the volume of trade, but a much larger proportion of the Latin American debt was contracted on a floating rate basis. Even official loans were not on concessional terms. A comparison of Tables 3 and 4 shows that the adverse rate effects of 1981 and 1982 were almost exclusively a Latin American phenomenon.[8] Other countries still enjoyed a preponderance of fixed rate obligations as well as larger offsetting earnings from foreign exchange reserves; the Latin American countries were forced to deplete their reserve after 1979.

But even this calculation of significant foreign exchange costs does not capture the full significance of the rise in the interest rate. It not only contributed to the current account deficit, but also had immediate adverse effects on the willingness of creditors to lend more. Between 1978 and 1981 interest payments on the debt rose from 19 billion dollars to 55 billion dollars for all non-oil developing countries, and the ratio to exports from 7.3 to 11.9 percent. The change for Latin American borrowers was much greater, as the interest service ratio climbed from 14.9 to 25.4 percent. Only an amortization profile skewed toward the future kept the overall debt-service ratio within bounds. It did not always register that the higher nominal rates at first were partially equivalent to shorter maturities, because they were compensating for inflation rather than signalling a deterioration in the capacity to pay. Spreads rose, loans were rationed, and maturities were shortened.

Such higher rates thus exacerbated the crisis through their implications for continuing the supply of capital and were a crucial factor in making developing country adjustment more difficult just when export receipts were falling off. Recession in the industrialized countries in the

Table 4

Sources of Deterioration in the Current Account
of Latin America,[a] 1979–1982 (billions of dollars)

	1978	1979	1980	1981	1982	CUMULATIVE 1979–82
Actual Trade Balance	-1.2	-4.1	-8.9	-10.0	5.5	
Adjusted Trade Balance		-3.2	-8.3	-1.3	13.3	
Oil Effect[b]		.9	.6	-1.1	-3.6	
Recession Effect		—	—	9.8	11.4	21.2
Export Volume		—	—	—	—	—
Terms of Trade		—	—	9.8	11.4	21.2
Interest Payments on Debt						
Service (gross)	7.9	12.4	19.5	28.7	35.3	
Interest Rate Effect (gross)[c]		-1.1	1.5	12.8	21.0	34.2
Interest Rate Effect (net)[d]		-.6	.5	8.6	15.9	24.4
Actual Current Account	-13.3	-21.4	-33.4	-45.4	-34.9	
Adjusted Current Account		-21.1	-32.2	-28.1	-11.2	

Source: IMF, *World Economic Outlook*, 1983; IMF, *Balance of Payments Yearbook*, 1983; Economic Commission for Latin America, *Annual Economic Survey, 1982*.

[a]Excluding Venezuela.

[b]Export prices of Latin American non-oil exporters, import prices of Latin American oil exporters, both from Economic Commission of Latin America, *Annual Survey*, 1982.

[c]Weights of .7 for prime rate and .3 for OECD multilateral non-concessional loan rates were used for long and medium term debt.

[d]Actual earnings of interest income reduced by ration of hypothetical real prime to actual and subtracted from gross payments.

past had at least been partially offset by more abundant and cheaper loanable funds.

The new positive real interest rate regime was largely the consequence of conscious policy in the industrialized countries. Tighter money became the principal instrument to reduce inflation. Reaganomics carried the process a step further by marrying lax fiscal policy to an insistence on lower inflation; the predictable consequence was higher deficits, interest rates and unemployment. Restrictive policy also yielded indirect effects that reinforced the tendency for interest rates to rise. Reduced surpluses were progressively realized by oil producers facing a softer and more competitive market, and those surpluses, formerly a source of savings to finance the deficits of the oil importers, were no longer available.

International capital markets thus magnified, rather than dampened, the oil shock of 1979–1980. Banks, concerned about their exposure, raised premiums to oil importer borrowers and, more importantly, became reluctant to lend at all. They began to prefer shorter loans, ostensibly trade credits, but in reality, like all lending, balance of payments finance. The differential effect on Latin American borrowers is clear. Estimated debt of less than a year rose 111 percent between 1979 and 1982 while medium-and long-term finance increased by 51 percent for all non-oil debtors. The corresponding regional statistics are 192 percent and 61 percent. Short-term loans to Latin American countries amounted to almost a quarter of their outstanding obligations at the end of 1982.

As Table 3 suggests, the cumulative effects of the external shocks experienced after 1979 were sufficient, for non-oil developing countries as a whole, to convert the large 1982 deficit of 87 billion to one of 12 billion dollars. That is, the sometimes drastic efforts on the part of these countries to curtail their imports could have led to significant improvement in their payments situation rather than the continuing difficulty actually experienced.

For the Latin American countries, per Table 4, the shock had a different, non-oil composition, originating primarily from rising interest rates. That enforced a radical reduction of imports beginning in 1982 that has continued to be the principal factor in the region's improved balance of payments. Clearly for those countries in the region like Brazil and Chile, that were both oil importers and large debtors to commercial banks, circumstances were even more trying.

But Tables 3 and 4 also make abundantly clear that the sharp initial raise in the deficit from its 1978 level must be explained on other grounds. By 1980, even abstracting from the oil price shock and the price of exports, the current account deficit of non-oil developing countries had risen by 75 percent over its 1978 level. The increase for Latin America is even greater. It is a mistake to blame the oil price and recession shocks alone for what was also an inadequacy of domestic policy and an excessive readiness on the part of the banks to lend.

For one thing, as Table 1 shows, there was much increased borrowing by Chile and Argentina as they pursued more open capital markets as an integral part of their new international monetarist stabilization experiments. Between 1978 and 1981 their previously moderate debt almost trebled, as they alone accounted for some 12 percent of increased developing country indebtedness. High domestic interest rates in conjunction with pre-announced, and in the case of Chile, fixed exchange rates encouraged rapid capital inflows that were translated into larger imports, but without the same proportion saved as was true of the earlier NIC borrowing in the aftermath of the 1973 oil shock. For another, oil exporters, and in particular Mexico, relied heavily on external finance to sustain high rates of growth of product and, disproportionately, of imports. The very initial shock of higher oil prices worked to their advantage. They borrowed not to accommodate to adverse external circumstances, but rather to exploit their new riches. Needless to say, they were attractive clients for banks again flush with Euro-deposits in search of application.

In both groups of countries, moreover, increased indebtedness did not fully translate into net increases in resource transfers. Indirect calculations from the recipients' balances of payments show that between 1978 and 1981 Argentina experienced a capital outflow equivalent to 60 percent of incremental indebtedness; Mexico, 40 percent; and Venezuela, more than 100 percent.[9] Contractual obligations, primarily publicly guaranteed, brought foreign exchange into the countries only to make it available for residents to send right back out. Chile, despite claims of critics to the contrary, does not seem to have fallen victim to this exchange of national liabilities for private assets held abroad; nor does Brazil.

A third category of continuing borrowers can also be identified. Some oil-importing countries, prominently Brazil, habituated to debt-financed adjustment, understated the different and more persistent international recession and took few precautionary measures. Brazil chose, for internal political reasons, to expand in 1980 at the expense of a deteriorating payments position. This expansion was checked early on by an increasingly inelastic supply of credit. As a consequence, Brazil's debt expanded relatively less than that of its Latin American neighbors. It also averted the hemorrhage of capital flight that afflicted some of the others.

Between 1978 and 1981, the principal debtors in Latin American were responsible for more than 40 percent of the increased debt tabulated in Table 1, compared to an initial participation of 30 percent. Almost all of the new debt was accumulated on a floating rate basis, and progressively, no longer at the rates previously available. For many, prudent import policies might have averted some of the later grief. A prominent exception was Brazil, whose large outstanding debt absorbed virtually all of the foreign exchange borrowed, and whose real imports remained compressed.

This country variability is lost in the aggregation of Tables 3 and 4. The countries with relatively large reserves that gained from higher interest rates are not those most affected by payments problems because of lagging exports. Nor did prices for all products move uniformly. The terms of trade of Asian oil-importing countries fell by 5.5 percent between 1980 and 1982; those of the Latin American countries by 13.6 percent. But however much external events impinged, as they impressively did, domestic policies and international negligence were also components of the seriously deteriorating situation that finally became patent in 1982.

Global equilibrium in response to the second oil shock was achieved at lower levels of real income. Instead of buffering the impact as before, developing country debt now transmitted it. Only so long as growth-led debt was compatible with developed country aversion to recession and OPEC willingness to hold Euro-currency deposits yielding low or negative real rates, could the strategy be effective. It made little difference that current account deficits in the early 1980s would have been in line with the trend of modest improvement had the external environment remained stable. What counted was that the strategy chosen was no longer viable, and also not easily reversible. Once in debt, it was more difficult to maneuver. Growth-led debt, especially for Latin America, had been converted to debt-led debt.

2. A Liquidity Crisis?

By the fall of 1982 there was widespread agreement that there was a debt problem. *Time* magazine, perhaps overeager to sell copies, made the situation a cover story and christened it a "debt bomb." Others more sober and analytically inclined differentiated between a liquidity crisis and a solvency problem: a short-term interruption of cash flow versus a long-term inability to repay debt. The majority view, including bankers, government officials and independent observers, inclined to the former. The World Bank, in its 1983 report on external debt stated it as follows:

There is no generalized debt crisis: rather, the mutual difficulties of developing countries in servicing foreign borrowing and of commercial banks in obtaining service payments on foreign lending are an outgrowth of the broader economic problems that grip all of the world's economies. The resolution of these difficulties lies in a restoration of economic health to the global economy and a resumption of strong growth in international trade.[10]

There is basis for such a characterization in the magnitude of the effects set in motion by the oil price shock in late 1979 and the policy response to it, as Tables 3 and 4 have already brought out. There is also persuasive evidence from casting the perspective forward rather than backward. As the IMF's medium-term scenarios show, Morgan Guaranty's balance of payments model confirms, and William Cline's more recent projections for 19 of the largest debtors reemphasize, "If this growth rate [3 percent annually for industrialized countries] can be achieved, the debt problems of the developing countries should be manageable and should show considerable improvement. . . . The central result of this analysis is that the debt problem can be managed, and that it is essentially a problem of illiquidity, not insolvency."[11]

I am partial to this assessment. Yet at the same time, it requires qualification in two important respects. For one, the analogy of countries to firms is not entirely adequate. Solvency for a firm is defined by an excess of assets over liabilities; otherwise it is bankrupt, and its creditors may benefit from its dissolution. Countries, on the other hand, do not cease to exist, nor can their assets, at least any more, be seized for distribution. Their technical requirement for solvency is a zero cumulative balance of payments over a very long time-horizon, in order to guarantee repayment of accumulated intervening debt. It is of limited practical significance. Since policies are variable, such a condition in principle could always be met over a suitably long period. So can the additional requirement that the real return on borrowing repay its cost, since capital in the developing countries remains relatively scarce.

A more relevant solvency criterion is therefore not the eventual capacity to pay, but the medium-term prospect for decelerating the increase in debt relative to exports. Such a criterion incorporates availability of foreign exchange rather than saving as the determining constraint in meeting obligations.[12] It also substitutes the existence of a limiting debt/export ratio, with continuingly growing debt, for the condition of its full repayment.

For the debt/export ratio to converge to a maximum, with developing countries still recipients of a net resource transfer from the industri-

alized countries, requires that export growth exceed the interest rate.[13] If it does not, the further borrowing necessary to cover both interest payments and import purchases will exceed the increase in exports, and force the debt/export ratio to continuously higher levels. An example, assuming balanced trade, illustrates the process. With imports and exports exactly equal, the rate of growth of the debt is simply equal to the uncovered interest costs that must be borrowed. If exports do not grow at the interest rate, the debt/export ratio rises.

Only by running a merchandise surplus, i.e., transferring real resources to creditor countries, can debtors prevent the debt/export ratio rising when interest rates exceed export growth. That, of course, is what many such countries have been forced to do since 1982, but that does not make them solvent. Rather, it accepts the present disequilibrium as a permanent state and refuses to see beyond the temporary favorable balance of payments to the longer term implications. Estimates suggest that such a transfer from the Latin American countries amounted to 20 billion dollars in 1982 and 30 billion dollars in 1983, representing 19 and 27 percent respectively of the value of exports of goods and services. "Thus was prolonged a situation that, taking into account the relative degree of development of the region, can only be qualified as perverse."[14] More generally, for all the countries in the World Bank reporting system, the positive net transfer of 16 billion dollars in 1981 was converted to a negative 7 billion dollars in 1982 and a larger negative 21 billion dollars in 1983.[15]

Favorable medium-term projections of the balance of payments, without regard to the transfer of resources to the developing countries required to sustain adequate rates of growth, are thus no *ipso facto* guarantee of solvency. Nor are even demonstrations of declining debt/export ratios, if they are achieved through premature graduation to export of real resources. Such exercises ignore the magnitude of the sacrifice entailed for the developing countries. They assume that ability to pay is equivalent to willingness to pay regardless of the costs. The caution of bankers in the face of such positive results and forecasts show that they, at least, understand the distinction.

But the forecasts themselves may be too rosy. That is my second objection to the prevalent characterization of the debt problem as a simple liquidity crisis. My concern is that the balance of payments calculations underlying such a diagnosis are overly optimistic. They place an undue emphasis upon economic recovery in the industrialized countries as a solution to the debt problem of the developing countries.

There are two reasons for a more cautious stance. One is the possible overstatement of the responsiveness of developing country exports, and especially those of the Latin American countries, to income growth in the OECD countries. The other is the distinct possibility that future global development may show a less trade-intensive pattern than that of the past on which the estimates are based.

Estimates of the elasticity of export volume of non-oil developing countries, and of the Latin American countries more particularly, vary. Most, however, fall short of the value of 3 used by William Cline in his influential study already cited. Calculations reproduced in Appendix Table A suggest a value of 1.7 for the aggregate, and a lesser 1.5 for the region. Cline reaches higher values because he looks at the relationship of total OECD imports with respect to OECD growth, and subsequently makes allowance for increasing participation of developing countries in this trade.

In the second instance, favorable trends in the prices of developing country exports may be overstated in the optimistic scenarios. In particular, the relationship with projected depreciation of the dollar may be flawed. If export prices responded exactly proportionally to currency changes, then dollar depreciation could improve the ratio of debt to export earnings; it would simulate the effects of inflation in reducing the burden of the debt, without inducing a compensating rise in interest rates. Some studies even report more than proportional effects on commodity prices from dollar appreciation. The IMF reports a more than unitary relationship between dollar prices and value of the dollar for quarterly commodity exports, thus implying a decline in real terms. In addition, a recent Federal Reserve study, covering all developing country exports, finds an elasticity of .5 between change in deflated export unit value and change in the dollar exchange rate.[16]

Yet the results are very sensitive to the statistical specification adopted. If terms of trade are related to changes in the rates of growth of income and prices, as an accelerationist view suggests, then the results are quite different. Appendix Table B reports a number of significant, but wrong sign associations between the rate of change of deflated annual export prices of non-oil countries and the value of the dollar. It also shows how it is possible to obtain the opposite result for a different specification of the relationship. For quarterly Latin American commodity export prices since 1973, no satisfactory statistical relationship was found, and *a fortiori*, no inverse correlation with the dollar.

These findings confirm the absence of any *a priori* reason why demand and supply relationships should produce a proportional outcome. In 1978, for example, when the dollar depreciated, dollar export prices actually fell, despite a growth rate of 4.1 percent in the income of the industrialized countries. The results depend upon the role played by dollar and non-dollar buyers and sellers in world markets. If non-dollar buyers' demands for commodities are price-inelastic, and supply is denominated in dollars, then dollar depreciation will have little effect on prices.

Dollar depreciation is anticipated to be the major source of higher export prices in a period of moderate international inflation. Terms of trade improvement in response to recovery is another, but secondary, contributor. Such an effect we have already encountered in gauging the extent of its opposite impact during the 1979–82 recession. Once again there are differences in statistical estimates of the strength of the terms of trade effect, differences that are compounded because of the differential export composition of individual countries. One can choose more or less optimistically.

The critical element in the most favorable balance of payments projections is this rise in developing country export prices. Morgan Guaranty's 1983 forecast assumed a 25 percent increase in the prices of non-oil commodities between 1982 and 1985; Cline, an annual rate of more than 20 percent for the exports of large, oil-importing debtors between 1983 and 1985. Substituting different responses to similar assumptions can yield significant revisions in the calculations, as I have demonstrated elsewhere.[17] Moreover, assumptions of dollar depreciation and continuing interest rate reduction have not been realized, and there is even doubt about the continuity of the economic recovery through 1985. Thus, very reasonable arguments can be constructed for uncertainty about the medium term, uncertainty that comes down predominantly on the side of more cautious expectations. The IMF medium-term base scenario prepared for the *1984 World Economic Report* was appropriately more measured: it predicted a decline in the debt-export ratio of major borrowers from 1.94 in 1983 to 1.65 in 1987, compared to Cline's reduction (for net debt-export for large oil-importing debtors) from 1.88 in 1983 to 1.28 in 1986.

There is equally good reason even to question whether the experience of the last two decades is an accurate guide to the near future. The world has emerged from an exceptional post-1945 period in which trade growth has been unusually responsive to increases in productive capacity. Trade intensity has exceeded that found in the 19th-century Pax Britannia. Some characteristics of the present situation argue against automatic resumption of past trends:

1. Protectionist sentiments are stronger. Advocates of freer trade barely prevailed in passing a new trade act in the United States that was stripped at the last moment of a number of potential new restrictions. Even that act makes it easier to file new dumping and countervailing-duty actions. Developing countries competing with basic industries in

the United States have become a special target and they are largely the NIC debtors. The real complaint is about competition, not subsidies.

A further factor has been the unevenness of the recovery coupled with easier entry into the American market. The fact that European countries have lagged behind, and the persistence of higher unemployment rates, have strengthened the tendencies toward protectionist policies. Japan continues to be difficult to penetrate, arousing increasing resentments among its Asian neighbors.

While cyclical factors contribute to this upsurge in protectionism, and especially to the overvalued dollar, it would be wrong to ignore the more permanent changes in the world economy that have occurred. Industrialization is no longer limited to the rich countries, and comparative advantage in many standardized products has shifted. There has been limited recognition of this reality, or the parallel reality of progressively more restricted market access. Pious words in favor of free trade and a new round of trade talks are becoming more dubious guarantors of opportunity for the debtor countries.

2. The present commitment to restrain inflation reduces the likelihood of replicating the commodity booms of the last decade, and with them, periods of much improved developing country terms of trade. Demands for stocks will be moderated since inventories are no longer a valuable hedge against inflation. High real interest rates reinforce this conclusion. We already see some evidence. Commodity prices, in SDRs and not appreciating dollars, have already reversed their earlier ascent. The Economist Index, after a rise in 1983 and the beginning of 1984, has now fallen below year-earlier levels in October by 7 percent. Prices of industrial inputs have declined by 13 percent. This dampens the likelihood of realizing further expected improvements for developing country terms of trade in 1984.

3. Emphasis upon the magical effects of recovery in the industrialized countries ignores the consequences of debt-imposed depression upon Third World trade growth. Trade among developing countries as a whole rose to about a quarter of developing country exports by the end of the 1970s. The decline in demand from other developing countries has been pronounced. For Latin American countries, excluding Venezuela, intra-Latin American trade that amounted to 19.0 percent of exports in 1980 fell to 14.9 percent by 1982.[18] While the principal market will continue to be the industrial countries, it is wrong to presume that the slowdown in growth that has been experienced, most overtly in Latin America, will not have adverse implications for export earnings.

These three alterations in the economic environment add to a concern over optimistic projections that seem to permit significant reductions in debt exposure along with a return to adequate growth rates of developing countries. The apparently favorable results thus far achieved by Mexico and Brazil in 1984 do not nullify a legitimate preoccupation.

For one, their accomplishment has come via a higher volume of real exports than had been anticipated, not through the more favorable vehicle of higher prices. Favorable terms of trade reduce the real burden of the debt by reducing its real resource cost, and hence make the needed export targets more easily attainable over an extended period. Less has to be given up in domestic expenditure.

Second, an eased foreign exchange constraint has benefited in both cases from continuing restraints on growth and imports that have swollen trade surpluses and has made possible the continuation of very large interest payments. The compatibility of a real decline in indebtedness and resumed growth, the basic scenario, has yet to be proved. Morgan Guaranty calculates that Mexico can achieve a 3 percent per capita income increase by the end of the 1980s although nominal debt is rising by only 3–4 percent. [19] For Mexico to save enough and import-substitute enough to grow at such rates implies domestic savings out of gross national product of about 30 percent and an import ratio of about 8 percent. While the latter does not differ greatly from the pre-oil boom years, the former is about 50 percent higher.

Third, the experience is not a generalized one. Small Latin American countries will show little improvement in 1984. Chile, Peru, Bolivia, etc., remain serious problems, not to speak of the poorer African countries. In its revaluation of likely trade volumes for 1984 in September, the IMF raised the target for the industrialized countries significantly more than for the developing countries.

The conclusion, therefore, is that it is too early to characterize the problems of the last several years as a mere liquidity crisis that has already largely been resolved. This is especially the case if high real interest rates persist, and it is well to remember that they actually increased in 1984. Such rates increase the burden of debt service and obligate import restraint, with adverse growth consequences, to equilibrate the balance of payments. Among the Latin American debtors, only Brazil, and not even Mexico, will probably satisfy in 1984 the criterion that export growth exceed the effective interest rate on debt.

This exclusively balance-of-payments-centered approach ignores another important consequence of high real interest rates. The higher the rate, the more resources must be transferred abroad, and the lower is national income. Interest payments must be made at the expense of potential domestic applications of national saving. Smaller countries, with their higher ratios of debt to national product, are especially vulnerable.

Recovery, along with high interest rates, may not therefore be as positive as Cline, for example, has continued to emphasize. His claim that a one percentage point increase in growth is worth seven times as much as a one percentage decline in interest rates is dubious.[20] Alternative, and equally reasonable, elasticities halve that margin of superiority, as I have shown. Because growth effects are cumulative, moreover, recovery requires time, while the effects of interest rate reductions are immediate. Favorable rates can be negotiated directly with banks, as the Mexican restructuring has shown; recovery, and export growth, cannot. The adverse economic consequences of elevated interest rates are therefore legitimately high on the agenda, especially when their real resource costs are also reckoned.

To these considerations must be added political sensitivity. Interest rate variations are viewed as a direct consequence of United States policy decisions and priorities, rather than as a market phenomenon. As such, they take on a significance beyond the direct foreign exchange or resource costs entailed. The extremely adverse reactions of debtors countries to the two-point rise in the prime rate experienced between January and June of 1984 is illustrative. Even though exports were expanding at rapid rates for some debtors so that the balance of payments effects were limited, their hostility was aimed at United States' preoccupation with domestic objectives at their expense.

Instead of satisfaction with the present and prospective effect from industrialized country recovery, my message is that a disproportionate share of the adjustment burden has already fallen, and may continue to fall, upon the debtor countries. The liquidity crisis, if that is what it turns out to be, has not been eased by the provision of adequate liquidity, but rather by a sharp reduction in developing country growth. From 1981 through 1984, non-oil countries grew at an average rate of 2.3 percent a year, compared to 5.6 percent between 1967 and 1980. For Latin America the decline has been even more dramatic: from 6.3 percent to a decline of 2.4 percent. Many countries in the region will not attain their 1980 standard of living again until the end of the decade, if then.

The IMF said as much in their 1983 report: "the results of Scenario A are less favorable as far as growth is concerned, and imply stronger adjustment efforts, than those presented last year. In part because of a lower flow of bank lending, the new Scenario A envisages . . . a lower deficit . . . despite conditions that would be less favorable for exports. The result is that the aggregate real GDP of non-oil developing countries in 1986 is now expected to be about 5.5 percent less than previously estimated. The volume of their imports is projected to be nearly 13 percent less."[21]

Under these circumstances, it is incorrect to focus exclusively on favorable trade projections. Solvency depends on assessments made by debtors as well as creditors. For the developing countries the greatest real cost of the debt has been the growth foregone, and the vulnerability to its repetition. If they have resisted more drastic actions, it has been both because of the belief that the sacrifice is temporary and that capital flows will resume, as well as the uncertain consequences of unilateral default. The idea of a debtors' cartel has not caught on for two reasons. One is that it has come after the principal costs have seemingly been paid, and rewards are imminent; the other is that, even within Latin America, the situation of individual countries is distinct. Both factors would diminish in intensity were there another generalized downturn.

In the concluding section, we therefore ask whether the institutional response to the debt crisis of 1982 adequately ensures against a repetition and provides a basis for sound recovery of the developing countries.

3. The Present Policy Matrix

At the end of 1984, the structure in place to deal with the debt problem is formally little altered from what it was in August 1982. Yet significant change has been registered. What has been added are additional resources from the quota increase of the IMF; the considerable experience of the repeated tasks of renegotiating debt and of hammering out country adjustment packages on a case-by-case basis; the new authority of the IMF (and national central banks) in imposing conditionality on the banks by requiring them to make new lending commitments as part of the overall program; and the organization of the private banks into smaller and more effective decision units. The latest outcome is a multiyear restructuring of Mexican and Venezuelan debt on more favorable terms, a process in which official pressures played a tangible role.

Have the modifications been sufficiently far-reaching? Financial circles, despite an official optimism, still have reason to agree with the June 1983 assessment of *World Financial Markets*. It found wanting the "relatively optimistic, laissez-faire school that assumes the current debt situation is a fairly short-term liquidity issue" to be solved primarily through LDC adjustment along with some OECD recovery. "By ignoring long-term structural elements of the international debt problem or overstating the prospects for global recovery, this approach risks forcing excessive deflationary costs on borrowers. It is also overly optimistic about market forces providing ample new borrowing."[22]

Debtor countries are not enthusiastic advocates of the status quo.

Internal dissatisfaction with austerity strategies persists. Despite recent more favorable borrowing terms, the new flows of resources have been minimal. Increased international reserves have derived from imposition of the single policy priority of large merchandise trade surpluses. That singlemindedness has had its own costs in the design of more effective domestic medium-term strategy. In the last analysis, as such documents as the moderate Declaration of Quito and the communiqués of the Cartagena Groupe emphasize, the debt crisis has been the occasion of a Latin American depression that rivals that of 1929.

The present situation derives its stability less from the assurance that it is adequate to the problem than from the fact that it has worked up to now. There is always a preference for marginal policy changes. In this case it has been reinforced by the demonstrated capacity of the present negotiating framework to evolve to meet new demands. The latest confirmations are the Argentine agreement with the IMF in anticipation of a new round of rescheduling discussions with the banks, and the multi-year restructurings noted above.

The Fund has performed three essential functions in structuring the present arrangements. On the one side, it has offset individual bank prudence that would call for a reduced commitment and shorter maturity by imposing proportional lending targets. This new conditionality imposed on the banks defeats the free rider problem inherent in a pure market relationship. Each bank would hope the others would participate, making it better off; such behavior, because none would, would make them all worse off. On the other side, the Fund has devised adjustment programs that assure the lenders that the developing countries will continue to make efforts to meet their obligations, and thereby avoid the moral hazard of countries simply borrowing more without an intention to repay. Finally, the IMF, in conjunction with the BIS, central banks and industrial country governments, has made available public resources to satisfy immediate liquidity requirements and supplement the private market. Central authority has thus been indispensable to a continuing bank-country relationship.

Yet for all its apparent success, this case-by-case framework suffers from serious deficiencies. In the first place, bank participation is largely on an involuntary basis. They make loans to cover interest payments and thereby avert default, buying an option for return of principal in better days ahead. While a rational decision, since lending to cover interest payments that otherwise would not be made involves no additional cost, the banks have on the whole obtained the best of the bargain. New lending has in fact fallen short of return interest payments, and even of the original expectations of the Fund. From bank financing of about 50 billion dollars a year in 1980 and 1981, borrowing of non-oil developing countries declined to 25 billion dollars in 1982 and 17 million dollars in 1983. The growth rate of bank claims plummeted from an annual average of about 25 percent in 1979–1982 to 9 percent in 1982 and 4 percent in 1983.[23]

Faced with more perilous assets, and a reduced market price for equity reflecting skeptical investor evaluations, banks pressed through the summer of 1984 for better terms and consequent higher earnings-flows to mollify shareholders. These decisions meant increased margins, both in the form of one-time fees and on-going premiums over the cost of funds. For the reschedulings completed for Latin America, amounting to some 44 billion dollars for seven countries, banks have obtained commissions of between 1 and 1.25 percentage points, as well as revised spreads that have usually added about a full percentage point to previous ones. By pegging interest rates to the U.S. prime, moreover, they have selected a base that has recently run about one percentage point higher than LIBOR. These efforts might have added between 70 and 130 million dollars to the profits of the largest nine U.S. banks, depending on the relevant marginal tax rates. They translate into an increased return on loans to those countries of about 25 percent in comparison with previous terms, quite independently of higher spreads being charged on new loans.[24]

Ironically, the absolute effect on total bank profits is relatively small, as is the effect on the borrowers. The cost of the higher premium over LIBOR to Mexico is less than 1 percent of foreign exchange earnings, for example, since what is relevant to the country is the total interest rate and not the margin. But the ill will of imposing, arbitrarily, increased costs of servicing an already burdensome debt is considerable. Such charges are not market-determined because the lending is involuntary.

At the same time, of course, the large money market banks find themselves under assault. They are being forced to set aside larger loan reserves to satisfy bank examiners and a Congress concerned with excessive bank exposure. They must also cope with second-tier banks who have much less to gain from a continued lending relationship with developing countries and do not want to renew outstanding loans, even at higher spreads. Michigan National Bank has even taken Citicorp to court over the involuntary extension of a 5 million dollars participation in a Pemex loan. For new money, the money market banks can no longer count on tapping their regional colleagues and must rely on the suasion of the Federal Reserve to pressure the smaller banks into staying in the game.

This short-term mentality provoked an increased country resistance, and an increased emphasis upon injecting larger political considerations, and elements of systematic stability, into the discussion. Banks logically preferred a minimum amount of additional lending or renegotiation. They, and even the Fund, want the country on a short leash and constantly accountable. While this surveillance may reduce the moral hazard problem, it does so at the risk of miscalculating the provocation to country default and to more concerted organization among debtors. The widening perception, particularly as interest rates rose in the first half of 1984, that the negotiating structure was inadequate precipitated its latest modification, the Mexican multi-year restructuring.

The agreement included a significant concession on terms. Interest rates were to be based exclusively on LIBOR, spreads were lowered, and no commission charges were imposed. For the first time the banks implicitly recognized that there could be no appeal to market forces in determining the cost of involuntary lending. They accepted reduced profits, before tax, of about 500 million dollars, and a corresponding Mexican benefit, fully reversing their previous strategy. In addition, the public debt was restructured over a 14-year term, explicitly accepting the necessity of a longer time-horizon for meaningful resolution of the debt crisis. Indeed, the only notable absence in the package, already a model for application to other countries, is the presence of an interest rate cap that would reduce susceptibility to market volatility. The agreement was thus a victory for those, like Paul Volcker, who from the beginning insisted upon a systemic, rather than a private perspective.

Yet it also raises fundamental institutional issues. The Mexican arrangement signalled another major step down the road of quasi-socialization of international lending inaugurated by the Fund's imposition of conditionality upon the banks. The international banks themselves, now centrally organized into negotiating committees, have conceded the inapplicability of simple market signals. The terms of the Mexican agreement call for the continued presence of the Fund even when the term of the present extended facility expires. It is therefore difficult to argue that one will soon see a return to normal, decentralized market borrowing as some bankers contend. Rather, the new institutional characteristics mirror the likely continued reluctance of bankers to play a major role in meeting current account deficit financing of developing countries as they did up to 1982.

Thus, for all the advance, current policies fail to address the adequacy of the long-term supply of capital. The inability to restore the past should not be unduly regretted. There is no reason to believe that the private profit calculus will produce the right amount of capital for the right developing countries. One of the causes of the present crisis is such market failure, failure that has had to be compensated by ever greater public intervention. But its continuing role is as yet still inadequately defined.

There is not even a clear policy direction should the present signs of improvement recede. This is far from an extreme hypothetical view. Recovery may not continue at its present pace. Rising social costs in one or more of the major developing countries may still lead to failure to live up to stabilization targets. The continuing pattern of adjustment via trade surpluses may provoke even more pronounced tendencies toward protectionism, with significant consequences for the structure of the trading system. Reaction against rapidly rising imports from the NICs can spill over to imports from industrial country competitors. Interest rates may resume an upward course, fed not merely by a continuing large budget deficit, but by threats of a sliding dollar. These possibilities, and with them slowed industrial country growth, are real. That reality contributes to pervasive uncertainty, itself a constraint on recuperation of the global economy in the 1980s.

The debt issue is thus far from definitive resolution. What we have is an evolving process that has averted financial disaster, but at a significant cost for the developing country debtors. Once the dangers of crisis recede, will even the present concern for these debtors survive? Will proper attention be focused upon the longer-term financial requirements of these countries? It is easier to respond to immediate pressure than to take the longer view. Financial collapse has its obvious costs. The costs of inaction are less tangible, but no less real: taxpayers pay through slower growth and increasing alienation of the developing world rather than by appropriations needed to underwrite public participation in financing development.

A few years ago, prior to the crisis of 1982, I wrote: "The principal danger is not the wholesale default by developing countries and the possibility that it may bring the world financial system crashing down. The principal danger is that available international finance will be inadequate to maintain a reasonable level of world economic growth in the 1980s. If the supply of funds proves inadequate, it will be the largest debtors — many of them Latin American countries — who will be most in danger. They will have to bear the brunt of the adjustment burden themselves. . . . The developed countries may not react to strengthen the system in time to avoid slowing of growth of their exports to the developing countries. The burden will fall primarily on the developing countries. Interdependence is still asymmetric."[25] That prognosis unfortunately proved accurate. I regret to say that there is little reason to amend it now.

In the last analysis, the debt problem is a development problem, not an isolated preoccupation with solvency or liquidity. It speaks not merely to the financial system, but equally to the future pattern of production and trade. Above all, it profoundly affects the lives of many hundreds of millions, the majority in this hemisphere. We do not escape its effects: interdependence is no less real for being asymmetric. The issue is not merely a technocratic problem, devoid of political content. Until these realizations become more pervasive, we shall continue merely to cope with the great debt crisis of 1982 rather than confronting and resolving it.

APPENDIX

TABLE A

Estimating Equations[a] for Export Volume Elasticity

PERCENTAGE CHANGE IN EXPORT VOLUME OF:	CONSTANT	PERCENTAGE GROWTH OF INDUSTRIALIZED COUNTRY PRODUCT	D-W	ADJUSTED R^2
Non-Oil Developing	2.5	1.08	1.61[b]	.10[b]
Countries, 1963–1982	(2.4)	(.52)		
Non-Oil, Oil Importing	1.5	1.73	1.50	.64
Countries, 1973–1982	(1.4)	(.42)		
Exporters of	2.1	2.46	1.71	.71
Manufactures	(1.7)	(.51)		
Low Income		[c]		-.10
Asia	3.9	2.29	1.95	.49
		(2.5)	(.74)	
Western	1.1	1.51	1.78[b]	.31
Hemisphere	(3.8)	(.73)		

Sources: Non-Oil Developing Countries, 1963–1982: IMF, *International Financial Statistics, Yearbook, 1983;* Non-oil, Oil Importing Countries, 1973–1982: IMF, *World Economic Outlook, 1983.*

[a]Standard errors in parentheses.

[b]One observation omitted to adjust for autocorrelation of the residuals.

[c]t-value less than one.

TABLE B

Estimating Equations[a] for Deflated Export Unit Value[b]

I. PERCENTAGE CHANGE IN DEFLATED EXPORT UNIT VALUE OF:	CONSTANT	OIL EFFECT (1973-74)	CHANGE IN INDUSTRIALIZED COUNTRY GROWTH RATE	CHANGE LAGGED	CHANGE IN INDUSTRIALIZED COUNTRY INFLATION RATE	DOLLAR APPRECIATION	D-W	ADJ. R^2
Non-Oil developing countries, 1964-82[c]	-1.59 (1.06)	13.0 (3.6)	1.04 (.43)	1.33 (.36)	2.74 (.65)	-.14 (.12)	1.96	.91
Non-Oil developing countries, 1971-82[c]	-1.13 (2.84)	11.5 (7.4)	1.33 (.56)	1.19 (.45)	3.19 (.97)	-.24 (.16)	1.03	.92
Non-Oil importing countries, 1974-82[c]	-1.72 (4.82)		1.06 (.53)	1.08 (.49)	3.12 (.77)	-.02 (.27)	2.43	.87
Exporters of Manufactures	.84 (.65)		1.26 (.32)	1.10 (.23)	1.85 (.37)	.76 (.13)	2.61	.91
Low Income[c]	-1.88 (2.89)		.95 (.30)	2.78 (.27)	.62 (.42)	1.06 (.16)	2.02	.95
Asia	.79 (1.81)		1.24 (.88)	1.33 (.64)	2.24 (1.01)	.86 (.36)	2.69	.58
Western Hemisphere	1.11 (10.06)		2.17 (.58)	1.83 (.54)	4.18 (.85)	1.36 (.30)	2.17	.95

II.
PERCENTAGE CHANGE IN
DEFLATED EXPORT UNIT
VALUE OF:

	CONSTANT	OIL EFFECT (1973-74)	INDUSTRIALIZED COUNTRY GROWTH RATE	DOLLAR APPRECIATION	D-W	ADJ. R^2
Non-Oil developing countries, 1971–82	-6.53 (4.09)	25.0 (5.6)	1.13 (1.19)	-.40 (.39)	2.17	.71
Non-Oil importing countries, 1974–82	-.89 (5.24)		1.13 (1.67)	-1.14 (.66)	2.08	.31

Source: As for Table A.

[a]Standard errors in parentheses.

[b]Increase in export unit values minus aggregate industrial country consumer price index increase.

[c]Corrected for autocorrelation.

NOTES

1. The basic sources for developing country debt and associated economic data are IMF, *World Economic Outlook*; World Bank, *World Debt Tables*; and OECD, *External Debt of Developing Countries*. All three are published annually. Coverages differ. This estimate comes from the World Bank.

2. For a recent review of bank debt restructurings, through June 1984, see IMF, Occasional Paper No. 31, *International Capital Markets, Developments and Prospects*, 1984, Appendix 3.

3. World Bank, *World Development Report, 1982*, p. 21.

4. See the article on Citibank in *Business Week*, May 16, 1983, pp. 124 ff.

5. These data cover the period 1965–81. During the interval the combination of export opportunities and access to credit gives reason to suppose that simple least squares captures a savings function unconstrained by foreign exchange shortage. To avoid problems of appropriate deflators, the functions are estimated in ratio form: $S/Y = a + b/Y_r + c_1CA + C_2CA$ where S is gross national savings, Y is gross national product, Y_r is real gross domestic product, and CA is the current account deficit. The coefficient $1-a$ is the estimated marginal propensity to consume out of gross national product, and c_1 and c_2 are the period specific propensities to consume out of the deficit for 1965–1978 and 1979–1981.

6. *World Economic Outlook*, 1983, p. 143.

7. IMF, Occasional Paper No. 3, *External Indebtedness of Developing Countries*, May 1981, p. 11.

8. Although Tables 3 and 4 use a similar methodology, they will not necessarily yield a set of Latin American estimates that are an exact proportion of the non-oil developing country total. Thus, the Latin American interest rate effect seems to exceed the total, when it cannot. Yet the conclusion that Latin America is responsible for the lion's share of the interest rate effect is surely valid.

9. For these estimates see Michael Dooley, et. al., "An Analysis of External Debt Positions of Eight Developing Countries through 1990," Federal Reserve Board International Finance Discussion Paper No. 227, August 1983.

10. World Bank, *World Debt Tables, 1982–83*, p. vii.

11. Willian R. Cline, *International Debt and the Stability of the World Economy*, Institute for International Economics, Sept. 1983, p. 71. *World Financial Markets*, June 1983.

12. That is, it takes as the appropriate constraint for developing country repayment the capacity to generate foreign exchange earnings rather than domestic saving. For an example of the latter, see *External Indebtedness of Developing Countries*, Appendix 3.

13. Specifying the following equations:

$$X_t = X_0 e^{gt}$$

$$M_t = (1+a)X_t$$

$$dD = M_t - X_t + iD_t$$

we can solve for debt, D_t, $= a/(g-i)X_0(e^{gt} - e^{it})$. Then the limiting debt/export ratio, $D(t)/X(t) = a/(g-i)$.

14. Economic Commission for Latin America, *Balance preliminar de la economia latinoamericana durante 1983*, Dec. 1983, p. 29.

15. World Bank estimates reported in the *New York Times*, January 26, 1984, p. 45 from *World Debt Tables, 1983*.

16. For the results reported by the IMF, see *World Economic Outlook, 1983*, Appendix A.9, pp. 154 ff. A different estimate, also for quarterly data, is found in Dooley, et. al., Appendix Table 17. The Latin American commodity price index in question can be found in Inter-American Development Bank, *Economic and Social Progress in Latin America*. Petroleum was excluded.

17. See Table 3 in my "The Debt Crisis: Round Two Ahead?" in R. Feinberg and V. Kallab, eds., *Adjustment Crisis in the Third World* (Overseas Development Council, 1984) illustrating the sensitivity of export earnings to key price assumptions.

18. INTAL, IDB, *The Latin American Integration Process in 1982*, Table 7, p. 35.

19. *World Financial Markets*, May 1984, p. 11.

20. Cline finds an elasticity as great as 7 based on the aggregation of country estimates, and a value of 5 derived from the elasticity estimates of his projection model (see p. 65). The actual simulations show a large effect because the sharp decline in the debt-export ratio reduces further the relative importance of interest payments.

21. *World Economic Outlook, 1983*, p. 20.

22. *World Financial Markets*, June 1983, pp. 11, 12.

23. See IMF, *International Capital Markets*, 1984, Chapter 3 and Appendix Table 42.

24. These estimates start from the terms and sums rescheduled reported in *Latin American Weekly Report*, 20 May 1983, plus subsequent news accounts. On average, spreads were one percent higher than during the period when the loans were initially contracted in the late 1970s, allowing for intervening grace periods. Commissions for rescheduling ranged between 1.25 and 1.50 percent, of which one percent was regarded as profit (taking into account the World Bank typical commission payment of 0.25 percent).

Commissions are presumed to be paid initially, even if not accounted in bank earnings in that fashion, and to yield a return of 10 percent a year. The average annual value, spread over the life of the loan, is therefore greater than the simple average (approximately twice as large).

To the before-tax annual earnings obtained by summing the incremental spreads and the average annual value of commissions, alternative marginal tax rates are applied to arrive at after-tax profits. These are then compared to the approximate share of loans to these countries in total bank assets to assess the increased returns on their holdings.

Equivalently, one can approximate the result, excluding commissions, by noting that the spread on rescheduled loans has doubled. Since such rescheduled loans are about one-quarter of the total extended by banks to these countries, the effect is about a 25 percent rise in after-tax earnings.

The calculations are reported in the *Wall Street Journal*, December 5, 1983.

25. *The Political Economy of the Western Hemisphere: Selected Issues for U.S. Policy*, Joint Economic Committee, 97th Congress, 1st Session, September 18, 1981, p. 163.

The External Debt Crisis in Latin America: Trends and Outlook*

Ricardo Ffrench-Davis

The past ten years witnessed substantial changes in the international economic relations of Latin America. Two most noteworthy changes were the accelerated growth in the deficits on current account of most of the countries in the region and the significant shifts in the sources for financing those deficits.

The composition of the external debt changed considerably during the decade. In the face of declining shares of loans from official creditors and foreign direct investment, the shares of private bank financing began to dominate in both the capital account and the balance of external debts. This phenomenon was not confined to the region, but was also shared by most developing countries. It was more pronounced in the semi-industrialized developing countries that include a large number of Latin American nations. The Latin American region accounts for more than 60 percent of the liabilities of the developing countries with private banking institutions (bank debt).

Section 1 begins with an examination of data and highlights the different picture that emerges when restricted or more complete definitions of the external debt are used. This has important implications for the analysis of the behavior of the debt, its servicing and the nature of the problems that arise in critical situations like the one prevailing today. The change in the sources of external financing has affected the countries of the region in various ways. This section focuses on two of them: (1) the terms of borrowing and their main consequences in the debtor countries; (2) the changing nature of external economic relations, their relations to national development, and their implications for macro-economic policies.

International private capital markets have expanded vigorously in the last fifteen years. A large number of developing countries, including Latin American countries, have gained increasing access to the lending facilities of banks in those markets. The following section first examines the peculiarities of both the world markets during the 1970s and the economic situation of the countries of the region, in particular those aspects that have a greater bearing on the accessibility to foreign bank lending; next, some of the currently important issues are outlined. Finally, some observations follow concerning the positive and negative consequences which could arise from the various alternatives of Latin American countries.

To sum up, the emergence of international private capital markets opened up new opportunities to the countries of the region and eased their adjustment to the critical situations they have faced since 1973. Worthwhile to note is the fact that funds were abundantly available in those markets throughout the mid-1970s, with fairly low real rates of interest. However, the outlook for the years to come remains ambiguous. The availability of funds and their cost will probably become less favorable within a framework of the international market that presumably will exhibit greater instability.

In these circumstances five factors seem crucial in determining the capability of the country in taking advantage of those markets. In the international sphere there is an economic factor as well as an institutional one. The economic factor relates to the evolution of the world economy in relation to the dynamism of the export markets of the countries of the region and to movements of real interest rates. The institutional factor relates to the volume and method of public financing. Importance will be attached to the restructuring of the maturity terms of the existing stock of external debts and to the compensation for the increased burden on the balance of payments caused by the interest on the debt.

Three other factors that are related to the domestic economy include the use of the external funds, and production and foreign exchange-generating potentials of them, and the capability of national economic policies to achieve an adjustment to changed equilibria consistent with an optimal use of national resources and investment. Many of the current adjustment processes involve an excessively high cost in employment and productive capacity. This is associated with a restrictive monetarist approach in the face of a general depression in the world economy.

Thus, this new international situation brings once again to the fore the issue of economic cooperation among developing countries.

1. Origins, Conditions and Objectives of External Financing

During the 1950s and 1960s the economic relations of the Latin American countries with the rest of the world were confined to trade, official financing and foreign direct investment. The net capital flow (deficit on current account) was relatively unimportant, accounting for 1 or 2 percent of the region's gross domestic product (GDP). In the 1950s direct investment was significant in magnitude, but the following decade saw a gradual decline in the net flow of funds (Table 1).

During the 1970s, with the emergence of bank flows, the privatization of fund flows to Latin America increased. In view of their predominant influence in external financing, the following discussion will focus on their characteristics and influences on the domestic economy. To provide a better perspective we shall examine the interrelationship of this type of financing with other financing sources for the countries of the region, and for the region as a whole compared with the developing countries as a whole.[1]

Composition of the Debt

One problem we had in analyzing external financing was the deficiency of data. Recently, the World Bank collected data for more than 100 countries.[2] As for the data on external debt, the principal defect is still the omission of two significant components: non-guaranteed debt and short-term debt. Both provide important information in the analysis of the recent behavior of external debt and its near-future prospects.[3] In addition, the Bank for International Settlements (BIS) data enable

Table 1

Public, Total, and Bank Debt of Latin America*, 1973–1982
(in billions of U.S. dollars)

	1973	1977	1980	1981	1982	ANNUAL GROWTH RATE 1973–1977	1977–1980	1981	1982
I. Public debt	27.0	71.9	124.1	142.3	166.9	27.7	20.0	14.7	17.3
II. Total debt	42.8	104.6	204.3	241.5	265.6	25.0	25.0	18.2	10.0
III. Bank debt	25.7	72.9	160.1	194.1	213.1	29.8	30.0	21.2	9.8

Sources: Prepared by the author on the basis of a World Bank documented *Debtor Reporting System;* UN, DIESA/DRPA; and BIS. The figures refer to the debt disbursed at the end of each year. Excludes liabilities with the IMF.

*Includes twenty-two countries

more complete estimates of the external debt which are used here.[4]

The evolution of external financing differs from country to country in the region. The status of oil production, economic strategies and policies, and economic structures of the particular country differently influence the country's behavior in its external debt relations. Despite great diversity, the behavior of bank lending in the countries of the region is quite similar. The same applies with respect to the critical debt problem facing most countries at present.

The composition of the capital account of the balance of payments of the countries of the region underwent substantial changes during the period 1960–1980. An examination of annual net flows shows that while direct foreign investment and official credits accounted for three-quarters of net capital flows during 1960–1970, they fell to one-third in 1980. At the same time, the share of bank sources grew from less than 7 percent to about 70 percent of the total in the same period. The remaining flows of private funds consisting of supplier credits and proceeds of bonds were at low levels and a decreasing share compared with the net flow of bank lending.

Similar behavior is found when the evolution of the balance of the external debt is examined. Tables 1 and 2 present the data and focus attention on the credit components. Table 1 contains data on two different external debt indicators at year-end 1973, 1977 and 1980–1982. Row I of the table shows the traditional measurement known as public external debt. Public debt includes only public or publicly guaranteed liabilities with a maturity of more than one year.[5] This is the debt on which more complete data are available, primarily since the beginning of the 1970s. Row II of Table 1 presents estimates of the total debt, i.e., public debt, non-guaranteed debt and bank loans with a maturity of one year or less.

The level of total debt is considerably higher than that of public debt. The gap between the two is much greater for Latin America than for the developing countries as a whole. In 1980, 40 percent of the debt of the region accounted for non-guaranteed and short-term loans whose terms of borrowing were much more unfavorable than those for public debt. The corresponding figure for the rest of the developing countries was only 22 percent.

Beginning with the suspension of crude oil shipments by the members of the Organization of Petroleum Exporting Countries (OPEC) in 1973, three subperiods in the composition of the debt may be distinguished. In the first period, 1973–1977, public debt grew more rapidly than total debt. This was due to the fact that while bank lending grew rapidly, it was the portion representing publicly guaranteed loans and loans with a maturity of more than one year that expanded most rapidly. In 1973 the outstanding proportion of bank debt to public debt was only 39 percent; by 1977 it had risen to 55 percent.[6] It fundamentally constituted syndicated Euroloans, a significant proportion of which went to public debtors in the borrowing countries. As a result, the public sector (or its plans in the case of publicly guaranteed investment credits to the private sector) has been favored with the reappearance of international private capital markets.

In the second period, the relationship was reversed. Total debt increased more quickly than public debt in all the developing regions. But the phenomenon was more pronounced in Latin America. In addition, bank debt is the most dynamic component of the debt. A large proportion of bank loans was not publicly guaranteed and had a short-term maturity; only 49 percent of the balance at the end of 1980 consisted of public debt. This trend was due to three factors. First, loans with longer maturities became relatively scarcer in the international capital market. For instance in 1980 reported Euroloans, whose average term was then 8 years, accounted for only one-fourth of new bank commitments to the

Table 2

Share of Bank Debt in Total Debt, for Selected Years, 1973–1982

COUNTRY GROUPS	1973	1975	1977	1980	1981	1982
1. Latin America (22)	60.0	68.6	69.7	78.4	80.4	80.2
2. Oil-exporting developing countries (16)	49.9	54.1	55.2	64.7	67.6	68.1
3. Oil-importing developing countries (69)	34.3	42.7	44.4	56.0	59.4	57.9
4. Total developing countries (85)	39.3	46.3	48.4	59.8	62.6	61.9

Sources: Prepared on the basis of data from World Bank documents, DRS; BIS; United Nations, DIESA & DRPA; and IDB. Total developing countries include twenty-two countries of the Latin American region; of these six countriees (Bolivia, Ecuador, Mexico, Peru, Trinidad and Tobago, and Venezuela) were classified among the sixteen net oil-exporting countries.

The figures in brackets beside the name of each group indicate the number of countries included.

developing countries. Second, in 1980 the second oil shock made itself felt in the context of a world economy in recession; many developing countries had to use their international reserves or short-term credit lines to finance their deficits on current account. Third, in a number of developing countries including some Latin American countries, new government economic programs gave the private sector a larger role in economic activity, which also involved the agents that participated in the contraction of external debt. Thus a considerable volume of credit flows took place without public guarantee in the debtor countries.

The third subperiod begins around 1981 with the halting of the expansive trend and with different reactions in various countries. The rate of expansion of total debt fell for the group of countries as a whole, and the change in the trend became dramatic in 1982. In this year the rate of expansion of the disbursed balance of the debt (at current prices) fell to a third of its former average rate in the previous period since the first oil shock. In addition, over 55 percent of the new credits were granted with maturities of up to one year. It should be noted, however, that the change did not involve a reduction in the nominal debt, but that its continued expansion was at a substantially lower rate than that of previous years. This meant a decrease in the financing of the deficits on current account. A part of the decrease was covered by the use of international reserves, and the rest was covered by an inevitable contraction in purchases abroad which will be discussed later.

Table 2 confirms the changes in the composition of the external debt. In all the country groups, the share of the bank debt increased throughout the period and in 1980 represented almost 60 percent in the developing nations as a whole and about 80 percent in Latin America.[7] If the period 1973–1977 is divided into two parts, it will be seen that the sharpest increase in bank lending took place immediately after the rise in the oil price in 1973. The recycling of petrodollars helped to place a number of developing countries that were not energy importers in a better position to face the external challenge. As is well known, it was the semi-industrialized countries that were able to obtain bank funds to correct the disequilibrium in their balances of payments earlier and in more adequate amounts.

Table 3 presents disaggregated information on the evolution and composition of the external debt for countries in the region in 1977 and 1981, the last year of fast debt growth.[8] In 1981, the seven principal borrowing countries accounted for 89 percent of the total debt and 93 percent of the bank debt of the region. In the group of the remaining fifteen countries, the share of bank loans is significantly smaller. However, the dispersion among them is very pronounced. For example, between

1977 and 1981 three of those countries had their access to bank loans abruptly reduced for various reasons. Table 3 presents separately the figures for Haiti, Jamaica and Nicaragua, whose bank liabilities decreased in that period. The remaining twelve countries show a percentage share of bank debt which, although significantly smaller than that of the seven major debtors, is greater than that of the remaining developing countries. If the seven larger countries of Latin America are excluded from

TABLE 3

Total Debt and Bank Share by Principal Borrowing Countries in Latin America, 1977 and 1981

	TOTAL DEBT			SHARE OF BANK DEBT IN TOTAL	
	U.S. $ Billions		Annual Growth Rate (percentages)	(Percentages)	
	1977	1981		1977	1981
COUNTRY	(1)	(2)	(3)	(4)	(5)
Argentina	7.8	30.8	41.0	62.4	80.7
Brazil	33.1	65.3	18.5	76.5	80.4
Chile	5.2	15.5	31.4	37.2	83.8
Colombia	3.9	8.4	21.1	45.1	65.0
Mexico	26.1	73.7	29.7	77.8	85.5
Peru	6.1	8.5	8.7	56.4	53.7
Venezuela	10.8	28.9	28.0	84.1	93.2
Haiti, Jamaica, Nicaragua	2.9	3.8	7.0	62.0	34.2
Remaining countries (12)	9.4	20.8	22.0	53.2	56.7
TOTAL	104.6	241.5	23.3	69.7	80.4
(Bank share)	(72.9)	(194.1)	(27.7)		

Sources: Prepared by the author from World Bank, DRS; United Nations, DIESA/DRPA; and CEPAL. Figures in cols (1) to (3) for Argentina, Brazil, Chile, Mexico, Peru and Venezuela are somewhat different from those implicit in Tables 1 and 2. The column 2 data are more comprehensive for these six countries. In the case of Chile, figures are total debt, as estimated by the Central Bank, minus liabilities with the IMF and those payable in domestic currency. The total for Latin American has not been adjusted, and is the same as in Table 1.

total developing countries, the remainder accounts for 43 percent in 1980 compared with around 54 per cent for the twelve smaller debtors in Latin America. Even the smaller debtors had relatively easier access to international private capital markets.

The predominant trend in the 1970s, of growing concentration in bank lenders, has had a number of consequences for the countries of the region. Its effects on financing terms are examined below.

Terms of Borrowing and Borrowing Activity

The terms on which the region borrowed have deteriorated as a result of both the hardening of bank lending terms and the increase in the share of bank debt to total debt. Indeed, in 1980 the nominal cost of bank credit was more than double the cost of official debt, so that its growing share in total debt has been a decisive factor in the increase in the average cost of the external debt. This can be seen in Table 4.

The rates of interest for all categories of creditors increased substantially between 1973 and 1981. However, the increase was not linear throughout the period. As a matter of fact in the middle of the period

TABLE 4

Interest Rates by Source of Debt (annual rates)

COUNTRY GROUPS	BANKS			OFFICIAL AND OTHER		TOTAL			
	1973 (1)	1980 (2)	1981–1982 (3)	1973 (4)	1980 (5)	1973 (6)	1977 (7)	1980 (8)	1981–1982 (9)
1. Latin America	9.0	14.2	16.5	5.3	7.0	7.3	7.4	12.5	14.2
2. Oil-exporting countries	9.0	13.5	16.0	3.9	5.4	6.1	7.0	10.5	12
3. Oil-importing countries	8.0	13.2	15.5	4.1	4.8	5.2	5.5	9.3	11
4. Total developing countries	8.4	13.4	15.8	4.0	5.0	5.5	6.0	9.7	11

Sources: Prepared from World Bank, DRS and United Nations, DIESA (1982) for 1973–1980. The figures for 1981–1982 are estimated from OECD (1982) and World Bank data.

the average interest rates charged by financial institutions had decreased. Nevertheless, the cost of the total debt increased somewhat because of the larger weight of the component of the debt with harder financing terms (compare columns 1, 6, and 7 in Table 4). In the second half of the period, rates sharply rose. This also continued in the years between 1977 to 1981, remaining in 1982 at the same high level of the preceding year. For Latin America the average bank rate (and commissions) rose by more than eight percentage points, and as already pointed out, its level was more than double the rate of non-bank credits.[9] The increase in bank costs, coupled with the privatization of the sources of debt, made the cost of external debt of the region significantly higher.

After remaining relatively stable from 1973 to 1977, the average interest rate on the total debt increased by seven percentage points between 1977 and 1981. The increase in the nominal rate brought in its wake an increase in the real rate, as the process of accommodation to the inflation that occurred in the 1970s speeded up towards the end of the decade. This process will be examined later. To sum up, the average interest rates rose by close to seven points; after 1977 the increase was generally much higher in the region compared to the rest of developing countries. Latin America paid an annual additional disbursement of approximately 8 billion dollars for increased interest in 1981.

The debt maturities also deteriorated in the same period. The annual amortization rate (annual payments as a proportion of outstanding debt at the beginning of the year) represented between 12 and 13 percent of the public debt in both 1973 and 1977 and rose to 15 percent towards the end of the period. As for the bank debt, maturities were considerably shorter with a higher amortization rate. This debt included commercial financing, medium-term Eurocredits, and short-term financial flows; short-term financial flows were caused by the balance-of-payments needs and speculative flows induced by differences in the financial rate of return. Annual amortization rates have been affected by fluctuations in the maturities of Eurocredits and changes in the composition of these flows. Despite the fluctuations, the amortization rate has been very high, with an average level of 42 percent in 1978–1980 and higher in subsequent years. In fact, information from the Bank of International Settlements shows an amortization rate of 46 percent in the period 1981–1982. In other words, nearly half of the bank debt existing at the beginning of each of these years had to be amortized or renewed during the corresponding year.

The World Bank and BIS data together reveal that around 1980 more than one-quarter of the total debt of the region had to be amortized or refinanced annually as opposed to 10 percent in the 1960s. This means that annual amortizations more than doubled, with a resulting increase in the gross indebtedness each year. This increase in "borrowing activity" had important consequences and helps to explain the acuteness of the problem of the external debt in the early 1980s. This is discussed in a subsequent section.

The increase in the debt and in its cost was reflected in the balance of payments through increases in interest payments. Between 1977 and 1980, interest payments tripled whereas in that period inflation was approximately 40 percent per annum. However, an important compensating factor emerged; namely, interest income was achieved as a result of investment of international reserves. During the period, there was a significant increase in reserves largely as a result of the inflow of private capital in larger amounts than those required for financing the deficit on current account. Concurrently, the management of reserves improved and in the financial markets an attractive source for investment was found; this investment began on a small scale in the mid-1960s. In net terms, around 1980, just over a third of the interest payments was offset by interest income — a situation similar to that in other developing countries as a whole. As in other cases, the differences among the countries were significant in Latin America, as shown by columns (3) and (4) of Table 5.

The relative weight of net interest payments in the current account has been strongly influenced by performance of the trade balance. For the countries of the region, interest payments represented more than half of the deficit on current account; for the oil-importing developing countries, the result was that the trade deficit doubled. So far in the 1980s the volume of net nominal interest payments has continued to grow because of the combined effect of higher rates, an increasing volume of debt, and smaller international reserves.

Table 6 presents the recent evolution of the main components of the balance of payments for the region. Between 1980 and 1982 there was a drop in exports but a much greater one in imports, as a result of the adjustment effort made in many countries. Hence, in spite of the fall of 6 percent in the terms of trade, Latin America achieved a major surplus in the trading account in 1982: it exported $10 billion more than it imported. Even so, the deficit on current account was high. The determining variable was the dramatic increase in net interest payments; this arose from a larger debt accumulated, abnormally high real interest rates, and a fall in the proceeds from the investment of international reserves. As a result, the interest payment on foreign loans accounted for virtually the entire deficit on current account in the region.

The increase in nominal interest rates was coupled with a deterioration in debt maturities, which substantially increased the total debt service. The result was a widening gap between the gross credits received annually and the funds available for financing the imports of the indebted countries. This evolution of financing terms has appreciably increased the vulnerability of the countries of the region to changes in the availability of financial resources in the international market in the recent past. Indeed, the gravity of the situation was dramatically revealed in 1982, when the total gross credits disbursed during the year fell below the level to cover adequately the amortizations and interest payments on the debt.

TABLE 5

Trade and Financial Deficits on Current Account, 1980
(in millions of dollars)

	Trade Deficit (1)	Financial Deficit (2)	INTEREST FLOWS Inflows (3)	Outflows (4)	CURRENT ACCOUNT DEFICIT (5)
I. Latin America	138	13,948	7,337	21,285	27,585
Argentina	1,373	946	1,229	2,175	4,774
Brazil	2,823	6,309	1,147	7,456	12,848
Chile	764	847	305	1,152	2,024
Colombia	238	156	471	627	159
Mexico	2,830	4,454	1,022	5,476	8,306
Peru	-837	542	201	743	72
Venezuela	-8,174	-650	2,263	1,613	-4,749
Remainder (15)	1,121	1,344	699	2,043	4,151
II. Oil-importing developing countries (69)	47,024	15,996	8,189	24,185	62,383
III. Total developing countries (85)	19,971	22,288	14,208	36,496	61,880

Sources: Section I based on CEPAL, *Statistical Yearbook for Latin America, 1983.* The minus sign in columns (1), (2) and (5) indicates a surplus. (5) is equal to (1) plus (2) plus the non-trade and non-interest balance in current account.
The current account is defined here as the sum of the balances of goods and services and private transfers.

The Relationship of External Financing to the National Economy

Changes in the volume, composition, and terms of external financing have a number of implications for the borrowing countries. Broadly speaking, the volume of net capital inflows has grown in real terms and as a proportion of GDP and exports. The increase was due in part to the fact that greater indebtedness was necessary to enable the Latin American countries to face the consequences of the shocks and the instability of external origin. The Latin American countries also appropriated external funds largely for capital formation. The rise in the rate of capital formation has been striking for oil-exporting countries as well as for the oil-importing countries.

Not every country took advantage of easier access to finance capital to strengthen the productive capacity. In some cases, the greater availability of credit in the international private capital markets has even induced the indebted countries to adopt exchange and trade policies that have in fact increased the size of deficits on current account and discouraged domestic production. These countries faced a more difficult payment situation and a more pronounced deterioration of their productive apparatus. Thus, the objectives and causes of indebtedness have varied from country to country, depending on their external situation and the nature of their domestic economic policies.

TABLE 6

Evolution of the External Account in Latin America, 1980–1982
(billions of US dollars)

	1980	1981	1982
1. Trade balance	-0.1	-0.7	10.5
(a) Exports	91.1	97.6	89.1
(b) Imports	91.2	98.3	78.6
2. Net profits and interest	18.4	27.9	36.8
(Interest net)	(13.9)	(22.6)	(32.0)
3. Deficit on current account	27.6	40.3	36.3
4. Balance of payments	-2.2	2.5	-19.9

Source: CEPAL, *Statistical Yearbook for Latin America, 1983.*

Concomitant with changes in the composition of the debt the nature of external sector relationships has also changed. For instance, the bank lender acted in a different way from the agents of public sources. Furthermore, some of the borrowing countries have modified their intermediaries, thus liberalizing movements of capital. The privatization of the sources and direct users of the loans has also made the national economies more vulnerable to fluctuations in international financial markets. Instability in the terms of trade has occurred along with instability in the terms of borrowing. The build-up of reserves during the 1970s has partially offset the global impact of external fluctuations on the foreign exchange balance; the repercussions of the external instability on the domestic economy in turn depended on the economic policy of each country. Nonetheless, the intensification of external instability and the lack of compensatory mechanisms adequate for the existing international financial order have made it difficult for the indebted countries to defend themselves against instability: both the excessive availability and the subsequent scarcity of funds have been main obstacles to a stable development.

The Relative Size of the Debt and of External Financing

Table 7 shows the evolution of the debt from several viewpoints, even after discounting the devaluation of the US dollar (line 5). Between 1973 and 1980 the dollar was depreciated by more than 100 percent; in 1981 by another 25 percent; and in 1982 by less than 10 percent. This magnitude reflected the intensity of the "financial shock" that many countries suffered in that year. Total debt increased by 111 percent relative to GDP from 1973–1982. The debt/exports coefficient for the Latin American region rose 27 percent between 1973 and 1980 with almost the entire increase occurring in the first half of the period (lines 11 and 12). In contrast, in the years of 1980–1982 the coefficient fell by 37 percent; in these years the rise in the nominal debt was coupled with an abrupt reversal of previously expansionary trends in exports. These indicators show the relative weights of the accumulated balance of the debt and the specific time it is measured. Two additional dimensions are pertinent. One is the terms on which the debt is serviced. The other is the amount for the country receiving net flows as reflected in the outstanding balance of the debt.

"Borrowing activity" has increased more sharply than the debt itself due to the deterioration in the terms of financing. In other words, the same net volume of external resources demands a much larger gross flow. In the foregoing subsection, the terms of borrowing and their evolution in the period 1973–1982 were examined. It is estimated that the annual service per unit of debt increased by over one-third between the beginning of that period and 1980. As a result, in addition to the increase in the debt itself, the debt service also rose by about one-third because of the deterioration in the terms of borrowing.[10]

TABLE 7

Evolution of the Current Account, Exports,
Production and Debt in Latin America, for Selected Years, 1973–1982

	1973	1977	1980	1981	1982
I. Amounts in billions of dollars at 1980 prices					
1. Deficit on current account (DCA)	7.4	16.7	27.1	39.5	34.7
2. Merchandise exports (Xg)	52.6	70.8	91.3	100.8	91.5
3. Exports of goods and services (Xgs)	66.7	87.4	118.1	132.6	118.4
4. Gross domestic product (GDP)	371.2	457.4	532.3	539.5	533.2
5. Total debt (TD)	92.6	151.0	204.3	254.5	285.6
6. International reserves (IR)[a]	25.3	35.9	34.9	35.4	29.0
7. Net debt (ND=TD–IR)	67.3	115.1	169.4	219.1	256.6
II. Percentage shares					
8. DCA/GDP	2.0	3.7	5.1	7.3	6.5
9. TD/GDP	24.9	33.0	38.4	47.2	53.6
10. ND/GDP	18.1	25.2	31.8	40.6	48.0
11. TD/Xg	176.0	213.3	223.8	252.5	312.1
12. TD/Xgs	138.8	172.8	173.0	191.9	241.2
13 TD/IR	366.0	420.6	585.4	718.9	984.8

[a]Includes gross official foreign exchange reserves.

Sources: IDB estimates for DCA, Xg, Xgs, and GDP. Table 1 for TD; IMF *International Financial Statistics,* for IR. The current United States dollar figures were deflated by the unit price index of manufacturing exports of the developed countries, published in United Nations, *Monthly Bulletin of Statistics.* The figures cover twenty-two countries.

The Real Cost of the Debt and International Inflation

The value of the debt is simply that of capital inflows less the amortizations paid in the course of the past years.[11] Inflation, therefore, influences the purchasing power or real value of capital for the borrowers. The international price level ruling at the time the funds are received determines the purchasing power received by the debtor and the price level prevailing when amortization is made determines the actual purchasing power transferred.[12]

In the 1970s the international economy faced an inflationary phenomenon of unprecedented persistence. During 1973–1980, inflation averaged about 12 percent compared with about 2 percent in the previous decade.[13] Moreover, it eroded the purchasing power of debt services. For example, 1 million dollars received in 1973, if repaid in 1980, was equivalent to the purchasing power of 462 thousand dollars at 1973 prices. This meant a real gain for the indebted countries; they received external credits with a specified purchasing power, repaying them with a reduced one. This fact often led to the false argument that it would be desirable to borrow as much as possible. The argument failed to foresee the transitory elements in this situation. For one thing, the "inflation effect" changed abruptly so that the international price index expressed in dollars fell in 1981 and again in 1982, which resulted from a lower rate of inflation in the industrialized countries and from the appreciation of the dollar. The unit value index of developed country manufacturing exports between 1980 and 1982, expressed in US dollars, fell 6 percent on average. The real value of the debt rose as a result of the general fall in the international prices of traded commodities.

The second transitory element, which tended to allay fears regarding the expansion of the debt and deficits on current account, related to real interest rates.[14] After 1973, with a soaring inflation, real interest rates declined. Nonetheless, in response to persistent inflation the nominal interest rate, and the bank rate much more vigorously, continued to rise. The trend was more pronounced from 1978 onwards. It is estimated that by 1980 about nine annual points of inflation had already been incorporated into the average rate paid by Latin American borrowers, and the process of accommodation continued throughout 1981 with the rise in bank rates and in their weight in the total debt. While inflation undoubtedly favored the indebted countries, the situation changed significantly in 1978, and already by 1981–1982 it became markedly unfavorable to the debtors.

Finally, the direct and indirect effects of capital flows on the domestic economy much be considered. The objectives sought with the loans and the means adopted to achieve them are as important as the real financial costs of the debt. The Latin American experience varied from country to country. Briefly, there are these factors in addition to any short-term financial cost of the debt that must be incorporated into the analysis to evaluate the effect of indebtedness during the 1970s. The first is the uses made of external funds; that is, to what extent did they supplement or substitute domestic savings and how did they affect the propensity to invest in productive activities? Second, what momentum did they achieve in the external sector? How much did they help to sustain a vigorous export base or open the way to a growing deficit on current account, possibly caused by excessive luxury imports and a deterioration in the real exchange rate? Third, to what extent did the national economy succeed in adjusting to the level and financing terms of external indebtedness and would it be affected by the outlook for the 1980s, an outlook likely to differ in key respects from the experience of the previous decade?

2. Emergence of the Crisis: A Recapitulation

In this section we recapitulate the most salient features of international credit markets and of the behavior of indebted countries. This will help to explain the nature and magnitude of the external debt problem.

The International and External Framework of the 1970s

The growing access of developing countries to international private capital markets took place in a special context in which external and internal factors came together to shape the trend observed in the 1970s. A linear extrapolation of that trend, even taking into account the presence of fluctuations, gives us an excessively optimistic view which is very different from the probable scenarios for the 1980s. The indiscriminate liberalization of capital movements and maximum possible indebtedness that had been proposed were based simply on the assumption that the trends present in the past decade would continue.

During the decade, the private international capital market expanded vigorously in an economic environment endowed with relatively abundant capital funds for the applicants that succeeded in acquiring the status of "clients." Indeed, during the course of the preceding years new debtors were being gradually incorporated into this market. By 1980 the borrowers of more than a hundred developing countries had access to bank loans. The balance of credits in sixty countries was larger than the respective overall national deposits in their respective financial institutions. The market was open to public and private users, and within relatively wide but not unlimited margins each country was able to choose the source of debt it preferred: the central bank, private enterprises, and private financial institutions acted as direct users or intermediaries. Finally, the growing access of developing countries to the international capital market meant a steady increase in their share in financial resources; although starting from a low level, the share increased at an average annual rate of 9 percent during the second half of the 1970s (see Williamson, 1983).

On average nominal interest rates were relatively low in relation to rates of national inflation, which increased from about 2 to 12 percent between the 1960s and the 1970s. However, as already stated, interest rates gradually adjusted to inflation. Furthermore, the operation of the international market has commonly followed a practice that has important implications for the evaluation of the future. Although bank loans are in principle for terms of various years, they are subject to floating interest rates plus some margins of financial intermediation. The most common practice is for the rates to be revised biannually in accordance with the levels they reach in the pre-established segment of the market. During the decade the market rates have fluctuated widely. Even the annual averages, which mask the abrupt changes characteristic of shorter periods, varied strongly; for example, between 1977 and 1979 they doubled. Although the spreads have also fluctuated widely, they have tended to be small and with a limited dispersion among countries and debtors. Therefore, the evolution of basic interest rates has been the main determinant of the cost of bank credit. The average maturity of external debts became shorter as the bank creditors increased their share in total. However, owing to the abundance of funds the latent problem of short maturities remained hidden. Indeed, the renewal of credits was a swift and apparently a sure process.

This short review shows that four important factors must be taken into account in an assessment of prospects for the coming years. First, the greater volume of funds obtained by developing countries was possible because the overall supply of funds expanded rapidly at the expense of a decrease in the share of other borrowers. Second, real interest rates were low and the dispersion of spreads was limited. Third, a major proportion of debt incurred by the regional countries is subject to floating interest rates: both the new flows and the balances of the earlier flows are continuously affected by the periodic changes in the market. Fourth, the periods of amortization were greatly reduced, placing countries whose debt renewal was automatic in a precarious position.

During the past decade, the countries in the region attained a substantial economic growth rate and a vigorous expansion of exports. During the period 1973–1980, GDP and exports grew in real terms by 5.3 and 8.5 percent respectively. To a large extent the availability of external financing contributed to this rapid growth. In addition, the region had an export potential based on its earlier import substitution industrialization.

The adequate economic performance of the countries in the region helped them to gain or widen their access to financial markets. From 1970 through 1979, the region as a whole had a balance of payments surplus. It received external credits in excess of its deficits on current account, enabling it to continuously increase its international reserves. These three characteristics — growth of GDP, of exports, and of reserves — permitted many countries of the region to acquire a status of creditworthiness.

The existence of an international private capital market has undoubtedly been a potentially positive factor for the region's economic development. As a result of the availability of funds, the countries were better placed to face fluctuations in the terms of trade and the subsequent oil shocks and to supplement domestic investment resources. Although on less favorable terms than accorded by official credits during the 1970s, private lending was relatively abundant and accessible with low cost. *Short maturities, the instability in interest rates, and certain problems of access of the poorer countries or countries in critical situations have been some negative external factors.* The principal problem at the national level in certain cases was the unproductive use of external savings. Sometimes, instead of helping to increase domestic investment it was used to discourage import substitution and to impede exports through the exchange lag caused by an excess of foreign exchange inflows.[15] However, it should be emphasized that the lag was mainly caused by the design of national economic policies. In my view, the determining factor was the absence of a debt strategy closely linked to public or private investment programs.

Problems in Perspective and Issues in Facing the Crisis

The evolution of international private capital markets in the 1970s was not linear. In particular, at the beginning of the 1980s symptoms of deterioration in various indicators could be observed. Real interest rates rose abruptly with considerable fluctuations, the average terms shortened, and the rate of expansion of credit to developing countries was less in 1980 than in the two previous years, forcing many of the developing countries to use their reserves. Whereas in 1978–1979 the countries of the region used 30 percent of capital flows to build up reserves, in 1980, 7 percent of the deficit on current account was covered by drawing from international reserves.

Some of the most important issues that emerged at the beginning of the 1980s were: (1) How capable was the capital market to achieve continued expansion? If expansion were to occur, what would be the amount obtainable by developing countries? (2) How will the terms of borrowing change and how easy will access be to the market? (3) How capable are the borrowing countries of adjusting to new situations? Within the limited bounds of this paper some observations on these points can be presented.

For many years, fears had been expressed about the capacity of the international private capital market to respond to the financing needs of the deficit countries. Although with important defects and gaps, the international private capital market had expanded dramatically for almost fifteen years and had played a key role in the process of adjustment to the oil shocks. A wide range of scenarios was envisaged by specialists with different perspectives, ranging from the complacent to the catastrophic. Without taking a catastrophic view, it could be argued that there are good reasons to expect a much bleaker view for the coming years during the 1980s than the 1970s in several crucial aspects. Even if the financial market were to continue to expand, it is foreseeable that the international financial market would do so at a much slower rate. A high growth rate, typical of a burgeoning market, naturally decreases as it matures. In addition, the economies of the industrialized countries hold out prospects of a very slow growth that might continue for some years, with the resulting sluggish growth in the domestic financial markets of these countries. A foreseeable climax then was that the international private capital market changes from a "borrower's" market to a "lender's" market. The course of these processes would normally be disquieting. The strains may be alleviated with the emergence of new banking institutions in the capital-surplus countries that operate directly with non-industrialized nations. A more vigorous role for public financing would also alleviate some of the principal causes of strain that affect international private capital markets. Aside from the alleviation of strains, the probable slower expansion of the financial market would also make it more difficult to increase the share of the developing countries; thus, increased supplies of credit to these countries would be restrained by the overall growth rate of the market. The significance of this point is clear if we remember that one-third of the increase in the total bank debt by the developing countries during the second half of the 1970s represented their increased share in the financing provided by the banks of industrialized countries.

The hypothetical change in international private capital markets would have a number of consequences for user countries. Overall, the real cost of financing could exceed the average of the previous decade, and there could be a greater dispersion of the spreads. These financial mechanisms that regulate demand are usually not the only ones in play. In situations of greater stringency, rationing by the lenders would tend to have greater weight through a reduction in the quotas or the limits they fix for each country or for each individual borrower.

In other words, the abrupt inelasticity of supply, which some developing countries faced in recent years, could become somewhat more frequent. This could represent a source of instability for the countries that have made heavy use of international private capital markets. Instability in access is not associated as much with the renewal of the debt as with the continuing increase in it, and it is on this point that attention should be focused.

The financial reforms effected in some industrialized nations and the profound disruptions in the international economy would help make interest rates unstable; the greater uncertainty prevailing would exert pressure towards reducing the average maturities of the debt, unless long-term public loans were revived. As noted above, the operating procedure of the bulk of the bank credits would mean that fluctuations in the interest rate would affect not only the new credits but also a predominant portion of the outstanding debt.

The intensity of the negative consequences of possible changes in the external financial framework for the economies of debtor countries would be closely associated with the use made of external financing, the development of adjustment capacity, and the mechanisms available for regulating the shifting of external instability to the national economy.

In this respect, the region offers a diversity of possibilities. A study of the country-by-country situation suggests that the less vulnerable countries are those that : (1) have made their external indebtedness conditional upon its use in public or private investment programs; (2) have endeavored to ensure that excessive flows of funds during the "borrower's" market period do not exert pressures to drive up the exchange rate and to favor heavy imports that compete with domestic production; and (3) have maintained flexible adjustment mechanisms, such as an active exchange rate policy. On the other hand, the indiscriminate openness to indebtedness, the practice of having growing deficits on current account covered by bank loans, and the loss of regulatory mechanisms lead to greater vulnerability to deterioration in the external market.

3. Actions in the Face of the Crisis

In 1981–1982 the earlier prognosis of serious financial problems for the developing countries was realized with virulent intensity. Many factors which appeared to have developed favorably in the preceding years changed their course. In this section I first examine the situation that affected the region toward the end of 1982. Next I note some of the existing estimates of the international macroeconomic variables that influence the servicing capacity of debtor nations. Finally, I consider some national, international, and regional measures for dealing with the problem of the debt so as to reconcile short-term with long-term aims and external equilibrium with national development.

The Financial and Trade Crisis in 1981–1982

The gravity of the debt problem in 1982 was due to the simultaneous deteriorations of several variables. The tables presented in section 1 provide the statistical support for the analysis which follows.

Regarding trade, exports fell 9 percent in constant values, thereby halting the prolonged trend of continuous growth. Most countries of the region suffered a fall in the volume of goods exported, an effect reinforced by a worsened terms of trade which declined as much as 13 percent in the last two years.

In the financial field, the rise in nominal interest rates contributed to increased deficits on current account. Here too, the deterioration of this variable was accompanied by the negative trend of other indicators which heightened the effect of the impact.

In fact, the level of international trade prices fell about 6 percent between 1980 and 1982, so that the real interest rate exceeded the nominal rate during this period.[16] The countries which were accustomed to abundant credits and low real interest rates began to suffer a sudden financial shock in addition to the trade shock. Under these circumstances, access to bank credit became more difficult. In other words, not only the financing costs rose but also the supply of fresh funds was reduced. This bears out the general hypothesis that the private financial market is procyclical in behavior: it tends to accentuate both the expansive and the recessive phases, without exercising any compensatory influences.[17]

With the emergence of signs of stringency in the financial market credits were no longer automatically renewable. This, of course, in view of the high amortization rates, made it very difficult for the countries which lost their "solvency" image to obtain new credits. In other words, the creditor was not only interested in the accumulated balance of the debt but also in the volume of gross flows being negotiated.

As I point out below, the countries have already made a great effort to cope with the resulting disequilibrium in the external sector. As a result of the effort to reduce imports by amounts greater than the fall in exports Latin America on the whole recorded a trade surplus equal to 2 percent of the region's GDP in 1982. The deficit on current account, however, still reached as high as 6.5 percent of the GDP. This is explained by a financial deficit (interests paid less those received) amounting to roughly 6 percent of the GDP; but there was also an additional element representing the negative balance in profits remitted as well as on the services account which has exceeded 2.5 percent over the last three years.

To sum up, despite the recessive situation existing in the region, in 1982 a large deficit on current account resulted mainly from interest payments. The distressing payment situation in Latin American countries was in turn aggravated by the high amortization rates they had to bear and by the difficulty in renewing existing credits. In 1982 the region had to use its reserves to pay for about 40 percent of its deficit on current account and, as already pointed out, the support obtained from financial capital inflows was negative: interest and amortization payments exceeded the gross revenue obtained from loans.

Some Projections

It is difficult to predict the future movements of such variables as inflation, the terms of trade, the volume of trade, rates of growth and interest rates. There is little doubt that their behavior will depend largely on the economic policies of industrialized countries. In recent years the econometric models have often erred in their forecasts, due both to changes in economic policies and to modifications in the parameters of behavior. Nonetheless, the models serve to indicate certain orders of magnitude, revealing interrelations among the key policy variables and the sensitivity to particular economic policies.

Based on different hypotheses, various regional or international institutions have made projections for the future. In general, the projections published were made with information applicable up to 1981. The projections for 1982 and 1983 showed large deviations from the actual values. Broadly speaking, inflation on the global scale has been less severe, exports and imports have been clearly lower, with the level of external debt increasing more rapidly. The most unfavorable aspect expected for the developing countries is the prolongation and intensification of the recession.

The basic result emerging from the projections made in respect to the debt problem is that the volume of exports, even under the *most optimistic* hypotheses, grows at an annual rate of nearly 6 percent, providing a contrast with the 9 percent attained by the region between 1973 and 1981. If the real interest rate were to settle at 6 percent, and its payment financed exactly by increased debt, the rate of debt to exports would remain at the high level reached at the beginning of the 1980s (2 in 1981 and 2.4 in 1982). And this implies that the financial capital would make no contribution to the availability of investment funds (gross loans are equal to the amortization plus interest payments). As a matter of fact, in 1982 there was a negative net transfer of funds; that is, net loans were less than interest payments. The negative balance was to be larger in 1983, and was projected to remain negative for the rest of the decade.

Furthermore, the borrowing activity could remain intense unless the debt maturities are rescheduled. The current debt renegotiations have brought some relief to developing countries but this is temporary. Indeed, for the bulk of the balance of the debt short maturities apply, so that as soon as the period covered by the renegotiated amortizations lapses, the problem of renewing the expiration dates will arise. In the probable context of sluggish world trade and capital markets, the profile of debt maturities may continue to remain a serious problem, as it has been in recent years. This would prolong the economic crisis in the developing countries.

From the above analysis, three factors emerge which have important implications. They are the financing terms (interest rates and amortization), access to new funds, and generation of foreign exchange through exports, which in turn depend on access to markets and the creation of domestic productive capacity. These being in short supply, alternative or complementary measures must be sought which call for the redynamization of import substitution on more efficient bases than in the past, and the intensification of regional and South-South cooperation.

Measures to Alleviate the Burden of the Debt

The gravity of the current debt problem calls for simultaneous actions on a number of fronts (see, for example, SELA, 1983). Measures to combat the debt problem can be identified at three different levels: national, international, and for the developing countries. These measures would aim at adjustment at the national level, the solution of conjunctural problems, the correction of structural deficiencies in the international financing system, and the exploitation of various mechanisms of cooperation among the countries of the region and the Third World.

The rapid growth of bank loans during the 1970s caused many

developing countries to incur excessive debts and to enlarge their external gap beyond what could be consistently sustained. To rehabilitate the respective national economies, domestic adjustment policies must be applied. Adjustment measures have been adopted in Latin America but their impact has been disproportionate. In fact, the region, in common with other developing countries, has found itself forced to resort to adjustment measures not only because of the excesses of the past years, but also because of the cyclical fall of its exports, the deterioration of its terms of trade, the rise in interest rates, and the abrupt cessation of the flow of funds.

In these circumstances the adjustment policies recommended by the International Monetary Fund seem inappropriate. There have been frequent — and justifiable — criticisms of the asymmetry and bias of the adjustments advocated by the Fund: asymmetry because it acts only on the deficit countries; bias because it emphasizes the short term and the seeking of equilibrium through restriction of demand instead of creation of supply. These characteristics can be defended in an overexpanded world economy with high employment. But in a world in recession with high unemployment, the imposition of restrictive policies on the countries with severe balance-of-payments difficulties can be self-defeating since it would only deepen the world crisis.

The countries which borrowed in excess would obviously see the need for the devaluation of their currencies. Indeed, many countries in the region have already substantially depreciated their currencies. Even with it, the adjustment to the external equilibrium seems to require, aside from modifications in domestic policies of the deficit countries, a strong recovery in the world market. Various projections show the important impact on the current account balance of the volume and price of exports as well as the impact of the rates of interest imposed on debtor countries. Hence, the level of economic activities and the evolution of the financial markets in the industrialized countries seem to play a key role in the level of external debt.

Another dimension of the current crisis relates to the striking structural imperfections in the international financing system. In recent years, problems have arisen in connection with the method of creating liquidity, the scarcity of funds with long maturities, the fall in the share of official loans, the insufficiency of compensatory financing, and the lack of mechanisms capable to refinance the external debt effectively. An integral solution obviously calls for actions to be taken in all four areas.

Despite all the declarations and agreements reached regarding the leading role of the SDRs in the creation of international liquidity, in the course of the last ten years their share actually fell by 50 percent (from

8 percent of the non-gold reserves to approximately 4 percent). Something similar has occurred with the quotas of the IMF as a percentage of annual world imports, which also decreased by a similar percentage (from 10 percent to less than 5 percent), even after taking into account the recent resolution (Eighth Revision) that increased the quotas by 47.5 percent.

Under the present conditions market forces will probably exert pressures for a further shortening of maturity and there will be increased difficulties of access to weak bond markets (on annual average during the second half of the 1970s less than ten developing countries succeeded in placing bonds in industrialized nations). A reversal of this trend requires a deliberate and decisive action aimed at new structures and market diversification. The strengthening of the multilateral, international, and regional institutions is essential in this process, along with the restoration of access to them for the countries which were in the process of "graduating."

As for the funds allocated to compensate transitory disequilibria of external origin, despite many improvements made by the Compensatory Financing Facility (CFF), its coverage is still limited; it is particularly noteworthy that the items that can be compensated by the CFF do not include outflows of interest payments, which in many countries have reached an annual value exceeding that of main export products.

The new situation in regard to the external debt also involves a serious lagging problem caused by short maturity periods. A complete solution, going beyond the economic crisis, calls for a rescheduling of the maturities of a substantial part of the debt. Otherwise, until there is once again a financial market offering ample credits, the term structure of the debt is likely to remain a permanent obstacle to formulating stable domestic policies directed towards development.

Thus, the existing projection leads to the conclusion that in the coming years the region's countries should not perhaps look to the world economy to provide the motor-power for their development. There will be an increasing need for developing countries to cooperate among themselves.

Given the prospects of the world economy, a favorable framework for the revival and extension of economic cooperation in the region exists. The gravity and persistence of depressed international demand should provide a propitious atmosphere for the strengthening of commercial and financial integration in the region. In other words, the existing crisis should provide a stimulus to apply the system of regional preference margins at the ALADI level as a mechanism to facilitate the expansion of intraregional export opportunities. At the outset this could basically cover the productive capacities currently underutilized, especially in the manufacturing sector. It could also provide a larger market for new products. There is no doubt that in order to resume the development process, the countries of the region will have to reconsider the adoption of import-substitution projects. Projects with economies of scale transcending the national market should be launched with a view to the regional market. To realize this option, more than mere reciprocal tariff concessions would be needed. Some type of mechanism must be set up for reaching agreements among the countries, enforced with criteria for selecting priority sectors and methods of guaranteeing a fair distribution among the participating countries. Otherwise, any agreement will remain only a paper one. Previous studies on industrialization have offered useful lessons on the appropriate criteria for identifying sectors of integrated development. Additionally, the experiences, negative and positive, gained in the Cartagena Agreement, LAFTA, and CACM might serve as guidelines in the search for mechanisms that would effectively ensure a fair distribution among countries.

In the financial and payment field there are numerous mechanisms in operation. The multilateral compensation agreements have functioned successfully. Even so, their efficacy can be increased, particularly through the intercommunication of three existing mechanisms (those of ALADI, Central America, and the Caribbean Community) and an expansion of reciprocal credit margins. The ALADI Reciprocal Payments and Credits Agreement channels a larger part of interchanges among member countries. The credit margins agreed between pairs of countries are often exhausted before the compensation periods of 120 days have elapsed, making it necessary to transfer funds in advance. The expansion of trade would probably create need for even larger credit margins. It is significant to note that according to the studies on the compensation agreements these mechanisms have been efficient in fostering reciprocal trade exchanges, have facilitated the establishment of direct financial relations among the countries of the region, and by avoiding a triangulation with the financial centers of the North have contributed to the saving of foreign exchange.

There are other financing mechanisms which have functioned more modestly or tentatively in pursuit of various aims. Without claiming to be exhaustive, one can mention the institutions which operate as reserve funds and/or a support for the balance of payments, the subregional development banks, the special intraregional credit lines of central and commercial banks and the Latin American bank acceptances. These offer ample possibilities for improvement as well as subregional linkages. Membership in both the ALADI Reciprocal Payments and Credits Agreement and the Santo Domingo Agreement have been open since 1981 to other countries of the region; thus there exists in principle the institutional framework for intercommunication through these channels.

In time of crisis, much of the future of the nation is at stake. In the present crisis, an effort to find the solution to the national problems solely in the recovery of the world economy may prove unwise.[18] The result would probably be a further weakening of the economies of the region, as they would be faced with a world market of limited dynamism, unreceptive to Latin American exports. In contrast, cooperation within Latin America in production and interchange of goods and services may help to overcome the crisis and to strengthen the bargaining position of the region in negotiations with the developed world.

NOTES

*This paper is an extended version of an earlier study entitled "External Debt and Balance of Payments of Latin America: Recent Trends and Outlook," published in IDB, *Economic and Social Progress in Latin America*, 1982. For a Spanish version, see *Integracion Latinoamericana* (Buenos Aires: INTAL, September 1983). This paper was finished in April 1983. Only some figures have been updated later.

1. The coverage of these groups of developing countries, which excludes net capital exporters, is that used by the United Nations, Department of International Economic and Social Affairs (DIESA) (1982). It includes 85 countries, of which 16 are net oil exporters.

2. These efforts are primarily reflected in its publication entitled *World Debt Tables*.

3. A detailed study covering the developing world as a whole and a sample of 14 countries on a disaggregated basis is to be found in DIESA (1982).

4. For various estimates whose debt and country coverage varies in Massad and Zahler (1977), International Monetary Fund (IMF) (1981a), and *World Debt Tables*. An examination of the problems of estimates appear in DIESA (1982). The IMF, in its International Financial Statistics, has started recently to publish disaggregated data or bank lending.

5. For further information on public debt coverage, see World Bank, DRS (1981).

6. In 1973 a predominant portion of the non-public bank debt represented international trade financing.

7. Latin America showed a percentage increase in bank debt similar to that of the developing countries as a whole during 1973–1981, but its non-public debt increased more rapidly, especially during the second half of the period.

8. Bank-of-International Settlements' (BIS) information on the bank debt is more complete and standardised. The analysis for the years prior to 1977 is limited to country groups.

9. Note that the interest rate of non-bank credits also rose, although more moderately.

10. The increase in debt service is reflected in part in the balance of payment figures. The interest payment component is consistent with our estimate; as for the amortization, this cannot be substantiated because in the balance of payment accounts only the net movement of short-term loans is recorded. See UN, DIESA (1982).

11. In addition, changes in the exchange rate of the currencies in which the debt is expressed should be taken into account. Since the figures usually published are reconverted into United States dollars, a devaluation of this currency relative to other currencies increases the value of the debt at the time the exchange adjustment is made.

12. An analysis of this aspect and references are to be found in Bacha and Díaz-Alejandro (1983) and Fishlow (1983).

13. The changes in the unit-value index of manufacturing exports of industrialized countries were used as an indicator of international inflation for the countries of the region.

14. The existence of floating interest rates to some extent causes the two elements to have much in common.

15. Not infrequently, the exchange lag was due to monetary problems caused by excessive inflows of external funds. Indeed, instead of restricting the inflow of capital, some countries appreciated the real exchange rate in order to increase the absorption of excess external funds.

16. Note that this is a different argument from that of the evolution of the terms of trade.

17. An exceptional situation, for reasons known, occurred in 1974–1975.

18. It is probable that in the absence of an agreement on the effective reactivation of integration, there will be a series of unilateral decisions that impede intraregional trade.

REFERENCES

Bacha, E., M. Bruno, R. Dornbusch and A. Fishlow. 1983. Panel on "Apertura financiera exterior y sus efectos sobre la economía nacional." In *Relaciones financieras externas. See* Ffrench-Davis 1983.

Bacha, E., and C. Díaz-Alejandro. 1983. "Mercados financieros: una visión desde la semiperiferia." In Ffrench-Davis 1983.

Bank for International Settlements. 1983. Annual Report, Basel.

_____. *International banking: liabilities, maturity distribution of assets and undispersed commitments,* bi-annual publication.

Devlin, R. 1978. "El financiamiento externo y los bancos internacionales: su papel en la capacidad para importar en América Latina en 1951–75." CEPAL, *Revista de la CEPAL,* no. 5, Santiago.

_____. 1983. "Renegociación de la deuda latinoamericana." *Revista de la CEPAL*, no. 20, Santiago.

Ffrench-Davis, R., and E. Tironi, eds. 1981. *Hacia un nuevo orden económico internacional: temas prioritarios para América Latina*. Fondo de Cultura Económica, Mexico, and *Latin America and the international economic order*, London: Macmillan, 1982.

Ffrench-Davis, R. ed. 1983. *Relaciones financieras externas y desarrollo nacional*, Fondo de Cultura Económica, Serie Lecturas no. 47, Mexico.

Fishlow, A., "La deuda externa latinoamericana: problema o solución." In Ffrench-Davis 1983.

Group of Thirty. 1981. *The outlook for international bank lending*. Edited by M. S. Mendelsohn for the study group on "Capital movements and the growth of international indebtedness" of the Group of Thirty, New York.

Helleiner, G., G. Pfeffermann and J. Williamson. 1981. Panel on "Mercados internacionales y dueda de los paises en desarrollo en los ochenta." In Ffrench-Davis 1983.

Hope, N. 1981. "Developments in and prospects for the external debt of the developing countries: 1970–80 and beyond." *World Bank Staff Working Paper*, no. 488.

IBRD. 1982. *World Development Report*, Washington, D.C.

IBRD/DRS. *World Debt Tables*. EC/167, Washington, D.C., annual publication.

INTAL. 1983. *El proceso de integración en América Latina en 1982*. Buenos Aires.

Inter-American Development Bank. 1982a. *Economic and social progress in Latin America*. Washington, D.C.

_____.1982b. *Deuda pública externa de los paises de América Latina*. Washington, D.C.

International Monetary Fund. 1981a. "External indebtedness of developing countries." Occasional Paper, no. 3, Washington, D.C.

_____.1981b. "International capital markets: recent developments and short-term prospects." Occasional Paper, no. 7.

_____.1983a. "Aspects of the international banking safety net." Occasional Paper, no. 17.

_____.1983b. "World economic outlook," Occasional Paper, no. 21.

Massad, C. and R. Zahler, 1977. "Dos Estudios sobre Endeudamiento Externo." CEPAL, *Cuadernos de la CEPAL*, no. 19, Santiago.

Morgan Guaranty. *World financial markets*. Several issues.

OECD. *Development Cooperation*. Annual report, Paris.

OECD. *Financial market trends*.

OECD. 1982. *External debt of developing countries*, 1982 Survey, Paris.

SELA. 1980. "Evolución de los mercados internacionales de capitales y la deuda externa de los paises latinoamericanos." Caracas.

SELA, 1983. "Análisis de la situación del financiamiento y la deuda externa de América Latina." Mimeo.

UN. 1982. "World economic recovery: the priority of international monetary and financial cooperation." DIESA, Committee for Development Planning, New York.

UNCTAD. 1980. "Financial resources for development: review of financial flows to and from developing countries." TB/B/C.3/166, mimeo.

UNCTAD. 1982. *Trade and development report.* Geneva.

United Nations, Department of International Economic and Social Affairs (DIESA). 1983. *World Economic Survey, 1983,* New York.

_____.1982. "International private lending and development strategies in developing countries." Study prepared by R. Ffrench-Davis, *Journal of Development Planning,* no. 14, 1984.

Williamson, J. 1981. *Exchange rate rules and crawling peg.* London: Macmillan.

Exchange Rate Regimes and the Real Rate of Interest

Larry A. Sjaastad

This paper examines the relationship between a specific type of external shock and the real interest rate in small open economies. In particular, it investigates the ability of alternative exchange rate regimes (including baskets) to insulate, partially or completely, a small open economy from the effects of *external* exchange rate instability. As such, it is a contribution to the macroeconomic stability-exchange rate regime literature that in its modern form was pioneered by Fischer (1977), with more recent contributions by Dornbusch (1981) and Weber (1981). Many of the contributions to this literature focus on two-country models and, as a consequence, can say nothing about the issue of *external* exchange rate instability (i.e., the consequences for a small open economy of fluctuations of the exchange rate between the monies of two or more large countries). Another strand of the literature has examined optimum currency baskets (for example, Bhandari, 1982, and Connolly, 1981, have considered a multi-country world). This paper is in accord with the latter approach.

The particular stimulus for this paper derives from the recent experience of a number of small open economies that permitted their domestic financial sectors to become highly integrated with world capital markets during the 1970s while maintaining some form of a (unilateral) fixed exchange rate with the U.S. dollar. These economies, of which Chile and Uruguay are outstanding examples, have gone from boom to bust in almost perfect step with the strength of the dollar. The central hypothesis is that, owing to certain asymmetries in the degree to which purchasing power holds in the short run, fluctuations in the value of the dollar vis-à-vis other major currencies leads to corresponding fluctuations in real rates of interest in the small, pegging economies that are greater in amplitude than those in the larger countries. That real interest rates in Chile and Uruguay have been subject to enormous variation is beyond doubt; Table 1 presents monthly data (at annual rates) on the

163

real rate of interest paid on short-term Chilean peso deposits for a five-and-one-half-year period ending with the abandonment of the fixed exchange rate regime in mid-1982. From January 1978 until the end of June 1979 the Chilean peso was being devalued at a preannounced rate (the now-famous "tablita"), but the exchange rate was fixed from July 1979 until 1982. While the month-to-month movements in the real rate of interest were often large, what is most striking about the data in Table 1 is the annual variation, and the clear correlation of the annual variation with the behavior of the dollar. During 1979 and 1980 when the dollar was particularly weak, Chilean real rates of interest were very low — just over 5 percent — but they began to increase almost immediately with the recovery of the dollar in late 1980.

The Uruguayan data, presented in slightly different form in Table 2, reveal a similar picture, although the timing is rather different than

TABLE 1

Chilean Short-Term Bank Deposit Rates on Annual Basis in Real Terms[a]

	1977	1978	1979	1980	1981	1982
January	24.60	63.08	24.60	22.42	15.66	34.49
February	13.80	30.45	16.35	22.56	44.25	52.51
March	0.96	0.96	0.84	4.41	32.30	26.08
April	11.75	9.12	1.45	0.48	20.13	30.30
May	17.46	33.08	9.12	0.24	18.02	40.92
June	17.74	17.04	9.77	4.78	44.75	—
July	7.06	8.21	−5.04	3.78	36.55	—
August	13.22	12.01	−18.40	2.18	20.41	—
September	12.42	17.32	−10.50	2.18	17.74	—
October	17.32	37.03	5.16	−7.86	30.91	—
November	57.17	41.42	12.68	−3.77	29.84	—
December	40.92	44.75	18.86	13.49	38.80	—
Annual Average:	19.54	26.20	5.41	5.41	29.11	36.86[b]

[a]Nominal rates are converted to real terms by adjusting for inflation as measured by the consumer price index. Source: *Boletin Mensual*, Banco Central de Chile (various issues).

[b]Average for first five months only.

TABLE 2

Inflation and Exchange Rates: Uruguay, 1977–1983

DATE	INFLATION[a]			EXCHANGE RATE[c]	DEVALUATION		REAL RATE OF INTEREST[e]
	WPI	12 Month	Quarter[b]		12 Month	Quarter[d]	
1977 Dec.	100.0	—	—	5.39	35.4	—	—
1978 March	107.7	—	34.5	—	—	—	—
June	120.2	—	55.2	—	—	—	—
Sept.	139.4	—	80.9	—	—	—	—
Dec.	159.6	59.6	71.8	6.98	29.5	—	-7.53
1979 March	183.6	70.5	75.1	—	—	—	—
June	222.0	84.7	113.8	—	—	—	—
Sept.	262.8	88.5	96.4	—	—	—	—
Dec.	282.6	77.1	33.7	8.43	20.8	—	-19.85
1980 March	299.0	62.9	25.3	—	—	—	—
June	312.0	40.5	18.6	—	—	—	—
Sept.	343.4	30.7	46.8	—	—	—	—
Dec.	363.3	28.6	25.3	9.95	18.0	—	16.68
1981 March	378.1	26.5	17.3	10.38	—	18.4	—
June	390.0	25.0	13.2	10.75	—	15.0	—
Sept.	429.9	25.2	47.6	11.13	—	14.9	—
Dec.	417.6	14.9	-11.0	11.53	15.9	15.2	27.13
1982 March	423.1	11.9	5.4	11.94	15.0	15.0	—
June	444.6	14.0	21.9	12.42	15.5	17.1	—
Sept.	469.7	9.3	24.6	13.12	17.9	24.5	—
Dec.	557.5	33.5	98.5	28.51	147.3	—	29.83
1983 March	676.9	60.0	117.3	32.14	169.2	—	—
June	742.6	67.0	44.6	—	—	—	—

[a]Rate of change of WPI.
[b]Rate for previous quarter expressed in annual terms.
[c]Selling rate in Mercado de Cambios.
[d]Rate for previous quarter expressed in annual terms.
[e]Short-term deposit (pasivo) rate deflated by rate of change in WPI.

in the Chilean case. A plausible explanation for that difference lies in the behavior of the Argentine exchange rates and the degree to which the Uruguayan economy is integrated with that of Argentina.

Argentina is a very important trading partner for Uruguay; indeed, the fact that the Argentine economy is huge relative to that of Uruguay and the ready (physical) access that Argentines have to the Uruguayan market indicates that most goods as well as services have to be treated as internationally tradeable (at least for analytical purposes). Thus, demand from Argentina can strongly influence prices in Uruguay.

In January 1979, Argentina embarked upon a "tablita" exchange rate policy, but the Argentine rate of inflation remained, for at least a semester, double her rate of devaluation.[1] Given that both Argentina and Uruguay established their "tablitas" with respect to the dollar, it was as if the Uruguayan tablita were defined relative to the Argentina peso. During 1979, the devaluation rates were such that the Uruguayan peso was being *re*valued at a rate of 2.5 percent per month with respect to the Argentine peso, which would imply — if purchasing power parity held exactly — that the rate of inflation in Uruguay would be about 2.5 points per months *less* than in Argentina.[2] And so it was; the Argentine inflation during 1979 (measured by wholesale prices) was at a monthly rate of 7.5 percent, whereas in Uruguay it was 4.8 percent. But the fact that the Argentine inflation did not "converge" to the rate of devaluation (plus external inflation) until late 1979–early 1980 meant that the Uruguayan inflation rate could not do so either due to the high degree of integration of the Uruguayan market with that of Argentina. Uruguay devalued during 1979 by only 21 percent, but wholesale prices rose by 77 percent (see Table 2).

The Argentine influence on the Uruguayan inflation rate — and hence real rates of interest — was reinforced by the weakness of the U.S. dollar during 1979 vis-à-vis other major currencies. The net result was that Uruguayan real rates of interest were very substantially negative during that year.

During 1980 the picture was modified considerably. The Argentine rate of inflation fell sharply towards the rate of devaluation of the Argentina peso, and the dollar stabilized; indeed, during the second half it appreciated against other key currencies. Apart from the U.S. inflation itself (which ran at 12.6 percent during 1980), the external inflationary elements disappeared from the Uruguayan scene. The result is evident. Uruguay devalued by 18 percent during 1980, and wholesale prices rose by 29 percent, the excess amounting almost exactly to the U.S. inflation rate. The undesirable consequence was a major increase in real rates of interest in Uruguay.

The year 1981 was exactly the opposite of 1979 for Uruguay, insofar as external effects are concerned. A series of major devaluations in Argentina caused the exchange rate to run far ahead of prices, imparting *de*flationary effects on Uruguay. While Argentina devalued by more than 250 percent, her wholesale prices rose by less than 160 percent. The major appreciation of the U.S. dollar (approximately 30 percent) in the last months of 1980 and the first quarter of 1981 actually drove down dollar prices of traded commodities, thus adding further to deflationary pressures in Uruguay. Despite a 16 percent devaluation of the Uruguayan peso and a 7.5 percent increase in wholesale prices in the U.S., Uruguayan wholesale prices rose by only 15 percent. The good news on the inflation front was exactly balanced by the bad news for the real rate of interest: the real rate on short-term deposits rose to nearly 30 percent, and that for loans was substantially higher.

The central idea of this paper, then, is that in small open economies that are well-integrated into international financial and real markets, domestic nominal interest rates are fairly well arbitraged with external rates; however, resulting real rates of interest are destabilized by external exchange rate shocks which are transmitted by the actual (or expected) behavior of the prices of traded goods.

1. Interest Arbitrage

There is strong factual evidence supporting the arbitrage assumption for both Chile and Uruguay. In the Chilean case, there has been a consistent spread between dollar (LIBOR) and internal peso rates that has caused Chilean real rates of interest to be generally higher than those in Uruguay. This spread between LIBOR and peso interest rates has fluctuated considerably, but exhibited no trend during the fixed exchange rate period (July 1979–June 1982). As is shown in Table 3, the spread between LIBOR and short-term peso deposit rates averaged (during the fixed-rate period) 1.5 percent per month, or about 20 per annum. The result is that Chilean interest rates were in nominal terms more than double dollar rates, despite the fixed exchange rate between the peso and the dollar.

There are several aspects of the interest rate spread that are puzzling. First, the spread does not appear to have declined significantly despite considerable relaxation of controls over international capital movements.[3] Second, the spread was unaffected by an enormous increase in both the stock and inflow of dollar loans; peso and dollar credit do not seem to have been close substitutes. Finally, the spread persisted despite an ex-

TABLE 3

Average "Spread" between Bank Deposit Rates in Chile and Libor[a]

	1975	1976	1977	1978	1979	1980	1981	1982
January	-7.69	-1.66	1.77	2.50	2.05	2.67	1.48	2.02
February	-6.97	-0.23	1.34	1.34	0.48	2.27	2.07	1.49
March	-10.62	2.77	9.96	0.11	0.48	1.87	1.98	1.17
April	-11.87	2.66	3.01	0.28	0.28	1.18	1.58	0.92
May	-0.51	2.42	0.94	1.54	1.06	1.39	1.28	1.28
June	1.69	2.91	-0.12	0.96	0.97	1.49	1.88	1.28
July	-1.79	13.37	0.37	0.97	-3.60	1.49	1.87	—
August	3.23	2.15	-0.78	1.66	1.98	1.49	1.28	—
September	2.01	1.19	-4.25	2.45	1.88	1.29	0.89	—
October	-2.31	1.57	1.32	2.95	1.58	1.09	1.28	—
November	-1.87	1.66	1.61	2.45	1.88	1.09	1.29	—
December	-1.40	2.90	-1.89	2.84	2.57	1.58	2.18	—
Annual Average	-3.17	2.64	1.02	1.67	0.97[b]	1.49	1.59	1.36[c]

[a]Calculated as $(1 + i_t)/[(1 + i*_t)(1 + e_t)] - 1$, where i_t is the domestic deposit rate (for pesos), $i*_t$ is LIBOR, and e_t is the rate of devaluation for month t. Source: *Boletin Mensual*, op. cit.

[b]Excluding July 1979, when there was an unscheduled devaluation of 6 percent, the annual average was 1.38 points per month.

[c]Refers to first six months only, excluding the period following the devaluation of June 1982 and the subsequent changes in the financial system.

traordinary expansion in the volume of peso deposits and loans (more than 200 percent in real terms during the 1979–1980 period).

There are at least two (complementary) explanations for that spread. First, due to phobias peculiar to Chile, the commercial banking system was never permitted to engage in arbitrage; regulations prohibited Chilean banks from holding net foreign currency positions. This regulation must have increased the cost of arbitrage by escalating the number of transactions. Second, regulations increased devaluation risk. During the period in question, banks were not allowed to borrow abroad for maturities under 2.5 years, and for maturities less than five years non-interest bearing reserves were mandatory. Although it is generally conceded that devaluation risk was virtually non-existent for the short term during 1979 and 1980, that risk was certainly not negligible for someone committing himself to a dollar liability with a minimum maturity of 2.5 years. Whatever may be the explanation for the spread, it was clearly responsible for the elevated real rates of interest on peso assets. The lack of a trend in that spread, nevertheless, supports the arbitrage hypotheses made above.

In Uruguay during the relevant period, there were virtually no regulations concerning bank transactions with the exterior, with the result that interest rates were highly arbitraged during most of the period. As Uruguay is essentially a dual currency economy (half of deposits and loans being denominated in dollars), this could hardly fail to be the case. Consider the possibility of an Uruguayan borrowing dollars locally on short term (one month), converting them to pesos, and then depositing the pesos for the short term. The cost of that operation is the dollar lending rate plus the rate of devaluation; the return, of course, is the peso deposit rate of interest. The individual undertaking this operation invests no capital of his own, although presumably he must have assets to place as security to obtain the initial dollar loan. The operation is not riskless as the rate of devaluation might turn out to be different from that announced in the tablita; indeed, the fact that the tablita was not violated until November 1983 does not mean that there was no risk. To the extent that such risk is perceived, some profit would have to be expected in order to induce individuals to accept the risk.

The results of this hypothetical exercise for 1978–1982 are presented in Table 4. The first column contains the actual dollar lending rates obtained from the data bank of the Banco Central.[4] The second column is the actual rate of devaluation (end of December to end of December) for the corresponding year, and the third column contains the peso deposit rate of interest. The final column indicates the percentage rate of profit on the operation, ignoring any difference between the buying and selling price of dollars.

Note that only during 1980 were any significant profits available (ex post) on this operation, and that by 1982 (first ten months only), the profit rate had fallen to a mere 3 percent. Of course, a 3 percent rate of profit on pure (e.g., costless) arbitrage is very high *if there is no risk.*[5] But obviously risk was present, particularly during 1980 when the widely anticipated devaluation in Argentina could well have raised fears of unscheduled devaluation in Uruguay as well. Even during the first ten months of 1982, the *ex post* profits from arbitrage were consistent with a high degree of confidence in the tablita.[6]

One might quarrel with the above, arguing that the relevant arbitrage from the point of view of banker, is between LIBOR and the local deposit rate, as LIBOR (plus some premium) represents the cost of the alternative source of funds for lending in Uruguay. A calculation based on that "spread" would of course result in a higher profit rate, but the increase would be more or less uniform for all years, so the *fluctuations* in the real rate of interest in Uruguay would be preserved.

TABLE 4

Interest Arbitrage: Uruguay, 1978-1982

Year	Dollar Lending Rate (%)[a]	Devaluation Rate (%)	Peso Deposit Rate (%)	Profit Made (%)[a]
1978	14.49	29.5	47.58	-0.5
1979	15.39	20.8	41.95	1.8
1980	17.43	18.0	50.05	8.3
1981	19.51	15.9	46.07	5.5
1982[b]	18.97	19.9	47.64	3.5
1982[c]	19.10	25.9	54.73	3.2

[a]See text for definition.

[b]Annual rate for January–October only.

[c]Annual rates for July–October only.

2. Price Behavior

The enormous fluctuations in the real rates of interest in Chile and Uruguay obviously stem more from changes in the devaluation rate/inflation relationship than from changes in (external) dollar rates of interest. From Tables 1 and 2 above, it can be seen that real rates in Uruguay fluctuated nearly 50 points (from minus 20 percent in 1979 to plus 30 percent in 1982), and that in Chile the fluctuations reached 30 points.[7] No such variation occurred in dollar rates of interest.

The behavior of Uruguayan inflation was reported in Table 2. Note that during 1978 and 1979 the rate of inflation exceeded the rate of devaluation by a margin far in excess of the U.S. rate of inflation, whereas in 1981 and 1982, the rate of inflation fell below the devaluation rate (even ignoring the last quarter of 1982 when the Uruguayan peso was floated and depreciated heavily). These two pairs of years are precisely those for which Uruguayan real interest rates were far out of line with real interest rates in the United States.

A similar story for Chile emerges from Table 5. During 1978 and 1979, inflation was much above the devaluation rate; but by late 1980, the inflation rate had dropped below the U.S. rate of inflation (in the face of a fixed exchange rate) and then became negative. At the same point in time the real rate of interest on peso deposits shot up by about 30 points.

The speed with which the Chilean inflation disappeared in late 1980 and early 1981 is truly impressive. During the first three quarters of 1980, wholesale prices were rising at a stable annual rate of about 35 percent; in the fourth quarter that rate suddenly fell to 12 percent and during the course of 1981 that price index actually fell by 4 percent. The collapse of the Chilean inflation coincided precisely with the major appreciation of the U.S. dollar against other major currencies during late 1980. In table 6 we present a three-month-centered moving average of the rate of change of Chilean wholesale prices at both monthly and annual rates. That tabulation indicates that the collapse began in November 1980 and that by February 1981 deflation had become the norm.

This dramatic change in the Chilean rate of inflation was not in response to any policy action in Chile; there was no change in Central Bank behavior or in exchange rates during the period in question. Rather, it came from abroad. In Table 7 we present data on external (dollar) prices of Chilean tradeables and dollar interest rates.

Unfortunately, data on the price behavior of Chilean tradeables is not available monthly, but it is clear from Table 7 that there was a dramatic change in the "external" inflation as measured by the behavior

TABLE 5

Price Level and Exchange Rate
Chile, 1975-1981

		Wholesale Price Index[a]			Exchange Rate[b]		
		Level	Rate of Inflation (%)		Pesos/$	Rate of Change (%)	
			Quarterly[c]	Annual[d]		Quarterly[c]	Annual[d]
1977	March	1,013	26	128	18.38	8[e]	71
	June	1,145	13	83	20.23	10	49
	Sept.	1,246	5	65	23.86	18	66
	Dec.	1,331	7	65	27.59	16	62
1978	March	1,473	11	45	29.86	8	63
	June	1,617	10	41	31.83	7	57
	Sept.	1,770	9	42	33.05	4	38
	Dec.	1,846	4	39	33.84	2	23
1979	March	2,026	10	38	35.24	4	18
	June	2,307	14	43	36.76	4	16
	Sept.	2,850	24	61	39.00	6[f]	18
	Dec.	2,922	3	58	39.00	—	15
1980	March	3,142	8	55	39.00	—	11
	June	3,356	7	45	39.00	—	6
	Sept.	3,622	8	27	39.00	—	—
	Dec.	3,744	3	28	39.00	—	—
1981	March	3,736	0	19	39.00	—	—
	June	3,700	-1	10	39.00	—	—
	Sept.	3,700	0	2	39.00	—	—
	Dec.	3,597	-3	-4	39.00	—	—

[a]Source: *Boletin Mensual*, op. cit.

[b]Source: *Indicadores Economicos 1960–80*, Banco Central de Chile, April, 1981. Monthly averages of bank rate.

[c]Change from end of previous quarter.

[d]Change from end of quarter 12 months earlier.

[e]Revaluation occurred during quarter ending in this month.

[f]The actual devalution during the third quarter of 1979 was zero, as the exchange rate was fixed at 39 at the end of June, 1979.

of the prices of Chilean tradeables. The inflation rate of dollar prices fell 22 points from 1980 to 1981, even though the U.S. rate of inflation as measured by the consumer price index actually increased. This evidence strongly suggests that it was the behavior of *dollar* prices of tradeables that introduced the gyrations in the Chilean inflation rate and therefore in real interest rates. Although the evidence is not readily at hand it appears that the same was true for Uruguay. It is equally clear that the U.S. rate of inflation is not, in the short run, a reliable guide to the *external* rate of inflation; nor are the more vulgar measures of the so-called real exchange very relevant.[8] The issue, then, is what determines the departures of a country's *external* inflation from the rate in the country to which it links its currency.

3. Exchange Rate Fluctuations and Relative Prices

An appreciation of a major currency, say the U.S. dollar, with respect to other major currencies (represented by the German DM) clearly

TABLE 6

Three-Month Moving Average of Chilean Inflation Measured by Wholesale Prices

PERIOD		MONTHLY RATE (%)	ANNUAL RATE (%)
1980	July	2.47	34.0
	August	2.60	36.1
	September	2.06	27.7
	October	2.07	27.9
	November	1.13	14.4
	December	0.90	11.4
1981	January	0.03	0.4
	February	−0.07	−0.8
	March	−0.33	−3.9
	April	0.03	0.4
	May	−0.33	−3.9
	June	−0.30	−3.5

Source: *Boletin Mensual,* op. cit.

will cause the dollar prices of (homogeneous) traded goods to be depressed (assuming underlying demand and supply factors for that commodity remain unchanged), and the DM price to rise. If the law of one price holds exactly, the decline in the dollar prices plus the increase in the DM price, both in percentage terms, must sum to the percentage appreciation of the dollar. For certain highly homogeous goods (metals, certain agricultural products, etc.), there is ample casual evidence that the law of one price holds quite well, and that the phenomenon described above does indeed occur.

For a small country pegging to the dollar and engaging heavily in the international commodity trade, an appreciation (depreciation) of the dollar vis-à-vis other major currencies will immediately experience deflationary (inflationary) pressures transmitted by changes in the dollar prices of its tradeables. This is in fact what appears to have happened in the cases of Chile and Uruguay (and perhaps other countries as well) during the 1978–1982 period of extreme dollar instability. Certainly these forces were at work on U.S. prices (and in the opposite direction in Europe and Japan) as well, but presumably with less speed and intensity. This

TABLE 7

External Prices of Chilean Tradeables and Interest Rates[a]

Period	Annual Rate of Change of Prices[b]	U.S. $ Interest Rate[c]	U.S. $ Real Interest Rate[d]
1977	5.1	7.0	1.8
1978	6.1	6.4	0.3
1979	26.8	11.2	-12.3
1980	16.6	13.9	-2.3
1981	-5.5	15.7	22.4
1982	-8.6	13.3	24.0

[a]Taken from Jose Gil-Diaz, "Del Ajuste a la Deflacion: La Politica Economica Entre 1977 y 1981 (Chile)," mimeo, November 1983.

[b]Rate of change of a simple average of unit values of Chilean imports and exports as calculated by the United Nations Economic Commission for Latin America.

[c]Annual averages of six month LIBOR rates.

[d]Defined against the prices of Chilean tradeables.

asymmetry comes about because the commodity trade—for which the law of one price holds well even in the short run—is much less important for the large developed economies.[9] If changes in the prices of tradeables impact more rapidly on small economies than on large ones, as appears to be the case, then an appreciation of the dollar will impose stronger deflationary pressures on countries such as Chile and Uruguay than on the U.S., and consequently real interest rates in the former countries will rise relative to those in the U.S.

A Formal Model

To develop the behavior of the price of traded goods for a small country, consider the case of a homogeneous commodity, the price of which obeys the "law of one price." We will assume a four-country world, three of the countries having large economies and major currencies, and the fourth being a "small" country in the sense that it is a price taker in both the goods and asset markets. All variables expressed in capital letters will be natural logarithms: $X = \ln x$.

Without loss of generality, we assume that country A is an exporter of the good in question, and countries B and C are importers. Country D, the "small" country, can be either an importer or exporter but is assumed to be sufficiently small that it does not influence the world price.[10] This permits us the following approximation:

$$q_A^s (P_A - \overline{P}_A) \cong q_B^d (P_B - \overline{P}_B) + q_C^d (P_C - \overline{P}_C), \tag{1}$$

as the equilibrium condition for the world market for a particular traded good. q_A^s is the excess supply of the good in country A, and the q^d's are the excess demands. P_j is the logarithm of the nominal price (in domestic currency) in country j, and $\overline{P}_j$ is the logarithm of the price level in that country. For simplicity, all other variables affecting excess demands and supplies are suppressed; these would, of course, have to be taken into account in empirical implementation of the model.

Prices are linked through exchange rates:

$$P_A = P_B + E_B = P_C + E_C, \tag{2}$$

where E_j is the logarithm of price of the jth currency in terms of A's currency. As usual, import duties, transport costs, etc., are ignored as we will focus on *movements in* rather than the *level* of the price of the good in question.

Substituting (2) into (1) and using the time derivative operator for variable x denoted by dx, we have:

$$dP_A = \rho_B(dE_B) + \rho_C(dE_C) + \rho_A\pi_A + \rho_B\pi_B + \rho_C\pi_C, \qquad (3)$$

where:

$$\rho_A = q_{\bar{A}}^{s'}/(q_{\bar{A}}^{s'} - q_B^{d'} - q_C^{d'}) > 0,$$

$$\rho_B = q_B^{d'}/ (\ '' \ '' \ '' \ ) > 0,$$

$$\rho_C = 1 - \rho_A - \rho_B > 0,$$

$$\pi_j = d\bar{P}_j \text{ (rate of inflation in country } j),$$

and ($'$) indicates the first derivative of the excess supply and demand functions. Clearly the ρ_j sum to unity, and their magnitudes reflect the degree of market power a country possesses in the world market for the good in question. In this context, the "small" country has a ρ of zero — as it is a price taker, changes in its exchange rate will not affect the major currency prices of the good in question. At the other extreme, a "price making" country will have a ρ of unity — it alone determines the world price of the good.

Equation (3) indicates that the rate of change of the dollar price of a homogeneous traded good is a weighted average of the rates of inflation in the large countries that trade the good internationally *plus* the sum of two positive fractions of the change in the major currency exchanges rates.[11]

If purchasing power parity held across all countries at all points in time:

$$\pi_A = \pi_B + dE_B = \pi_C + dE_C,$$

then obviously $dP_A = \pi_A$. The point, however, is that purchasing power parity does *not* hold between the major currency countries in the short run, so that exchange rate changes alone are sufficient to introduce large variations in the relative prices of traded goods. In terms of equation (3), it is clear that a depreciation of the dollar (currency A) against, say, the DM (currency B), will generate a stepwise change in the dollar price of the good in question quite independently of underlying inflation rates. To the extent that the good is somewhat heterogeneous (e.g., motor cars), the law of one price would hold only over time, and the change would be gradual rather than stepwise. In either case, the change in the dollar price of the good would be a positive fraction of the amount of dollar depreciation.

Taking into account exchange rate changes in the small country, we have:

$$dP_D = dP_A - dE_D \qquad (4)$$

as the rate of change of the internal price in country D of the good in question.

Let us now generalize the above results to all goods traded internationally by country D. Define:

$$dP_t = \sum_i \omega_i dP_{Di}, \tag{5}$$

where P_t is an appropriate index of the logarithms of internal prices of traded goods in country D, and P_{Di} is the logarithm of the internal price of the ith traded good, the movements of which follow equation (4) above. The ω_i's are the relevant weights, and sum to unity. Inserting "i" subscripts into equation (3) and combining it with equations (4) and (5), we obtain:

$$dP_t = \sum_i (\omega_i \rho_{Bi}) dE_B + \sum_i (\omega_i \rho_{Ci}) dE_C + \sum_i (\omega_i \rho_{Ai}) \pi_A + \sum_i (\omega_i \rho_{Bi}) \pi_B$$

$$+ \sum_i (\omega_i \rho_{Ci}) \pi_C - dE_D, \tag{6}$$

where dE_D is the rate of the *revaluation* of D's currency against the dollar. Note that the magnitude of the ρ_{ji}'s depends upon the structure of the world market for good i, and that of the ω_i's depends upon the nature of the internal market in country D.[12] Given that $\sum_j \rho_{ji} = \sum_i \omega_i = 1$, we can rewrite (6) as:

$$dP_t = K_B(dE_B) + K_C(dE_C) + \pi_w - dE_D \tag{7}$$

where: $K_j = \sum_i (\omega_i \rho_{ji}) > 0$,

$$\sum_j K_j = 1, \text{ and}$$

$$\pi_w = K_A \pi_A + K_B \pi_B + K_C \pi_C.$$

The term π_w will be referred to as the rate of "world" inflation (from the point of view of country D), and is a weighted average of individual country rates.

Equation (7) is the centerpiece of the analysis. Note that, in the face of external exchange rate instability, the internal prices of trade goods can move quite differently from what would be indicated by that country's exchange rate behavior and the inflation rate in the country to which it pegs its currency. Indeed, the naive versions of the so-called real exchange rate (referred to earlier) implicitly assume $K_A = 1$ and $K_B = K_C = 0$ (taking A as the country to which D pegs its currency). From the definitions of the K_j, this would be true only if $\rho_{Ai} = 1$ for all i, and $\rho_{Bi} = \rho_{Ci} = 0$, again for those goods traded internationally by country D. In terms of the interpretation of the ρ_{ji} given earlier, this implies that country A is an absolute price maker (for all relevant goods) and that countries B and C are price takers. If that were true of course, a one-country model of the world would be quite sufficient.

In principle, equation (3) could be estimated from time series data for all countries and all relevant traded goods, and the summary equation (7) could also be estimated for all relevant countries; the only difficulty that one might anticipate is that the underlying parameters might themselves depend upon the exchange rate system prevailing among the major currencies, and worse, on the degree of instability in major currency exchange rates. That is, market structures, particularly those of traded commodities, may well depend upon the world financial structure in which they operate. This point will not be explored in this paper.

Note also that equations (3) and (7) do not take into account many variables that might affect prices of traded goods. Agricultural products, for example, are subject to supply shocks arising from climatic conditions; these are not captured in the equations but clearly can be introduced. In what follows, we will ignore those difficulties and focus only on the price effects arising from exchange rate instability.

4. Currency Baskets vs. Exchange Rate Rules

In Equation (7), the variable for controlling the domestic rate of inflation (of traded goods, at least) is the exchange rate. That is, a country can adopt an exchange rate rule based on equation (7) that will permit it to achieve whatever is the desired behavior of internal prices of traded goods. Suppose for example that country D wished to minimize the variance of its internal inflation rate relative to that of the rest of the world (e.g., with respect to π_w). To do so, it would establish an exchange rate rule defined as follows:

$$dE_D = \sum_j (dE_j) K_j, \tag{8}$$

which, in terms of the level of the exchange rate, implies

$$e_D = K_0 (\prod_j e_j^K), \tag{9}$$

where $E_j = \ln e_j$, and K_0 is an arbitrary constant.

Equation (9), written in terms of spot exchange rates, also holds implicitly for forward rates, thereby generating an implicit forward exchange market for the small country and permitting normal hedging operations on the part of traders in that country. In addition, other exchange rate rules are readily designed; the "tablita," for example, would result from merely adding a constant term to equation (8). It is clearly possible then, to devise a simple and workable exchange rate policy that will insulate a small country's rate of inflation from the effects of instability in external exchange rates.

It is intuitively obvious that exchange rate rules and currency baskets are analytically quite similar; indeed we will now show that they can be virtually identical in operation. Let us define the exchange rate in the form of a basket as follows:

$$e_D = x_A + e_B x_B + e_C x_C, \tag{10}$$

where e_D is the nominal exchange rate in terms of, say dollars per peso, x_A is the number of dollars in the basket, x_B the number of DM, and x_C the number of yen, and e_B and e_C the dollar prices of DM and yen respectively. The choice of the dollar as the "reference" currency is purely arbitrary, as is the restriction of the number of currencies in the basket to three.

Suppose that we wanted e_D to adjust so that the internal prices of tradeables follow the world rate of inflation π_w; that is, we simply equate equations (8) and (10). In general this will not be possible with constant weights (the x_j's); when external exchange rates fluctuate, the weights must also change:

$$\partial e_D/\partial e_B = \partial x_A/\partial x_B + x_B + e_B(\partial x_B/\partial e_B) + e_C(\partial x_C/\partial e_B) = K_B e_D/e_B, \tag{11}$$

the extreme righthand side being the partial derivative of equation (9) with respect to e_B. A similar equation can be written for $\partial e_D/\partial e_C$. The two equations will have a total of six unknowns ($\partial x_j/\partial e_k$) for $j = A, B, C$ and $k = B,C$; the interpretation is that there exists an infinite number of ways in which the weights of the basket can be adjusted to accommodate changes in external exchange rates. The implication is that we can arbitrarily fix any four of the six variables and solve for the remaining two; the simplest solution is to set $(\partial x_j/\partial e_k) = 0$ for $j = B,C$ and $k = B,C$. That is, we hold constant the number of DM and yen in the basket and alter the number of dollars in response to a change in external rates.

Solving equation (11) and its counterpart under this arrangement, we obtain the following variations for the dollar weight:

$$\partial x_A/\partial e_B = (e_D/e_B)(K_B - e_B x_B/e_D) = (e_D/e_B)(K_B - f_B),$$
$$\partial x_A/\partial e_C = (e_D/e_C)(K_C - e_C x_C/e_D) = (e_D/e_C)(K_C - f_C), \tag{12}$$

where $f_B = e_B x_B/e_D$ is the fraction of the basket made up by B's currency, and similarly for f_C. If only the dollar weight is adjusted in accordance with equation (12), the exchange rate will behave exactly according to the rule described by equation (9). Any other rule could also be accommodated by the basket.

Of course a basket with fluctuating weights is self-defeating. The whole point of the basket is to reduce the effects of external exchange rate fluctuations in as *simple* a manner as possible; if the weights are continuously changing, that simplicity is lost. But the basket can be made to behave approximately the same as the exchange rate rule by choosing the weights such that $f_B \cong K_B$, and $f_C \cong K_C$ (assuming that the K's have been estimated). This will indeed be possible if external exchange rates behave as stationary variables; we firmly fix x_A arbitrarily and then choose x_B and x_C as follows:

$$x_B = K_B \overline{e}_D / \overline{e}_B,$$
$$x_C = K_C \overline{e}_D / \overline{e}_C$$

where $\overline{e}_j$ *is the mean dollar price of the* jth currency. As $\overline{e}_D$ incorporates both x_B and x_C, it can be solved out to obtain the following weights:

$$x_B = x_A (K_B / \overline{e}_B K_A),$$
$$x_C = x_A (K_C / \overline{e}_C K_A). \tag{13}$$

The weights (relative to x_A which is arbitrarily chosen) are proportional to the K_j — the jth currency's influence on D's prices — and inversely proportional to both the value of the currency being included and to country A's weight in the price equation. A basket so composed will yield results highly similar to the exchange rate rule, even with constant weights.

Note that the weights defined by equation (13) have little to do with country D's trading pattern; indeed, D might include a substantial amount of a given currency in its basket even if it had no trade with the corresponding country, and the converse is true as well. What matters is the ability of the country in question to influence the international prices of traded goods, not the volume of trade that one might have with it.

5. The Real Rate of Interest

Let us now suppose that a small country pegging to currency A chooses to adopt an exchange rate rule (such as defined by equation [8]), or an equivalent basket (as defined by [13]); will that policy result in a stable real rate of interest? To answer this, we will assume that the rule (or basket) is sufficiently well defined to permit strong interest rate parity between A's and D's currencies:

$$i_D = i_A - dE_D, \tag{14}$$

where i_j is the nominal rate of interest in the jth currency. No account of any interest rate spread is explicitly included, but it could be without changing the nature of the results. As noted earlier, there is considerable evidence that equation (14) holds roughly for countries with a well-defined exchange rate rule, as had Chile and Uruguay during the 1978–1981 period, once the spread is taken into account. Assuming that the domestic rate of inflation is governed by dP_t, we define the real rate of interest in country D as:

$$r_D \equiv i_D - dP_t. \tag{15}$$

Substituting equation (7) and (14) into (15), we obtain:

$$r_D = i_A - \pi_w - K_B(dE_B) - K_C(dE_C),$$

and noting that

$$r_A = i_A - \pi_A,$$

we obtain:

$$r_D = r_A + K_B(\pi_A - \pi_B - dE_B) + K_C(\pi_A - \pi_C - dE_C). \tag{16}$$

Equation (16) indicates that the real rate of interest in country D will equal that in A plus some fraction of departures from purchasing power parity in the rest of the world.

Alternatively, we define the "world" real rate of interest as:

$$r_w \equiv K_A r_A + K_B r_B + K_C r_C$$

and hence r_A as:

$$r_A = r_w + K_B(r_A - r_B) + K_C(r_A - r_C). \tag{17}$$

Upon substituting equation (17) into (16), we obtain:

$$r_D = r_w + K_B(i_A - i_B - dE_B) + K_C(i_A - i_C - dE_C); \tag{18}$$

that is, the real rate of interest in country D can also be expressed as that in the rest of the world (r_w) plus some fraction of departures from interest rate parity in the rest of the world.

The upshot is that if *strong* purchasing parity holds continuously among the major currency blocks, then $r_D = r_A$. If *strong* interest rate parity holds among the major currencies (i.e., $i_j = i_k + dE_K$), then $r_D = r_w$; if both hold, we have $r_D = r_A = r_w$ (there is only "one" market). Clearly either would improve the stability of the real rate of interest (r_D), as both r_A and r_w have been substantially less volatile than Chilean and Uruguayan real interest rates over the past decade.[13]

There are two problems with the above. First, the derivation of the above results do not depend upon specification of any particular exchange rate rule (or basket); from the definition of the real rate of interest in country D:

$$r_D = i_D - dP_t$$
$$= (i_A - dE_D) - dP_t \qquad (19)$$
$$r_D = i_A - (dP_t + dE_D),$$

we see that the results depend only upon the existence of a rule that is sufficiently well-specified, understood, and believed to permit arbitrage. Moreover, we can see from equation (7) that the term in brackets of (19) does not depend upon any specification of dE_D, only that whatever behavior we have in dE_D be fully reflected (with opposite sign) in dP_t. Thus the results for both cases described above will occur with *any* exchange rate rule, including a fixed rate, a "tablita," or even a rule based on the forward premia between the major currencies.

The second problem arises because it is now well-known that purchasing power parity does not hold among major currency areas (with floating rates) in the short run, and also that strong interest rate parity fails to hold across the major currencies. Actual interest rate differentials explain but a tiny fraction of subsequent changes in spot rates among the major currencies even though the forward premia are virtually identical with the interest rate differentials. Without either strong interest rate parity or continuous purchasing power parity among the major currencies, one well-defined exchange rate rule (or basket) would appear to be as good as any other.

The Case of Floating Rate

It has frequently been suggested, particularly in Chile, that the exchange rate be floated; that is, that there be *no* exchange rate rule of basket. This case is difficult to analyze, as it requires specification of the behavior of a floating rate. We do not attempt that, but rather we will build on empirically established *weak* interest rate parity:

$$i_k = i_j + F_j, \qquad (20)$$

where F_j is the forward premium on country j's currency in terms of k's currency.[14] Further, we make the heroic assumption that weak interest rate parity would also hold between currency D and the major currencies if D were to float its currency.[15] In that case, equation (14) is replaced by:

$$i_D^* = i_A - F_D \qquad (14')$$

and equation (15) can be written as:

$$r_D^* = i_A - (F_D + dP_t)$$
$$= r_A + (\pi_A - dP_t - F_D), \tag{15'}$$

where (*) indicates interest rates in country D under the floating rate regime. Thus we see that country D's real rate of interest is that of country A plus the error in country D's forward rate as a predictor of the inflation rate differential between A and D.

How does equation (15') compare with the results in (16)? That comparison is difficult because to arrive at (16) we assumed that purchasing power parity, in the form of equation (7), held between currencies A and D. Such an assumption is reasonable if D is following an exchange rate rule, but less so if D's currency is floating. If economic agents in D treated F_D as a good indicator of the actual (future) change in the spot rate, then equations (15') and (16) would be one and the same.

Alternatively, we might assume that equation (7) would continue to hold—that actual changes in P_t would be governed by the behavior of E_D. Introducing equation (7) into (15'), we obtain:

$$r_D^* = r_A + (\pi_A - \pi_w - K_B dE_B - K_C dE_C + dE_D - F_D),$$

which can be simplified to:

$$r_D^* = [r_A + K_B(\pi_A - \pi_B - dE_B) + K_C(\pi_A - \pi_C - dE_C)] + (dE_D - F_D)$$
$$= r_D - (F_D - dE_D).$$

Under our assumptions, the real rate of interest in D, given a floating rate, is the same as that with a fixed rule but less the forecast error made by the futures market for currency D. If that market is efficient, the expected values of the real rate will be the same under the two different arrangements.

In terms of variance—and it is the variance which concerns us here—the variance of r_D^* will exceed that of r_D if there is a negative covariance between r_D and the forecast error. To get some notion about this, note that by assuming weak interest rate parity, equation (18) can be rewritten as:

$$r_D = r_w + K_B(F_B - dE_B) + K_C(F_C - dE_C);$$

that is, r_D is the world rate plus some fraction of forecast errors for the spot rates between the major currencies. Defining these errors as

$$z_j \equiv (F_j - dE_j), \text{ we have:}$$

$$r_D = r_w + K_B Z_B + K_C Z_C, \tag{18'}$$

and:

$$r_D^* = r_w + K_B Z_B + K_C Z_C - Z_D. \tag{21}$$

Defining deviations of r_D and r_D^* from r_w as x and y respectively, and assuming for expositional purposes that the variance of all (percentage) forecast errors are the same and equal to σ^2, we have:

$$\sigma_x^2 = (K_B^2 + K_C^2)\sigma^2 + 2K_B K_C [Cov(Z_B, Z_C)],$$

and:

$$\sigma_y^2 = (1 + K_B^2 + K_C^2)\sigma^2 + 2[K_B^2 K_C Cov(Z_B, Z_C) - K_B \, Cov(Z_B, Z_D) - K_C \, Cov(Z_C, Z_D)].$$

Hence:

$$\sigma_y^2 - \sigma_x^2 = \sigma^2 - 2[K_B Cov(Z_B, Z_D) + K_C \, Cov(Z_C, Z_D)]. \tag{22}$$

We can say nothing about the sign of equation (22) on *a priori* grounds; however, if shocks to the international market are distributed symmetrically, it is reasonable to assume that $Cov(Z_B, Z_D) = Cov(Z_C, Z_D) = (\frac{1}{2})\sigma^2$. Recalling the definition of E_j and F_j, the forecast error between D and B is given by $(F_B - F_D) - (dE_B - dE_D)$, whose variance is assumed to be σ^2; that is, the same as the variance of the forecast error between A and B, on the one hand, and A and C, on the other. Thus:

$$\sigma^2 = \sigma^2 + \sigma^2 - 2[Cov(Z_B, Z_D)],$$

so:

$$Cov(Z_B, Z_D) = (\frac{1}{2}) \, \sigma^2,$$

and similarly for $Cov(Z_C, Z_D)$. Consequently, equation (22) reduces to:

$$\sigma_y^2 - \sigma_x^2 = \sigma^2[1 - K_B - K_C]$$
$$= K_A \sigma^2 > 0.$$

Thus there is a weak presumption that if country D were to pursue a floating rate rather than an exchange rate rule (or basket), the variance of her real rate of interest would be increased.

6. Concluding Remarks

During 1973–1983, the business cycles in a number of Latin American countries have been far more severe than in the United States or Europe. From 1978 through 1980, many Latin countries experienced growth rates well above "normal," only to fall on extremely hard times in the course of 1981, experiencing massive declines in real output and record unemployment rates. Nowhere have these fluctuations been more severe than in Chile and in Uruguay. In both countries real rates of interest have swung violently. As their capital markets have become (until recently) increasingly integrated with world markets, one suspects that external shocks might well have played a role in determining the interest rate movements that they have experienced.

This paper has examined such a hypothesis and found supporting evidence at both the theoretical and empirical levels. In particular, the strength of the U.S. dollar vis-à-vis other major currencies seems to be highly correlated with real interest rates in at least some of the countries that have pegged to the dollar. On the theoretical side, a model of world markets for traded goods provides a basis for understanding how this phenomenon might come about, of which the mechanisms are the effects of exchange rate movements among major currencies on dollar prices of traded goods.

The second part of the paper examined the possibility of devising an exchange rate regime — either an exchange rate rule or a basket — that would insulate small, open economies from the real interest rate effects of fluctuating external parities. The conclusion is that no such regime exists unless either (a) purchasing power parity holds rigidly among the major currency areas, and/or (b) strong interest rate parity holds among the major currencies. Obviously, neither condition is satisfied in practice in the short run. In the absence of either condition, all that can be accomplished with alternative exchange rate regimes is to switch the source of the variance. With a fixed rate regime, for example, most of the variance in the real rate of interest is introduced by swings in the rate of inflation in the small country. Under a rule such as is indicated by equation (9), the variance in the rate of inflation will be attenuated, but to do so will introduce additional (and compensating) variance into nominal interest rates leaving the variance in the real rate unaffected.[16]

The floating rate alternative was also investigated. That case is intrinsically more difficult; the tentative conclusion is that there is little reason to expect that such a regime would result in a smaller variance in the real rate of interest than would prevail with an exchange rate rule or basket.

The dismal conclusion is that real interest stability, in a world of floating rates among the major currencies, is a distant goal for small economies that are integrated with world markets. Financial (or real) autarky seems to be the only viable (but attractive) alternative. Unfortunately, the most attractive solution — restoration of stability to the world monetary system — is beyond the realm of the smaller countries.

NOTES

1. During 1979, wholesale prices rose by 130 percent, whereas the Argentine peso was devalued by only 61 percent. A higher degree of "convergence" was realized during 1980, when wholesale prices rose by 57 percent in the face of a cumulated devaluation of 23 percent.

2. From the fourth quarter 1978 through the fourth quarter 1979, the average monthly rate of devaluation in Argentina was 4.1 percent; for Uruguay, it was 1.6 percent.

3. Until the end of 1980, short-term foreign currency liabilities of the Central Bank of Chile were included in net foreign assets of that institution; thereafter, they were excluded. Therefore, the period from July 1979 through March 1982 was divided into July 1979–December 1980 and January 1971–March 1982. For the first period, the correlation coefficient between capital inflows (measured as the change in the net foreign liabilities of the monetary system on a monthly basis) and the spread (as reported in Table 3) was -0.53, marginally significant. For the period January 1981 through March 1982, that coefficient was merely -0.122, which is not significantly different from zero at the 10 percent level. While the results indicate that during the first period (when short-term Central Bank foreign borrowing was included in the series) there is a weak inverse correlation between capital inflows and the spread, that relationship does not appear during the second subperiod. The explanation may lie in either the removal of capital controls, or the change in the manner in which net foreign assets are reported.

4. Let i_{tj} be the actual short-term (one-month) rate of interest for the jth month of year t, expressed at an annual rate. The rates appearing in Table 4 are calculated as:

$$[(1+i_{t1})(1+i_{t2})(1+i_{t3}) \ldots (1+i_{t12})]^{\cdot 12} - 1.$$

5. Note that the risk associated with the operation described in the text is clearly *one-sided*; no one in his right mind would have worried about an unscheduled *re*valuation of the Uruguay peso.

6. Apparently the abrupt rupture of exchange rate policy in November 1982 came unexpectedly; see the final row of Table 4, which refers to an operation conducted only during July–October of 1982. The implication is that the increase in peso rates of interest during the second devaluation beginning in mid-1982 were entirely due to the increase in the scheduled rate of devaluation against the dollar.

7. One reason for the larger amplitude in Uruguay is because Table 2 defines real rates against the Uruguayan wholesale price index, whereas in the Chilean case the deflator was the consumer price index, which has a smaller variance than the WPI.

8. The simplest version of the "real" exchange rate is $ER = EP^*/P$, where ER is the nominal exchange rate, P^* the price level in the country on whose currency ER is defined, and P the domestic price level. Note that the U.S. price level behaved very differently than did dollar prices of Chilean tradeables as reported in Table 7.

9. The reference here is to currency areas rather than countries per se. While German trade is enormous (approaching 40 percent of GDP), the external trade of the European Common Market, which roughly corresponds geographically with the European System, is far smaller as a fraction of the EEC's combined production.

10. This assumption is made for exposition simplicity only; the qualitative nature of the results are preserved even if country D has monopoly or monopsony power in the world market.

11. The above analysis is intended to convey the flavor of a world in which the major currencies are the dollar, the DM (representing the EMS countries); and the yen. Clearly it generalizes to any number of countries and currencies.

12. The ω_i's could be defined arbitrarily, of course, so as to make P_t reflect whatever might be desired by policymakers.

13. Even if dP_t does not govern the overall inflation rate in country D, the above results will still hold for the tradeables sector.

14. $F_j \equiv (f_j - e_j)/e_j$, where f_j is the forward rate for currency j, defined for the same maturity as are i_j and i_k.

15. This presupposes that the float would result in a futures market for D's currency. Such a market did not emerge in the case of the float of the Uruguay peso, at least not during the first year of that float which began in late November 1982. Nor did it emerge during the brief float of the Chilean peso in August 1982. One supposes that the explanation lies in the small volume of transactions in those currencies.

16. This statement holds for certain cases only; if the adjustment process in the capital market is different from that in the real sector, the resulting variance in the real rate of interest might differ from the results obtained above. This poses an interesting line for further research.

References

Bhandari, Jagdeep S. "Determining the Optimal Currency Composite." Mimeo, 1982.

Connolly, Michael. "Optimum Currency Pegs in Latin America." Mimeo, 1981.

Dornbusch, Rudiger. "Exchange Rate Rules and Macroeconomic Stability." In *Exchange Rate Rules*, edited by John Williamson. 1981.

Fischer, Stanley. "Stability and Exchange Rate Systems in a Monetarist Model of the Balance of Payments." In *The Political Economy of Monetary Reform*, edited by Robert Aliber. 1977.

Weber, Warren. "Output Variability under Monetary Policy and Exchange Rate Rules," *Journal of Political Economy* (August 1981).

PART III

Strategies of Adjustment

Stabilization and Economic Justice: The Case of Nicaragua

E. V. K. Fitzgerald

The theme of this paper is stabilization policy, a term which has unfortunately earned itself a bad name in development economics in the past few years. In Latin America, however, stabilization policy has been a constant feature of economic debate at least since independence, precisely because of the effect of the world trade cycle on export earnings, and thus the need for politically sovereign governments frequently to adjust domestic economic policy to an exogenously determined balance of payments.

The modern debate on stabilization in Latin America really starts, however, in the Great Depression of the 1930s, when for the first time there was a general reaction against the principles of "sound finance" and an attempt to implement a strategy of counter-cyclical monetary intervention and import-substituting industrialization. Monetarism, of course, had been the current orthodoxy since the previous century, when it was felt by bankers (and Marx, incidentally) that the effect of the downswing of the trade cycle was to reduce wages to reasonable proportions, eliminate inefficient enterprises and restore profitable capital accumulation — the effect transmitted from center to periphery by the gold standard. It should also be remembered that the rest of what is now called the Third World was then largely colonized and thus part of enclosed currency areas. In other words, Latin America had developed, long before the present decade, a definite attitude toward stabilization based on the premise that industrialization and real wage maintenance were more important objectives than price stability or a fixed exchange rate.

In the present debate about stabilization, when the principles of "sound finance" are again popular not only with international bankers but with certain governments in the Continent, the disagreement starts not so much with the correct policy but with the causes of the problem. Briefly, the debtors' story is about the depression in the world economy, deterioration in the terms of trade, the need to sustain investment in production and social infrastructure, and rising interest rates. Just as briefly, the creditors' story is about irresponsible government borrowing, failure to adjust domestic policies to external realities, lack of business confidence and shortages of funds. But whatever the causes, and however much debt rescheduling the bankers can be persuaded to accept (for they too wish to avoid default), some sort of stabilization policy has to be adopted to bring imports into line with exports and to restore a country's creditworthiness. Again, no person would disagree that the only solution·in the long run is to expand exportable production and achieve higher world prices, although there might still be debate as to how this is to be managed.

In the short run, stabilization policy must act on demand; even in the long run, in a situation of supply constraint (particularly of imported producer goods but also often of food), demand must be kept roughly in line with the expansion of production capacity. The orthodox package of demand control is well known (budget cuts, real wage decline, devaluation, etc.) and is correctly criticized by all those concerned with issues of economic justice for having a greater impact on the incomes of the poor than on the rich and of sacrificing development to profitability. The bankers reply that this may well be so, but profitability must be restored if accumulation is to start on a balanced basis and full employment is to be achieved. The weakness of the critics' position is that they have very little to offer as an alternative for short-term demand management, which is what counts at any given moment. Moreover, when popular governments do gain power,[1] they often run into situations of balance of payments deficits and soaring inflation, which undermine their support among the very poor whom they are seeking to help.

It is this problem that I wish to address here. Is it possible to design and implement a demand management policy which combines stabilization with economic justice in a mixed economy? By "economic justice" in this context I do not mean anything very complex and Rawlsian; rather, my premise is that the real incomes of workers, artisans, and peasants should not fall in the process. In other words, the problem is to formulate a realistic alternative to IMF-style policies.

To put the same question in another form, why is it that popular governments seem to have so much trouble with finance? This is not only a problem in mixed economies; for even the socialist countries, when they decide to decentralize and restore a degree of enterprise initiative and consumer choice, seem to run rapidly into severe macroeconomic disequilibria and require a stabilization policy as well. Yugoslavia is a good example of this.

It is my contention that such an "economically just stabilization policy" is possible in principle. This belief is based on the approach to macroeconomic analysis developed by Kalecki, which itself derives from the tradition of the classic pillars of political economy, and which is more suitable to the peculiar economic structure of Latin America (and much of the semi-industrialized Third World for that matter) than either Keynes or Friedman. This approach places income distribution and price formation at the center of the stage, but works from the supply side, so that the fundamental determinant of the standard of living of workers and peasants is the supply of basic needs (or "necessities" as Kalecki calls them); if these basic needs are secured, then the effect of macroeconomic adjustment will automatically fall on the supply of other commodities. If, in turn, adequate profits are sustained (through price policy) and investment is stimulated (through the import of capital goods), there is no reason why production should suffer either. Of course, the necessary demand constraint will fall particularly on the middle class in the nonproductive sectors, such as commerce and services, which absorbs a very large slice of the pie in Latin America but does very little to justify it.

1. Basic Needs

I do not wish to dwell too long on the characteristics of the Nicaraguan economy, but rather to explain the sort of stabilization policy problems that faced the government in the first years after the revolution in 1979. I shall take the story up to mid-1983 because since then the increase in insurgency financed and supported by the present United States administration has forced Nicaragua into what is virtually a war economy. Very different considerations come into play about resource allocation and foreign finance under such conditions, even though macroeconomic disequilibrium is clearly just as undesirable, if not more so.

The economic situation in July in 1979, when the Sandinistas took power after a popular rebellion against Somoza, was critical. Gross domestic product (GDP) in that year fell by one-third, industry had been bombed and looted, crops had not been sown for the 1979–1980 harvests, cattle had been slaughtered, airplanes and ships stolen, wages left unpaid, hospitals destroyed and foreign debtors unpaid. The cost of the war was estimated by the United Nations to exceed 1 billion dollars, in an economy with a national income of little more than double that figure.[2] Somoza had run up an external debt of 1.6 billion dollars in the previous few years, but there was little evidence of productive investments; the funds had been used to finance capital flight, and only 3 million dollars were left in the reserves from these loans and the bumper 1978–1979 export harvest of cotton, coffee, and sugar.

The nationalization of the properties of Somoza and his "cronies" gave the new government direct ownership of about one-quarter of material production (that is, about one-half of big business in the country), all the banks, and most of the transportation system. To this was added strict state control over foreign trade because of the foreign exchange shortage, and over wholesale trade in basic consumer goods to avoid speculation. On the other hand, the private sector controlled (and still controls) three-quarters of production, almost all retail commerce, housing, and so on.[3] As we shall see, there was not only a commitment to maintain private productive enterprise so long as it contributed to development goals, paid fair wages, etc., but also to provide a positive stimulus to small farmers, artisans, and local organizations of social services such as health and education. On the international scene, political non-alignment was matched by trade and aid relations with all areas of the world economy. This is what the Sandinistas call a "mixed economy"; in terms of comparative economic institutions, it might be compared with, say, Mexico.

Finally, because the movement of Sandino and the resistance to Somoza had been essentially a "national liberation struggle," a clear strategic aim was to reduce economic dependence on the United States, but without going to the other extreme, as Cuba was forced to do. Nicaragua is lucky in that, since 1959, Latin America had developed very rapidly, so other semi-industrialized economies such as Mexico and Brazil were in a good position to help economically. Similarly Europe, the Arab world, Japan, etc., provided the possibility of trade and finance independent of the United States, but without excessive commitment to the socialist bloc which would be incongruent with geopolitical realities and inappropriate to the development needs of Nicaragua.

In this sort of situation, even with considerable foreign aid, it would not have been possible simply to expand the economy in a "Keynesian" fashion to restore income levels, because of the domestic supply constraints. Moreover, as income redistribution towards the poor was obviously necessary (otherwise why have a revolution?) some differential action was needed; but simply raising wages would be highly inflationary (as the Chilean experience had shown[4]) and would not benefit the really poor in the so-called informal sector. While credit to industry and agriculture had to be raised (with particular emphasis on small farmers for the first time, which had a considerable redistributive effect) to restore production, and the budget had to be expanded rapidly in response to the new health and education programs, some sort of stabilization policy was necessary to contain inflation. However, with three-quarters of the economy in private hands, it was not possible to control incomes or prices directly.

The only way to secure popular living standards was through the supply itself of basic needs, by removing them from the impact of market forces. That is, it was necessary to make access to food, clothing, housing, health, education, public transport, and so on independent of the actual monetary income of the family. If people's only access to basic needs is through the market, and you cannot control everybody's income, a stabilization policy will naturally fall most severely on the poorest. So the first stage in the stabilization policy, strange as it may seem, was to secure basic needs and not to adjust wages upwards.

Guaranteeing the food supply to the population is a problem of production and distribution. The main supply of stable items such as corn and beans, cheese and tomatoes, comes from small peasant farmers. There is a dilemma between low prices (which help the urban poor) and high ones (which help the peasants) which can only be resolved by higher productivity. Thus, the land reform program had to include the allocation of fertile lands to small farmers (in service cooperatives for the most part) and investment in irrigation on state farms — both in order to raise food output. Therefore, from the start, the economic plans included national food security as a key objective.[5]

The other problem is distribution: if distribution is left to the market in times of shortage, food prices will rise and the urban poor above all will suffer. But the dangers of rationing or state retailing are also considerable because of the bureaucratization that they entail. In the case of Nicaragua, it would also be politically and economically impossible to set up a chain of state stores replacing all the small shopkeepers. What was done, then, was to establish a minimum quota per capita for basic products (sugar, cooking oil, etc.) which is supplied through the neighborhood private shops; the shopkeeper receives from the state warehouses the amount that corresponds to the population of his area (about a thousand people on average) and the neighborhood committees see that he adheres to the rules. Other goods, and the surplus of basic products, are sold through the open market.[6]

The next step was taken in education, where the Literacy Crusade in 1980 reduced illiteracy from over 60 percent to approximately 12 percent; since then, the program has been continued in the form of adult education organized at the local level. At the moment, out of a population of 3 million persons, Nicaragua has one million participating in one form of education or another. This educational effort is largely independent of market forces, although private (religious) schools are still important in secondary education. The health system is not based on large hospitals and doctors but, rather, on local sanitation and preventive medicine centered on the family itself. The main cause of death in Nicaragua has traditionally been child gastroenteritis; this has been reduced enormously by teaching mothers simple methods of rehydration. Polio has been eliminated, and malaria controlled through mass sprayings and annual medication campaigns. These are all essentially community affairs. Similarly, the housing programs (after a false start with apartment buildings) are based on the "site and services" system where the local authority opens dirt streets and installs electricity and water connections to housing plots. Families then build their own houses, buying basic materials at a fixed price from the state and gradually improving the house over the years.

In sum, the "basic needs program" is based on popular organization. Politically and socially, the advantages of this are obvious; but economically too this has the effect of mobilizing underutilized labor without a large capital cost, raising living standards directly without paying inflationary wages. From the point of view of stabilization, this also protects popular living standards from market forces. This is *real* supply-side economics.

2. External Balance

The second step in the stabilization policy was to reduce as much as possible the exchange content of consumption, so as to release imports for exportable production and investment. The main objective of cutting consumption in a stabilization policy for a small developing economy is the reduction of imports to reduce the trade deficit. Normally this is done by cutting total consumption. However, an alternative is to reduce the import content of consumption itself, even if this requires changes in traditional patterns. There is a belief among many development economists (particularly of the structuralist ECLA — Economic Commission on Latin America — school) that the consumption of the poor (food, clothing, etc.) contains less foreign exchange than that of the rich (televisions, automobiles, etc.) Even though this is clearly true for some items, it became rapidly obvious in Nicaragua that popular consumption also relies heavily on foreign exchange. For example, beer bottles are imported from Guatemala, the tops from Canada, the hops from Europe, and so on. However, in cigarettes it was possible to eliminate cellophane in the wrappings and substitute tobacco stems for the filters. Again, housewives come to shop with a basket instead of receiving paper bags.

This process has been repeated throughout the consumption system, although it can sometimes have unexpected results. Imports of drinking glasses were halted to encourage use of local pottery; but the informal sector immediately started to fashion glasses out of bottles, thereby creating a bottle shortage. Imports of packaged soups were halted on the grounds that this was a middle-class luxury, until a delegation of agricultural workers pointed out that when peasant women are working on the harvest there is no time to prepare supper in the evening. Planners often forget these things. Another example is the ranking of basic needs themselves. In the case of Managua, for example, we put housing further up the list than public transport; the inhabitants of the barrios had the opposite opinion. This is simply because senior planners have their own cars and are shocked by informal housing which is "home" to someone else.

Having established basic needs consumption and reduced import content as much as possible, it was nonetheless necessary to cut non-basic consumption to the very minimum as the cutting edge of the stabilization program. The problem, of course, is to define non-basic consumption in order to act on it from the supply side, apply taxes, and so on. Imports of cars and televisions with official exchange supplies were quickly eliminated; taxes were raised on gasoline, and eventually rationing was introduced. However, the Ministry of Finance wanted beer, rum, and cigarettes defined as non-basic in order to raise taxes and reduce the fiscal deficit; the trades unions were of the opposite opinion. The effect of this, particularly the import controls, was to reduce sharply non-basic consumption to less than half the pre-1979 level, while basic consumption was restored to its previous level by 1981. Nonetheless, this basic consumption was more equally spread than before, so that urban employees in particular did not feel any great improvement, in marked contrast to the peasantry and the urban poor. One inevitable result has been that the competition in the market for the limited amount of free foreign exchange has pushed the parallel rate skywards.

In general, the effect of supply restraint without direct control over private sector incomes has inevitably been inflationary; but the inflation is differential — a combination of controlled prices for basic consumption goods and services and market-clearing prices for the rest. This is the monetary side of the "real" redistribution of income through differential access. Logically, if a different supply pattern is imposed on the existing income distribution in a market economy, price adjustment must take place.

The consumption policy obviously has a negative impact on the middle and upper classes, who are the beneficiaries of an "orthodox" stabilization policy but not of this sort of economic justice. This can, as in the case of Cuba, have as a consequence the emigration of key producers, technicians, and professionals. Therefore, an attempt has been made to give incentives to these people in the form of vehicles, housing, and so on — creating the problem that this tends to generate the sort of hierarchy known as "nomenklatura" in socialist countries. One of the major sources of internal opposition to the present government in Nicaragua is precisely this urban middle class in the commercial and services sectors, who have been badly hit by this stabilization policy. Someone has to bear the burden of a reduction in consumer demand, or in the case of Nicaragua, of a limited expansion after a war: in Nicaragua, this "someone" has been the better-off non-producers. (In other cases, such as that of Costa Rica, it has been the poor who bear the burden.) These are the political costs of economic justice. In consequence, the government has tried to explain to producers and professionals why they cannot expect any great improvement in their standard of living; as a whole, their reaction has been positive.

The planners felt that once a consumption policy had been worked out, the next task would be the balance of payments: if basic needs and foreign exchange could be arranged, then the financial balances could be safely worked out without endangering the "real side" of the economy. This, incidentally, turned out to be also the basis for effective economic planning in a mixed economy. In technical terms, foreign trade is the "Department One" of the economy while basic needs is the "Department Two," both of which must be brought into line for an effective economic plan.[7] The first task was to restore the level of export volume, particularly from agriculture, even though world prices had been declining; long-term restructuring towards semi-industrialized natural resource exports would depend upon heavy investments that would not bear fruit until the second half of the decade.

Naturally enough, there was a tendency to turn land over to food crops, so the land reform program had to emphasize restored productivity in cotton, coffee, sugar, and meat on the large farms, both state and private. Cotton posed a particular problem because of the ecological damage the existing system meant in terms of pesticides, etc., even though it is the most profitable crop for the country in terms of net foreign exchange earnings. Fortunately, with the help of an American volunteer entymologist, it was possible to discover a way of spraying around the edge of the cotton fields and killing off the bugs early on; this saved both foreign exchange and human lives, not to mention maintaining the ecological balance.

Recovery of meat production was very difficult because of the slaughter of the herds in 1979; it will take a decade to restore the previous level. In this case and that of sugar, moreover, the level of domestic demand began to rise dangerously, threatening export earnings and requiring domestic rationing. Generally speaking, however, the government managed to get export volumes up to something approaching pre-1979 volumes by 1983. Meanwhile, however, world prices had weakened and, more seriously, the prices of imported inputs and machinery had risen by over one-half. Thus, instead of a balance of about 600 million dollars in exports and imports, there was an export income of about 500 million dollars and imports of 900 million dollars, so that a deficit of 400 million dollars had to be financed internationally.

As stated above, the new government inherited from Somoza a debt of 1,600 million dollars and virtually no reserves. The servicing of that debt would have involved paying some 500 million dollars, which was quite impossible. There was a morally very strong position for refusing to pay at all; but this would have meant severing connections with the Western banking system, which was contrary to the strategy of non-alignment. The banks, more from a fear of the bad example to other countries than from altruism, agreed to an unprecedented restructuring on the basis of a five-year grace period on principal and a flat 7 percent interest rate meanwhile, the differential with the prime rate being capitalized.[8]

The next step was to negotiate new finance. By 1980 it was very clear that the United States government was not going to help and would put heavy pressure on the World Bank and the Inter-American Development Bank as well. The World Bank produced a very favorable report in 1981 ("The Challenge of Reconstruction"[9]) but since January 1982 did not make a single new loan, on the ostensible grounds of "inappropriate macroeconomic policy." The interesting development was that the major source of external finance since 1979 has in fact been Third World countries such as Mexico, Argentina, and Brazil, and Western Europe. The socialist countries have provided about one-quarter of all foreign aid. If we compare the case of Nicaragua with that of Cuba, for example, the Cubans had to choose between the USA and the USSR, and once they were cut off from the former, the latter was the only choice. In the case of Nicaragua, twenty years later and with a far less sophisticated economy, the choice of trading and financial partners is far wider, and the possibility of truly non-aligned international economic relations is possible.[10]

Every year, among donations, trade credits and development project loans, it has been possible to obtain the 400 million dollars or so necessary to balance the external accounts. About half of these resources have gone into essential supplies such as medicines, food, fertilizers, and spare parts; but the other half has gone into investment projects. This is because this deficit on external account is clearly not sustainable in the long run. The development projects emphasize the resolution of this problem through the industrialization of natural resources. On the export side, we may mention expansion of sugar (to be sold to socialist countries at fair prices), renovation of the coffee plantations, expansion of burley tobacco, the development of processed fruit and vegetables, exploration for new gold deposits, re-equipment of the fishing fleet and the sawmills, and the expansion of traditional crops such as cotton and sesame. All these projects are already financed and under way; they should come on board before the end of the decade.

The perils of import-substitution are well known in Latin America, so the strategy here has been to concentrate on basic needs (particularly food) and energy. Here we may mention irrigated grains (corn and beans), African palm oil, cotton spinning and textile mills (Nicaragua exports raw cotton and imports cloth at present!), on the one hand, and the generation of geothermal and hydroelectric power to substitute for imported oil, on the other. The geothermal is very interesting because it is based on tapping the heat of volcanoes for steam-driven turbines with Italian technology.

Thus, the long-term solution to stabilization is from production, and not just demand restraint. However, this will not be sufficient unless there is some improvement in the external terms of trade, particularly access to developed country markets at "just" prices — that is, prices which enable reasonable wages to be paid and leave enough to finance further expansion, once the imported inputs have been purchased. The present prices set by the world economy (that is, imposed by the developed economies) are not sufficient to allow this. This is not just a problem for Nicaragua, but for Latin America and the whole Third World, which is why the proposed New International Economic Order is so important. It is worth noting that this is essentially based on the concept of the "just price" discussed by Aquinas several centuries ago!

3. Financial Balance

The last step in stabilization was to construct and apply the internal financial balances that would be consistent with basic needs, on the one hand, and the external account, on the other. This, in a small way, was an innovation in planning technique, and derived in part from work done by Richard Stone at Cambridge in recent years. The method is based on the integration of the "sources and uses of funds" for the whole financial system with the national accounts upon which the annual economic program itself is based. The basic needs program determines the extent of government expenditure, while production targets the amount of domestic credit. Foreign finance, recuperation of credit from the previous year's agricultural cycle and savings deposits are the main sources of finance, along with a limited amount of monetary expansion in line with economic expansion and international inflation. Given these sources, and the need for production and investment credit in the economic program, the permissable government budget deficit emerges as a remainder.

Thus, the total supply of finance is kept in line with the expansion of the economy and the availability of external resources. In principle, therefore, it will not be inflationary. The point here is that a "monetarist" policy can be applied as long as the basic balances of the economy are controlled beforehand. Given the requirements of finance within the plan for production and investments (in both the public and private sectors), the permissable government deficit to be financed by the Central Bank is the residual. Once the minimum budget consistent with basic needs requirements is met, then the targets for fiscal income are derived, framing tax and tariff policy for the next year. This oversimplifies the procedure somewhat, as a process of mutual adjustment in the targets has to be undertaken to achieve the proper balance, but this is the basic logic.

4. Conclusion

Taking the first years of the Sandinista revolution as a whole, how successful has the policy been? As the figures in the Appendix indicate, GDP had recovered to about 85 percent of its pre-revolutionary level by 1983; this represents a considerable effort considering that the real volume of imports was 20 percent below its 1977 level and several sectors, such as fishing, mining, and construction, were seriously affected by military conditions, while the livestock sector still needed more time to recuperate from the 1978–1979 slaughtering. As the tables indicate, real export volume in 1983 was still below the historical level, but in fact in real terms (in 1980 prices) the trade gap had been gradually moving into balance between 1980 and 1983, though this was not reflected in the balance of payments because of the dollar price movements. In other words, if the prices of 1983 had been the same as those in 1977, there would only have been a modest deficit on current account, which could have been covered by normal development loans for the import of capital equipment.

Turning to the balance of internal demand, we see a rapid recovery of investment, which reached 1978 levels by 1981, but which had to be scaled back a bit to accommodate the expansion of military construction from 1982 onwards, which is not shown in the national accounts. With partial recovery of national income, a closing real trade gap, and rising investment, consumption was bound to suffer. Public consumption (that is, goods and services used by the government, mainly for health, education and other social services) has obviously expanded rapidly as part of that basic needs programs: the real level in 1983 was nearly three times that of 1977. Private consumption, therefore, although it recovered initially between 1979 and 1980, began to decline rapidly thereafter to make room for the other demand categories; in 1983 it was barely two-thirds of what it had been in 1977. Given that basic consumption (food, clothing, etc.) was maintained, what was actually happening was a drastic decline in non-basic consumption, as we have explained above.

In sum, this is the logic of a stabilization program with economic justice.

APPENDIX

Gross Domestic Product (millions of cordobas at 1980 prices)

	1977	1978	1979	1980	1981	1982	1983
G.D.P.	29,353	27,050	19,902	21,892	23,052	22,779	23,683
Gross Fixed Investment	6,831	2,897	-1,266	3,364	5,201	4,302	4,351
Fixed	6,183	3,431	1,203	2,883	4,694	3,801	3,830
Inventories	648	-534	-2,469	481	507	501	521
Consumption	23,805	22,841	17,640	22,488	20,665	19,424	19,904
Public	2,351	2,843	3,045	4,107	4,658	5,446	6,286
Private	21,454	19,998	14,595	18,381	16,007	13,978	13,618
Basic	—	10,000	—	10,587	10,905	10,362	10,920
Non-basic	—	9,998	—	7,794	5,102	3,616	2,698
Exports of Goods and Services	6,800	7,413	8,484	5,039	5,789	5,323	5,800
Imports of Goods and Services	8,083	6,101	4,956	8,999	8,603	6,269	6,372

Trade Balance (millions of US dollars)

	1977	1978	1979	1980	1981	1982	1983
Export (f.o.b.)	636.2	646.0	615.9	450.4	499.8	405.8	432.0
Imports (c.i.f.)	761.9	593.9	360.2	887.2	999.4	775.5	807.0
External Terms of Trade (change)	15.6	—	-3.8	3.6	-20.5	-14.4	-12.2

General Price Index (annual change)

	1977	1978	1979	1980	1981	1982	1983
	11.4	4.6	48.2	35.3	23.9	24.8	31.0

Source: UN/ECLA based on Nicaraguan national accounts.

EDITORS' NOTES

1. "Popular governments" may be defined as governments that draw their support from, and intend to benefit, the majority of the population: industrial and agricultural workers, peasants, and low-income urban groups.

2. See the report by the United Nations Economic Commission on Latin America, *Nicaragua: Repercusiones Económicas de los Acontecimientos Políticas Recientes* (August 1979).

3. See E. V. K. Fitzgerald, "The Economics of Revolution," in Thomas W. Walker, ed., *Nicaragua in Revolution* (New York: Praeger, 1982).

4. See Alain de Janvry's paper, this volume.

5. See Solon Barraclough, *A Preliminary Analysis of the Nicaraguan Food System* (Geneva: UNRISD, 1982).

6. See CIERA, *Distribución y Consumo Popular de Alimentos en Managua* (Managua: CIERA, 1983) and *La Situación del Abastecimiento* (Managua: CIERA/MIDINRA, 1983).

7. This model is developed more formally in E. V. K. Fitzgerald, "Planned Accumulation and Income Distribution in the Small Peripheral Economy," in K. Martin, ed., *Readings in Capitalist and Non-Capitalist Development* (London: Allen and Unwin, forthcoming).

8. See the references in the report by the International Monetary Fund, *Recent Multilateral Debt Restructurings with Official and Bank Creditors*, Occasional Paper 25 (December 1983).

9. World Bank, *Nicaragua: The Challenge of Reconstruction*, Report No. 3524-NI (October 9, 1981).

10. See Michael E. Conroy, *External Dependence, External Assistance, and "Economic Aggression" Against Nicaragua*, Helen Kellogg Institute for International Studies Working Paper No. 27 (July 1984).

Industrial Development in Mexico: Problems, Policy Issues, and Perspectives

Kwan S. Kim

Mexico is currently faced with the most serious economic and financial crisis in its modern history. The current crisis, however, has several historical parallels. While the solution of the current problems is evidently most urgent, at the same time there is now a real need to evaluate long-term development strategies for establishing a viable industrial structure in Mexico.

This paper concerns the longer-term industrial development strategies for Mexico. A careful evaluation of the government's industrial development strategies is undertaken from a historical perspective, so that the failures and successes of a policy strategy can be identified for future lessons. Although the focus is on the industrial sector, the analysis will take into account, as it must, the linkages between macroeconomic and sectoral behavior. In particular, special attention will be given to the relationships between sectoral and trade policies in Mexico.

The paper begins with a discussion of the origins of Mexico's industry, and its historical role in overall development. It proceeds to examine the current situation, to identify constraints on industrial development as well as possibilities of further development. The paper also discusses recommendations for future directions of Mexican industrial development.

1. Industrialization and Economic Development

Compared with other developing countries, Mexico already has a relatively well-developed industrial structure. At this level of development, it is hardly necessary to attempt to rationalize Mexico's efforts for industrialization.[1] The historically important roles played by the industrial sector in the overall development of advanced, industrialized countries are well known. One simply cannot find a developed economy in which the proportion of the labor force employed in industry is insignificant. Even in the country with the most advanced agricultural sector in the world (the U.S.), less than three percent of the labor force is engaged in agricultural activities.

This need not be taken to imply that agriculture or other primary-sector activities are relegated to a secondary role in *development planning*. Expansion of agricultural production and productivity requires the use of industrial inputs in the form of fertilizers, machinery, irrigation and electrification. On the other hand, increased agricultural production permits a more rapid industrial growth through the provision of primary inputs and through its contribution to the balance of payments. In sum a healthy expansion of the industrial sector seems to require a balanced growth in both sectors.

Nonetheless, while the production in agricultural and extractive activities is generally constrained by natural resource endowments, the development of the industrial sector is less restrained by these factors. Its growth essentially depends on the expansion of demand in the economy. The industrial sector, in addition to creating its own demand for intermediate and capital goods, also generates demands originating in sectors outside industry in the course of economic growth.

By contrast, for example, the service sector is more vulnerable to the activities in the rest of the economy and does not in general provide an autonomous force to stimulate other sectors. Manufacturing activities thus constitute a dynamic force in stimulating economic growth; they alter the technical foundation of the economy and increase the use of machinery. Thus, they not only provide necessary capital goods inputs to raise productivity and to generate employment and income in these and other sectors, but also accelerate their own growth as well as growth in other sectors. In particular, expansion of industrial activities leads to improved productivity in agriculture through the industrial inputs it provides and through the absorption of underemployed agricultural labor.[2] Productivity in the tertiary sector is similarly affected through increased demands for services and through the reduction of labor which otherwise is likely to be retained in that sector. Also, the expansion of industrial employment enhances the purchasing power of the lower-income groups, which is likely to stimulate increased demands for low-income-oriented basic goods.

As compared with manufacturing, agriculture and service industries generally experience fewer economies of scale as markets expand in size.[3] There is a reinforcing relationship between industry and market size. Manufacturing industries are generally affected by economies of scale that accompany market size. Some industries continue to improve their efficiency with larger scale.

Given the important role of industry in the overall development process, it seems that Mexico, with an industrial base servicing the domestic market industries, must continue to strive for a rapid industrialization if it desires to expand opportunities for employment and for the production of basic necessities for the working population. Also, exports of manufactures are more apt to be successful for a country such as Mexico.[4]

Of course, economic growth is not synonymous with economic development. However, one must not presume that it is possible to obtain equitable development without growth in the economy. Precisely because this objective cannot be automatically attained in a market-oriented economy, the state needs to intervene to favor less-privileged groups by means of fiscal and other economic policies. The capacity of the state to carry out this objective depends on the growth of output and of the economy. It is simply not feasible to redistribute income under conditions of economic stagnation.

2. Industrial Performance from a Historical Perspective

The performance of the industrial sector in Mexico in the post-war period has been generally impressive. As a consequence, Mexico is now the tenth largest country in the world in terms of gross domestic product originating in manufacturing. By 1980, it produced more than 10 percent of the total Third World manufacturing output. The industrial sector accounts for nearly a quarter of the gross domestic product and employs about 20 percent of the country's labor force. In terms of the dollar value of output,[5] the size of this sector is far greater than that in such developed countries as the Netherlands, Switzerland, Belgium, Denmark, or Norway. In absolute terms, it is about the size of Argentina or India, more than five times that of Israel, Colombia, or Chile, about twice that of South Korea, and a half that of Brazil (Table 1). The significant aspect in these comparisons is that industrialization in Mexico has been achieved primarily during the last three decades.

Mexico pursued the strategy of import-substitution industrialization in the postwar decades.[6] The basic framework of the protective system was in many ways strengthened from the early 1950s through the mid-1970s.[7] Criticisms against such a strategy aside, achievements in industrial development must be given due credit. Among the more significant achievements were:

1. During 1950–1980, the share of non-oil industrial activities in national income increased from 19 to 25 percent, and the proportion of labor employed in industry jumped from 12 to 20 percent, with labor productivity growing at 3 percent and employment at 4 pecent.

2. During the decades of the 1960s and 1970s, gross industrial output in real terms increased at an annual average of 8.3 percent and 7 percent, respectively (see Table 2).

3. Imports of manufactures as a proportion of the gross domestic product declined from 10.5 percent in 1956 to 5.5 percent in 1973, although in recent years they have risen to about 8 percent.

4. During the 1960s, Mexico's exports of manufactures grew at an annual rate of 8.5 percent (Table 2). In particular, from 1965 to 1973 they increased at an annual rate of 14 percent. This was

TABLE 1

The Share of Manufacturing Value Added (MVA)
in the Third World* Countries, 1973 and 1980

1973		1980	
Country	Share of MVA	Country	Share of MVA
Brazil	20.62	Brazil	22.66
Argentine	13.79	Mexico	10.85
Mexico	10.70	Argentine	9.86
India	8.76	India	8.27
Turkey	4.18	Republic of Korea	4.46
Venezuela	2.91	Turkey	3.73
Iran (Islamic Republic of)	2.76	Iran (Islamic Republic of)	3.02
Republic of Korea	2.71	Venezuela	2.61
Philippines	2.36	Philippines	2.51
Peru	2.25	Thailand	2.01
Total	71.04	Total	69.98

Source: UNIDO, *Industry In A Changing World* (New York, 1984).
*Excludes China and other Asian socialist countries.

slightly above the average performance of all developed countries and was 4 percentage points higher than the average growth rate in world manufactured goods trade. Manufactured exports continued to grow at an annual rate of 4.8 percent during the 1970s.

One must note in this connection the important contribution to export expansion made by Mexico's border industries which engage in processing imported materials for re-export, mainly to the United States.[8] Mexico's exports from border industries rose from practically nothing in the mid-1960s to 800 million U.S. dollars in 1980.[9] About 50 percent of this can be attributed to value added in Mexico. In gross terms, border-industry exports amounted to some two-thirds of Mexico's total manufactured exports in the same year.[10]

Investigation into structural changes in Mexican industry points to the important role played by a growing domestic demand in the development of the industrial sector. According to an available estimate (see Table 3), the percentage of the increase in industrial output related to the growth in domestic demand was about 90 percent during the 1960s, with the remainder explained by export expansion and progress in import-substitution. The share of the contribution by increased domestic demand was nearly 100 percent for the decade of the 1950s and exceeded 100

TABLE 2

Industrial Growth in Mexico, 1950–1980*: Average Annual Rates of Growth (%)

	GDP	GROSS MANUFACTURED OUTPUT	IMPORTS OF MANUFACTURES	EXPORTS OF MANUFACTURES
1950–1960	5.6	6.3	6.8	4.9
1960–1970	7.2	8.3	4.6	8.5
1970–1980	6.6	7.0	10.2	4.8
1970–1974	6.8	7.4	10.6	8.7
1974–1977	4.4	4.1	−7.2	0.6
1977–1980	8.6	8.8	32.2	9.9

Sources: National accounts data published by the Secretario de Programacion y Presupuesto and GDP data taken from *World Statistical Tables* (IBRD).

*Based on data in constant prices.

percent for the 1970s. Sustained growth in aggregate domestic demand contributed to reductions in the share of imports in the gross value output, and at the same time, to increases in the proportion of manufactured output exported.

As domestic demand expanded,[11] investment opportunities developed, followed by improved industrial organization, realization of scale economies, and incorporation of new technologies in production — all of which further led to increased productivity. This improved productivity with the resulting narrowing of the differences in internal and external prices, promoted further import-substitution industrialization as well as expansion of exports. Perhaps more importantly, this may have directly improved Mexico's industrial competitiveness in the world market.

3. Trade Liberalization and the Recent Setback

Beginning in the early 1970s, Mexico started to experience balance of payments difficulties which eventually led to the devaluation of 1976. However, it must not be presupposed that the worsened balance of payments situation was entirely caused by *import-substitution* industrialization policies. Rather, the secular deterioration in the non-oil external payments was due in part to a combination of various forces: (1)

TABLE 3

Sources of Industrial Growth in Mexico, 1950–1980*

	DOMESTIC DEMAND	EXPORT EXPANSION	IMPORT SUBSTITUTION
1950–1960	99.4	2.1	−1.5
1960–1970	89.0	2.6	8.4
1970–1980	104.0	3.3	−7.3

Source: *Mexico*, NAFINSA, *Future Directions of Industrial Strategy*, Mexico City, 1983 (mimeo), p. 35.

*The percentage of the increase in output related to the components: see Hollis B. Chenery, "Patterns of Industrial Growth," *American Economic Review* 50 (1960), 624-54.

a progressive stagnation of the agricultural sector with a gradual diminution of surpluses for export; (2) the worsening in the balance of payments in services; and (3) the increasing debt burden to the rest of the world. Thus, even before the process of import substitution could advance to the next stage, these forces virtually dimmed the prospects for a sustained industrial growth.

While the decelerated pace of industrialization in the first half of the 1970s was largely caused by balance of payments difficulties, the reasons for a slow-down in industrial growth in the second half were quite distinct and in good measure related to abrupt changes in economic policy. Although Mexico's industrial strategy over the past few decades had led to notable achievements in industrial development, it had certain weaknesses which became manifest during the early 1970s and reappeared in a more acute form during the recent crisis. It is important to account properly for these weaknesses.

Returning to the more recent episode, the sudden discovery of large oil reserves opened the possibility of quickly overcoming the balance of payments constraint and of undertaking expansionary economic policy. The policy framework during the period of 1976–1981 was comprised of two main elements, the first relating to the macroeconomic strategy and the second specifically to the industrial sector. The macroeconomic strategy called for expansionary government spending and trade liberalization. While maintaining a relatively stable nominal exchange rate regime, and low real interest rates,[12] the government resorted to subsidized prices of energy and other basic needs goods to moderate domestic inflationary pressures. Sector-oriented policies included an incentive system for promoting private investments as well as public-sector investments in "strategic" branches of the industrial sector.

A broad spectrum of industrial branches quickly benefitted from these sectoral policy measures. According to a government report, from 1975 to 1981 the production of crude oil increased 3.2 times; natural and refined oil products by 2 times; basic petrochemicals by 2.5 times; fertilizers by 2.3 times; steel and cement by 1.5 times; automobiles by 2 times; and electricity by 1.7 times. Once the depressive economic conditions that extended until 1977 were overcome, the real gross domestic product grew at an annual average rate of 8.5 percent, while industrial output grew at 9.6 percent between 1978 and 1982. The average annual rate of employment absorption in manufacturing achieved 5.4 percent, and real investment in industry increased by nearly 18 percent per annum. Private-sector investments, largely induced by a new input subsidy scheme, were particularly marked in industries producing intermediate goods which are intensive in the use of energy as well as capital goods. It is worth pointing out that in spite of the liberalization measures, effective protection levels, reflecting the effects of subsidized inputs to industry, still remained sufficiently high to provide incentives for industrial expansion.[13]

The manufacturing sector, however, after the initial expansion in 1978 and 1979 at 9.8 and 10.6 percent per annum respectively, slowed to a growth rate barely exceeding 7 percent in the following two years. This decelerated pace of growth was accompanied by increases in imports of industrial origin and the attendant balance of payments difficulties.[17] In real terms, imports rose by nearly three times between 1977 and 1981. This contrasts with the earlier 18 percent decrease registered between 1975 and 1977. It is remarkable to note that imports of consumer goods experienced the largest relative increase. Their share in total imports jumped from 6 percent in 1977 to 12 percent in 1981.[15]

An expansion of this magnitude quickly turned out to be untenable, even with a massive export of crude oil. In 1976 no one would have suspected that five years later (in 1981) as a result of the doubling of the world oil price, Mexico would be able to export 14 billion dollars worth of crude oil, an amount equal to four times the current account deficit in that year. Imports, however, continued to exceed any increases in oil revenue; consequently, substantial trade deficits persisted throughout these five years. For instance, in 1981 total imports reached 23.2 billion dollars with a current-account deficit of close to 12 billion dollars. Finally, precipitated by the rapid rise in interest payments on public debt as well as by destabilizing speculation on the peso, the financial crisis stemming from external payments problems culminated in 1982. At the same time, the influx of imports began to adversely affect growth of domestic industries.

Various reasons have been advanced for this explosive growth in imports. First of all, there is the hypothesis that as a result of expansionary demand management,[16] bottlenecks in certain sectors characterized by excess demand in relation to installed capacity quickly developed. But this still does not explain why there were substantial increases in income elasticities of import demand in a large number of industries that were not particularly constrained by capacity limits.

Above all, the period of 1977–1981 witnessed substantial investments in industries from both public and private sectors.[17] This should have reduced demand pressures on capacity utilization with the resulting reduction in elasticities of import demand. As is well known, the contrary happened: values of import demand elasticities increased greatly rather than diminished. There is also evidence that rates of capacity utilization in industry decreased during this period. This seems to contradict the hypothesis of bottlenecks as a factor primarily responsible for the explosive growth in imports.[18]

An alternative explanation seeks the answer in the deterioration of the competitive position of Mexican industry in the world market, caused largely by the accelerated inflationary trend seen during this period. Despite the exchange rate policy which permitted the peso to slowly appreciate in real terms following the initial devaluation in 1976, the average unit cost of Mexico's industries relative to its trading partners still remained at a comparable level until the late 1970s. Thus, the overvaluation of the peso and the rapid growth of the economy may have stimulated imports, but these two factors alone cannot explain the sudden explosive growth in imports.

A third explanation is that the import boom during the period stemmed from the abrupt shift in economic policy from protection to sudden liberalization. Although the alternative hypothesis relating to expansionary domestic demand cannot be ruled out, in view of the foregoing discussion the question still remains whether the observed increase in import elasticity did result from the bottlenecks in the economy.

The Mexican government turned to export promotion when it encountered increasing difficulties in the balance of payments. As a means to promote an export-conscious industrial sector, it resorted to various forms of subsidies to exporters, precluding the use of imported inputs in export production only when domestic substitutes were available. Thus, at the beginning of the 1970s, manufactured goods exports constituted only 4 percent of the gross value of industrial output with processed foodstuffs accounting for only about one-third of export sales. Exports of industrial goods rose to 5.5 percent of the value of industrial output by 1978.

This effort for export promotion was soon accompanied by policy measures that permitted increased imports. In particular, the dismantling of quantitative controls on imports processed rapidly during this period and equally embraced consumption, intermediate and capital goods. Even for industries subject to import controls, import licenses were issued automatically and indiscriminately. Quantitative controls were eventually to be replaced by tariffs yielding equivalent protection, but these were never implemented. The average level of tariff, net of subsidies, drastically declined over the period.

By mid-1981, the structure and level of industrial protection was not significantly different from that prevailing in the member states of GATT (General Agreement on Tariffs and Trade), the agreement Mexico had repeatedly boycotted. Moreover, unlike many of the signatory countries, Mexico lacked indirect, subtle mechanisms of protection such as anti-dumping legislation or other industrial or sanitary regulations.

4. Policy Issues on Liberalization Versus Protection

Although the performance of manufacturing industry under a protective regime in Mexico has in general been satisfactory, the protective policy has been criticized for promoting inefficiency in industry. Armed with the theory of comparative advantage, critics have often influenced policy decisions, and in a large measure were responsible for the progressive trade liberalization measures instituted since 1976. These critics' theoretical foundation is the orthodox proposition that free trade leads, in a static sense, to an optimal use of society's given resources.

In this connection a more important issue would be the dynamic effects of protection which unfortunately are difficult to gauge. The orthodox theory tells us that given the limited size of domestic markets in developing countries, protection creates monopolistic and oligopolistic market structures that may lead to inefficiencies in the allocation of resources among industries as well as to inefficiencies resulting from the loss of incentives for efficient operations.

The theoretical issues aside, there is no empirical evidence to suggest that the efficiency cost of protection would be particularly exorbitant for countries like Mexico. The studies show that for developing countries on average it amounted to less than 3 percent of the gross domestic product.[19] The cost of protection is likely to be much lower in a country such as Mexico which has a relatively large domestic market. In this regard, it is also significant to note that the government strategy of excessive protection in the past has encouraged private investors to industrialize the economy. There has recently been a concern that a sudden dismantling of the protective mechanism in Mexico would exert an adverse impact on investment in the industrial sector.[20]

Even though competition in the international market can eliminate many inefficient firms, there is little certainty that investments channeled into specific branches of industries will be the ones that turn out dynamically viable and efficient. Those industries judged to be efficient in the static sense of comparative advantage may not necessarily be the ones in which productivities and technical progress will advance most rapidly, nor will they become industries with large demand elasticities. In any case, as pointed out by many Mexican economists, if a greater degree of competition is necessary to promote industrial efficiency, this can be done through encouraging competition among firms operating within the context of the domestic market.

Other costs of protecting capital-intensive industries suggested by the traditional theory include adverse impacts on economic growth, in particular, on the growth in total productivity, which is effected through the transfer of labor from high-productivity to low-productivity industry. Although a few empirical studies have confirmed the presence of a positive correlation between output growth and export activities, it must be noted that these studies typically covered the period of a world trade boom in the 1960s and in the early 1970s.[21]

One argument supporting trade liberalization is that it aims at eliminating monopolistic gains that would accrue to the producers under a system of protection. It is also argued that trade liberalization, by expanding output of labor-intensive industries in Mexico, leads to increased employment of wage earners, and therefore, to a more even distribution of income.[22] Even if this were the case, realization of this effect would require an essentially long-term adjustment period. Over this period, as revealed by the recent Mexican experience, it will be necessary to continue to revalue the currency in real terms. Otherwise, the attendant inflationary pressure will set in motion the need for subsequent, nominal devaluations of the currency, larger every time, with the resulting reduction in the real wage rate and its adverse impact on income distribution. In the end, the distribution of income could possibly become more uneven.[23]

Other critics of protection have pointed out the high administrative costs of the import control system as well as the problems of corruption associated with it. Without doubt, these are a real disadvantage of the system. However, in the context of the Mexican economy, such costs may well turn out to be of secondary importance compared to the adverse impacts on the economy if protection were totally eliminated. In this connection, an important economic effect of the recent trade liberalization policy was to retard the development of intermediate- and capital-goods sectors. Within a few years following the policy of liberalization, the level of investment in these sectors drastically declined. At the same time, both the volume of imports and the share of intermediate- and capital-goods imports rose rapidly.

Thus, a relevant question to ask is: Had trade liberalization measures not been adopted, to what extent could these imports have been replaced by domestic production? It may well turn out that the security of the domestic market offers the best incentive for sustained investment in capital-goods industries in Mexico.

Proponents of trade liberalization have argued that the import effect of liberalization was transitory in nature, and that once the intital adjustment process was over, import behavior would return to a normal situation. The recent experience has already shown that the growth rate of imports, far from tapering off with time, accelerated during the period of unrestricted trade.

There is really no assurance that in the future the policy of restricting domestic aggregate demand, combined with a currency devaluation to maintain a realistic effective exchange rate, will provide a viable basis for industrial development in Mexico. More likely, the net effect of such a measure is to depress domestic industries more severely than the previous import restriction measures could have afflicted. There have been a number of precedents of such cases, including England, Chile, and Argentina. In those countries, the recession was combined with inflation and recurrent balance of payments problems. Mexico could find itself in a permanent crisis without the prospects for a sustained development process into the future.

5. Industrial Policies for the 1980s: A Synthesis

From the preceding discussion, it is clear that the principal problem facing Mexican industry is the difficulty in sustaining socially acceptable economic growth without incurring external deficits that exceed the financial capacity of the country. The acceptable growth rate can be understood to be the one that provides productive employment to the labor force which grows by 4 percent per annum, and that provides basic needs goods for a population that will reach 100 million by the end of this century.

In principle, policy measures for correcting external disequilibrium must be aimed at reducing the magnitude of import coefficients in import-substituting industries, at expanding exportable industries, or at implementing some combination of both measures. However, is it realistic to assume that Mexican industry will be capable of overcoming its tendency toward external disequilibrium through promotion of manufactured goods exports?

The answer to this question is not simple. The reason for this lies in the profound changes in the world economy that have taken place in recent years. If one considers the historical evolution of the world economy, the two decades following the Bretton Woods system until the oil crisis in the early 1970s can be viewed as a period of trade boom for the Western industrial economies as well as for the rest of the world. During this period many developed countries could attain and sustain a near full-employment growth rate. Several developing countries also achieved remarkable progress in industrialization. The developing country share of the total world industrial output climbed from 6 to 9 percent.

The rapid growth of developed countries during the decades of 1950–1970 stimulated expansion of the world market. The world trade volume in manufactured goods increased by more than 10 percent over the period. The fruits of this expansion were also shared by Newly Industrializing Countries (NICs), including Mexico. A few NICs registered as much as 14 to 16 percent annual growth rates.

This process came to an abrupt halt in the early 1970s. From 1974 to 1977 the total volume of world trade in manufactured goods grew by 5 percent annually, which was only about half of the trend growth rate of the period between 1950 and 1970. The industrial growth rate of advanced NICs declined to about 7 percent while Mexico's growth rate dropped to 4.1 percent.

More recently, during the years 1979–1983 world trade in manufactured goods has stagnated, which has affected the economies of NICs relatively more severely. The neo-protectionism in industrialized countries appears to have been particularly discriminating against exports from NICs. Mexico has been no exception to this trend. For instance, the United States, which accounts for the lion's share in Mexico's total trade, has recently imposed a number of restrictive measures against Mexican exportables. In 1980 the U.S. excluded some fifty Mexican export products from its generalized system of preferences. An additional forty-four products were added to the list the next year. The U.S. government is also obligated to impose a countervailing duty on Mexican export products benefitting from a subsidy. Thus, in the first four months of 1981 Mexico's trade deficit with the United States reached 1.4 billion US dollars, nearly twelve times the deficit for the same period in 1980.

The prospects of international trade for developing countries during the current decade are not that promising. The world economy is likely to grow much more slowly than it has in the past. Even if the recent recovery of industrialized nations is assumed to continue in the immediate future, it will not by itself be sufficient to return developing countries to economic growth rates comparable to the past. In addition, the adverse impact of the recent recession in the industrialized countries on developing country terms of trade has proven to be longer-lived.[24] In the absence of immediate prospects for a terms-of-trade reversal, worsened export prices in the world market are likely to impinge on developing country efforts for export expansion. Thus, there is a need for developing countries to reevaluate the relationship between growth and trade, and particularly the role of exports in overall development.

In this respect, the structuralist argument popular in the 1950s and 1960s in Latin America is likely to gain a new momentum in the 1980s. The argument focuses on two policy dimensions: renewed emphasis on import substitution by assigning to the domestic market a more important role in industrialization strategy, and policy priority on technical and economic cooperation among developing countries. The structuralist argument of course lost its cogency during the period of trade prosperity when the opening of the economy seemed a key to the success in industrialization.

Orthodox economists usually cite the experiences of the Southeast and East Asian countries during the 1960s and 1970s (South Korea, Taiwan, Singapore, and Hong Kong) as success stories of trade liberalization policy. It is important to note that their success was achieved under rather unusual circumstances. First of all, these countries are relatively small and had no options but to open their economies to the world market. The largest of the so-called "Gang of Four," South Korea, today has a manufacturing sector which is only a half of Mexico's. Secondly, a large share of their exports is accounted for by intra-firm transactions by multinational corporations. This places them in a position particularly vulnerable to changes in the economic activities in the parent countries of these multinational firms.

From a different point of view, the East Asian economies have structural characteristics very different from those of other industrializing countries of relatively large size. For example, Japan, whose success in manufacturing exports cannot be questioned, is an economy in which total exports constitute a relatively small proportion (12 percent) of the gross domestic product, and whose growth has depended mainly on the expansion of internal markets.

The principal conclusion emerging from the foregoing discussion is that during the current decade Third World countries, including Mexico, may have to rely, much more so than in the past, on the dynamics of their own internal markets and domestic competition for economic growth.[25] It will of course be easier for a relatively large developing country like Mexico to pursue a domestic market-oriented industrialization strategy. A large market is a prerequisite to the development of scale economies in production, which is indispensable for a sustained industrial growth. A recent study finds that Mexico's internal market is sufficiently large as to justify installation of a large number of industrial plants for producing capital goods.[26]

In this connection, account may be taken of another reason for the concern with trade liberalization for Mexico. A recent study shows that about half of Mexico's manufacturing exports are related to intra-firm transactions by the multinational firms in Mexico.[27] This leaves these exports vulnerable to the economic activities of parent firms in their countries of origin. The automobile industry in Mexico is a case in point. Despite large investments in plants in Mexico, export-oriented production has simply not materialized because of the recent depression of industries in the United States.

The industrial strategy described above by no means implies an economic autarky. Autarky is impracticable for any economic system, given a country's need for advanced technology. Internally oriented, industrial-sector development cannot, however, be expected to result in an immediate reduction in imports, nor can it be expected to quickly reduce the size of import coefficients. Expansion of industries oriented toward the domestic market is likely to generate, at least initially, an increased demand for capital-goods imports from abroad.

It is also important to note that for Mexico the easy stage of import substitution is over. Given the relative scarcity of physical and human capital in Mexico, an inward-oriented strategy is likely to entail rising costs, as requirements for skilled labor, for intermediate and capital goods tend to increase at the next stage of import substitution.[28]

Some critics have argued that Mexico's import-substitution-oriented policy in the past has largely discriminated against export expansion. A careful analysis, however, does not justify this assertion. As has been shown, it was precisely during the period when import controls were rigorously imposed that performance of exports was satisfactory on its own terms as well as in relation to other countries.

In the long run there does not have to be a conflict between an internal market-oriented development strategy and an export-oriented development strategy. History is replete with examples of industries developing with a growing domestic market, gradually expanding to markets abroad.[29] Indeed, the Mexican industrial structure, with its diversified products in a growing domestic market, provides a substantial base for future exports of manufactures.

Thus, in the future when the world economy recovers, a better strategy for promoting exports should still be based in large measure on a set of policies that is similar to the set of past policies which have succeeded in consolidating a basically viable and dynamic industrial structure. Evidently, Mexico's domestic market cannot support all industries. Reliance on protection gives rise to inefficient production in some industries. Thus, measures for export promotion must be industry-selective, based on the principle of complementarity to a viable industrial structure for the economy. At the same time, import-substitution possibilities must not be overlooked for industries where demand growth is expected to be more dynamic (engineering and durable consumer goods),[30] or where economy-wide linkage effects in production are substantial (capital goods).[31] In particular, despite Mexico's rapid industrial expansion over the three decades 1950–1980, its capital-goods industry is much less well developed, as compared with other industrialization countries like Brazil, South Korea, Taiwan, and India. Currently, capital-goods and intermediate-goods inputs account for close to 90 percent of total imports.[32] Thus substitution of capital-goods imports by domestic production may be one of the few remaining possibilities for Mexico.

Available studies indeed show that the domestic market size and technological capacity for producing capital goods should not provide real obstacles to sustained progress any more in Mexico than in other leading Newly Industrialising Countries.[33] At bottom, as the Japanese experience authentically demonstrates, there is fundamentally no contradiction between a domestic market-oriented import-substitution strategy and other complementary policies leaning toward export promotion.

6. Other Policy Options

Today, Mexican industry finds itself caught in a dilemma. The enterprises that spent heavily on capital goods for production of exportables are faced with a still-depressed world market. Likewise, those firms that invested in industries for domestic markets are faced with similar conditions. To this may be added the effects of the recent devaluations and high interest rates, which undoubtedly are generating further disincentives to investors. In these circumstances, the important issue is what policy measures must be adopted to encourage investment in plant and equipment required for strengthening the productive structure of industry.

There is no simple approach to this issue. It is clear, however, that in order to avoid a stagnation in investment, investors must be offered an assurance of healthy growth in the economy and reasonable rates of return on investment. The important question is: How can the domestic market be expanded without disproportionately stimulating aggregate demand and without incurring external payments deficits? Sufficient reductions in government spending are an obvious option, which is currently undertaken as part of economic stabilization measures. However, since the bulk of government spending in Mexico is on social welfare and on subsidies for production of basic needs goods, there is a real limit to the reduction in spending. Apparently the other inevitable option is to restore measures of restricting imports, at least during a transitional period of adjustment.[34]

In this regard, excluding the cases of manufactures trade that are highly sensitive to the real exchange rate,[35] a devaluation policy that relies on the working of the pricing mechanism to correct disequilibrium may not be effective for Mexico in view of the expected delay in the realization of its effects and the consequent inflationary impacts.[36] As argued by many Latin American structuralists, the developing economies are generally characterized by a structural rigidity. Thus, apart from the argument of price inelasticities in developing country trade sectors, the attempt to stimulate exports by changes in the nominal exchange rate may quickly precipitate inflationary pressures, rendering exchange rate policies largely ineffective. In addition, since many Mexican industries have been operating at an idle capacity of production, the economic rationale of seeking allocative efficiency through devaluation may be questioned.

The success of devaluation policy also depends on the tolerance of the trade unions and workers to accept the reduction in real wages that normally accompanies a devaluation in the short run. Apart from the question of whether or not Mexican workers will in the "national interest" accept any prolonged stagnation in the living standard, a policy of currency devaluations has its costs in terms of undue burden imposed on less-privileged classes of society.

Once adequate growth in the internal market is secured, other policy measures complementary to import restrictions can be instituted. Among these would be: legislation to redistribute monopolistic gains accruing to protected industries, industry-wide coordination in capital- and intermediate-goods production, expansion of consumer-goods production to accommodate a growing market, preferential financial terms for capital- and intermediate-goods industries which generally call for long-term investment, and selective use of subsidies to basic needs goods producers in lieu of price controls.

For Mexico, the question of exports need not be considered solely in the context of an undervalued domestic currency.[37] Empirical evidence shows that in the trade of manufactured goods international price differences are less important a factor compared to such factors as product quality or technological innovation. Moreover, in Mexico more than a half of total exports in manufactured goods and, in particular, more than three-quarters of metal mechanical products exported take the form of intra-firm transactions by multinational firms. In the capital-goods industry, subsidiaries of multinational firms mostly carry out capital-goods exports. Relatively few exports, mainly concentrated in equipment for the oil industry and agricultural implements, are exported by Mexican firms.[38] Since many multinational corporations resort to so-called transfer pricing, an overvalued domestic currency has relatively unimportant influences over their export activities.

If an overvaluation of the currency impedes export activities, other policy instruments are available for correcting distortions without subjecting the economy to inflationary or other repercussions. In this regard, it is worth noting that the total number of important manufacturing export firms in Mexico may not exceed 500, a relatively small number when considering financial and fiscal support, perhaps in the form of tax rebates. These sectoral policies clearly do not directly promote export activities. Nonetheless, their favorable impact on investment is conducive to indirectly stimulating expansion of the export sector.

The use of exchange rate variations as an instrument to correct external disequilibrium, particularly under a freely fluctuating exchange rate regime, has serious implications for the level and structure of investment. Frequent fluctuations of exchange rates make the planning difficult not only for the government but for the private sector. Likewise, as evident in the recent Mexican experience, a devaluation can lead to higher interest rates which, even under a sustained demand expansion, will discourage investment, particularly in heavy industrial projects.

7. Conclusions

The recent experience under the administration of President Portillo reveals the importance of implementing sectoral policy as an integrated part of an overall macroeconomic policy framework. Given the then prevailing international market conditions, import-liberalization measures, combined with expansionary domestic policy, proved to be incompatible with an externally oriented industrial-sector development.

Moreover, if the domestic productive structure is to be strengthened and the revitalization of industry is to be assured, it will be necessary to do so without resorting to an unrestricted trade and exchange-rate liberalization scheme for Mexico. Future sector-oriented policy must concern itself with sustained industrial growth in the face of uncertain external conditions. Thus the conventional infant industry argument still applies to sectors with a clear dynamic comparative advantage potential. Of course, extreme care must be exercised to ensure efficiency in encouraging development of domestic industry. For instance, the level of protection needs to be gradually diminished as industry develops. At the same time, one has to be aware of the limits of import substitution for Mexican industry as well as the potential contribution that can be made by certain branches of export industries. Thus, there is a need to take into consideration specific sectoral conditions in implementing any industrial development strategy.[39] The future industrial policy for Mexico needs to be based on a more "eclectic" approach combining the notion of maximally exploiting domestic market potentials on the one hand, and an emphasis on industry-selective export-promotion measures on the other.

NOTES

*An earlier version of this paper was presented at the 1983 Latin American Studies Association meeting in Mexico City. The author gratefully acknowledges a seed money grant from the Kellogg Institute of International Studies at the University of Notre Dame for collection of research materials. This work was inspired by Neo-Keynesian writings on development.

1. For a comparative performance analysis of semi-industrialized countries, see B. Balassa, et. al., *Development Strategies in Semi-industrial Economies* (Baltimore: Johns Hopkins Press for the World Bank, 1982), pp. 38–62.

2. For a discussion of the dynamic attributes of industry in the economic growth process, see A. Hirschman, *The Strategy of Economic Development* (New Haven: Yale University Press, 1958).

3. For an empirical study of the efficiency saving related to industrial firm size, see P. A. Yotopoulos and J. B. Nugent, *Economics of Development: Empirical Investigations* (New York: Harper & Row, 1976), pp. 149–53.

4. See J. N. Bhagwati and T. N. Srinavasan, "Trade Policy and Development," in R. Dornbusch and J. Frenkel, ed., *International Economic Policy* (Baltimore: Johns Hopkins Press, 1979).

5. See United Nations, *Growth of World Industry*, various issues.

6. In 1970 effective protection in Mexican industry averaged 60 percent with a significant rank correlation between the importance of import substitution in an industry and the level of protection. See A. Ten Kaate, et al., *Protection and Economic Development in Mexico* (Mexico City, 1981).

7. For instance, the value of controlled imports rose to 72 percent of total imports in 1974, from the prevailing level of 6 percent in the 1960s.

8. Duty-free treatment was accorded beginning in the mid-1960s and a tax rebate scheme on manufactured exports (11 percent) was introduced later in 1973.

9. These "maquiladora" industry activities are recorded in Mexican balance of payments data as "net income from tranformation services."

10. An important issue concerning the development of border industries is the problem of effectively integrating the maquiladora plants with the rest of the economy. Small-scale local industries have been shown to be particularly affected by maquiladora plants. Hence, despite increases in local value added

made possible by border industries, expansion of this trade entails complex issues to be resolved.

11. In recent years some industries, such as textiles and clothing, have been identified as the cases in which the lack of demand acted as a constraint on domestic production. However, there had recently developed a substantial import competition in demands for these products, which can be attributed to the latest import-liberalization measures.

12. It may be noted that these factors combined were largely responsible for the quickening of the "dollarization" of the Mexican economy during the period.

13. According to Nacional Financiera data, in 1979 an average effective subsidy rate in intermediate-goods industry in Mexico was about 25 percent, and 79 percent in a few capital-goods industries, in contrast to a negative rate in the food-processing industry.

14. A prevailing view has been that an "overheated Mexican economy" stemming from the expansionist government policy was the fundamental cause of balance of payments problems. A counter-argument is given in the discussion that follows.

15. Imports of machinery for manufacturing activities also experienced increases with their share in the total rising from 49.4 percent in 1977 to 52.1 percent in 1981 (SPFI estimates).

16. For instance, the public sector deficit rose from 5.7 percent of GDP in 1977 to 14.8 percent in 1981.

17. Note that foreign investment still represents only 4 percent of total investment in plant and equipment in Mexico, and is not significant.

18. For empirical evidence, see J. Eatwell and A. Singh, "Se Encuentra 'Sobrecalientada' la Economía Mexicana? — Un Análisis de los Problemas de Política Económica a Corto y Mediano Plazo y Post Scriptum," *Economía Mexicana* No. 3 (1981), pp. 253–78.

19. See J. Bergsman, "Commercial Policy, Allocative Efficiency and X-Efficiency," *Quarterly Journal of Economics* 88 (1974): 409–33, and World Bank, *Mexico, Manufacturing Sector — Situation, Prospects and Policies* (Washington, D.C., 1979).

20. That is, a large number of foreign firms have invested in Mexico, seeking the benefits of tax shelters under protection. They would be unable to penetrate the market in any other way. With the removal of tariffs, many foreign firms would be inclined to divert investments from Mexico.

21. See B. Balassa, et al., *Development Strategies in Semi-Industrialized Economies*, p. 56.

22. A recent study shows that the long-run effect of export promotion in Mexico is almost neutral in affecting the distribution of income. See K. S. Kim and G. Turrubiate, "Estructuras del Commercio Exterior y sus Efectos en el Contenido de los Factores, el Empleo y la Distribución del Ingreso en Mexico," *Trimestre Económico* (October-December 1983), pp. 2173–92.

23. Critics of Mexico's commercial policy often recommend replacement of quantitative controls by tariffs, since a tariff system allows gradual elimina-

tion of protection with planned precision. However, in a country such as Mexico where the income distribution is uneven, demands for luxury goods tend to be highly price-inelastic. Thus, tariff rates would have to be substantial to provide adequate protection. In this regard, other fiscal measures would be more appropriate. Moreover, the use of the pricing mechanism as a commercial policy, as compared with such alternative measures as quantitative controls, increases the propensity to consume in the economy and reduces the availability of savings for investment.

24. The terms of trade confronting the Latin American countries fell by 13.6 percent between 1980 and 1982. See International Monetary Fund, *World Economic Outlook, 1983*, Table 14, pp. 183–84.

25. This view is similarly subscribed to in the National Industrial Plan prepared by the Secretaria de Patrimonio y Fomento Industrial and the Global Plan formulated by the Secretaria de Programación y Presupuesto.

26. See NAFINSA-ONUDI, *A Strategy for Developing Capital Goods Industry in Mexico* (Mexico City, 1977).

27. R. de la Ramírez, "Mexico-U.S. Trade and Foreign Investment: A Firm Level Study of International Trade Patterns of American Firms in Mexico," Ph.D. dissertation, University of Cambridge, 1982.

28. Similar results are likely to follow even with an export-oriented industrialization strategy for Mexico. As a newly industrializing country, Mexico is unlikely to be able to continue to sustain export expansion in traditional, labor-intensive manufactured goods. Capital- or technology-intensive export efforts are likely to be costly for Mexico.

29. See, for example, the argument by S. B. Linder in *An Essay on Trade and Transformation* (New York: Wiley, 1961).

30. This refers to the case in which the income elasticities exceed one.

31. It is important to note that as shown by the historical experiences of many countries, export possibilities generally follow a full development of domestic market-oriented industrialization.

32. The recent balance of payments statistics show that Mexico's capital-goods imports during the first quarter of 1984 amounted to as much as 11 billion U.S. dollars, which represented an increase of 5.6 percent over the previous year.

33. See NAFINSA – UNIDO, *The Supply of Capital Goods in Mexico.* (Mexico, A.F., 1979).

34. Reliance on the pricing mechanism for correcting payments deficits is generally considered relatively ineffective in a developing country like Mexico. Some Mexican economists contend that a more effective method is to employ an innovative system of quantity controls on a selective and judicious basis.

35. For instance, textiles and clothing among non-durable consumer goods have been identified as tradeable goods generally sensitive to the real exchange rate.

36. For a rigorous estimation of the influences of exchange rate policy, we need to calculate real effective exchange rates — a measure of the real rate after adjusting for changes in export incentives. Because of the lack of data, no such estimates exist for Mexico. However, heuristic evidence exists that shows

a general ineffectiveness of exchange rate policy. For instance, between 1970 and 1977 Japan's world market share of manufacturing-goods exports increased by 4 percent, despite the fact that her unit cost, measured in dollars, increased at an annual rate of 24 percent. On the other hand, during the same period the share of the United States and England in the world's total manufactured-goods exports decreased by 3 and 2 percent respectively, although their respective unit costs increased by only 8 and 14 percent. See OECD, "The International Competitiveness of Selected OECD Countries," *Economic Outlook* (Paris, 1978).

37. Using the recent time-series data, Brailovsky found no significant correlations between Mexico's share of exports in the world markets and the real exchange rate. See V. Brailovsky, "Exchange Rate Policies, Manufactured Exports, and the Rate of Inflation," working paper for the Institute for Industrial Planning, Ministry of Natural Resources and Industrial Development (Mexico, 1981).

38. C. J. Dahlman and M. Cartes, "Technology Exports from Mexico as a Starting Point in the Study of Technological Capability". *World Development* 12 (1984), 601–24.

39. Some branches of industries (notably, light consumer goods) are known to have a saturated domestic market, limiting further possibilities of import substitution.